I0591485

Translating
Popular Fiction

NEW TRENDS IN TRANSLATION STUDIES

Volume 22

Series Editor:
Professor Jorge Díaz Cintas

Advisory Board:
Professor Susan Bassnett
Dr Lynne Bowker
Professor Frederic Chaume
Professor Aline Remael

PETER LANG

Oxford • Bern • Berlin • Bruxelles • New York • Wien

Translating Popular Fiction

Embracing Otherness in Japanese Translations

Kayoko Nohara

PETER LANG

Oxford • Bern • Berlin • Bruxelles • New York • Wien

Bibliographic information published by Die Deutsche Nationalbibliothek.
Die Deutsche Nationalbibliothek lists this publication in the Deutsche National-
bibliografie; detailed bibliographic data is available on the Internet at
http://dnb.d-nb.de.

A catalogue record for this book is available from the British Library.

Library of Congress Cataloging-in-Publication Data

Names: Nohara, Kayoko, 1964- author.
Title: Translating popular fiction : embracing otherness in Japanese
    translations / Kayoko Nohara.
Description: Oxford ; New York : Peter Lang, [2018] | Series: New Trends in
    Translation Studies ; 22 | Includes bibliographical references and index.
Identifiers: LCCN 2016008958 | ISBN 9783034319638 (alk. paper)
Subjects: LCSH: Translating and interpreting--Japan. | Fiction genres. |
    Japan--Foreign influences.
Classification: LCC P306.8.J3 N65 2016 | DDC 418/.020952--dc23 LC record
available at http://lccn.loc.gov/2016008958

Cover design by Peter Lang Ltd.

ISSN 1664-249X
ISBN 978-3-0343-1963-8 (print) • ISBN 978-1-78874-026-5 (ePDF)
ISBN 978-1-78874-027-2 (ePub) • ISBN 978-1-78874-028-9 (mobi)

© Peter Lang AG, International Academic Publishers, Bern 2018
Wabernstrasse 40, CH-3007 Bern, Switzerland
info@peterlang.com, www.peterlang.com, www.peterlang.net

All rights reserved.
All parts of this publication are protected by copyright.
Any utilisation outside the strict limits of the copyright law, without
the permission of the publisher, is forbidden and liable to prosecution.
This applies in particular to reproductions, translations, microfilming,
and storage and processing in electronic retrieval systems.

This publication has been peer reviewed.

Contents

Figures

Tables

Acknowledgements

First of all my deepest gratitude goes to all the translators of the literary works I have quoted in this book. The literary attraction of their works to a large extent resides in the stylistic features I have tried to detect, and thus this book is a tribute to their ingenuity and creativity. The book initially contained a much larger variety of examples from many more translations but only a modest number could be displayed because of the limited space.

I am especially indebted to Prof. Mike Norton for his support in improving the text throughout the finishing stages. Likewise, I am grateful to Ian Platt and to the Hon'yaku Plus editing team.

I would also like to thank Dr Phillip Harries for opening up the world of translation studies to me in Oxford, Prof. José Lambert for the opportunity to work as a post-doc in the irreplaceable Leuven environment, Prof. Lawrence Venuti for personal discussion at the early stages of the project, and Prof. Daniel Gile for his long-term encouragement to write this book. Speaking of encouragement, I must also mention Prof. Gideon Toury and Prof. Sándor Hervey. Nothing would have started without them. Prof. Tanaka Akio, Prof. Ōno Susumu and Prof. Naitō Yorihiro have taught me about both academic research and life more than I could ever give credit for.

My special thanks go to all my friends and colleagues who supported me, but especially to Katori Yayoi, Kawano Eriko, Tago Miyoko, Hiraki Megumi, Dr Amir Isamu and Dr Nakada Kazuyoshi who have been there for me, together with all the ex-research assistants and students for their devoted support. It has been great to run "Nohara Lab" for endless discussions with them all. Many thanks also to Prof. Tom Hope, Prof. Susa Masahiro, Prof. Yamaguchi Shinobu, Prof. Abe Naoya, Prof. Yanabu Akira, Prof. John Maher, Prof. Mizuno Akira, Prof. Ujiie Yōko, Prof. Nishina Kikuko, Prof. Kusakebe Osamu, Prof. Sanada Haruko, Tanaka Kukiko, Asaba Masaharu, Prof. Aizawa Masuo and of course Tsuda Hiroshi for their friendship and cooperation in this and other related projects.

This work would not have been possible without the financial support of the Shōyū Club and the JSPS. I am deeply grateful for that.

Special thanks also go to Prof. Jorge Díaz-Cintas for our extended talk in East Putney, for his precious suggestions and – together with the Advisory Board Members – for accepting my manuscript for his wonderful series. I am profoundly grateful to all the anonymous referees who worked on this book, not only by catching mistakes but also by suggesting important points that would have never occurred to me. Many thanks to Dr Laurel Plapp, Ben Goodwin and all the editors and technical staff members at Peter Lang for their patience and encouragement. I simply adore their office on St Giles in Oxford.

I give my heartfelt thanks to my mother, who I am sure is watching this and whose love and guidance are with me in whatever I pursue, and to my precious family members, especially Carola and Werner Ertl and Ella Donhauser.

Finally, I thank Prof. Wolfgang Ertl, for having patience with me and for taking on this challenge, providing support, excellent wine and philosophical quotations whenever difficulties arose.

Tokyo, January 2018

CHAPTER I

Introduction

Imagine yourself on an evening commuter train in Tokyo, packed (as goes the Western cliché) but highly organised. Many of the passengers, men and women, sitting or standing, are holding a book, a smartphone or a tablet in their hands. Some are playing online games, some are glancing at a blog, some are reading a novel, and others are flicking through a weekly *manga*, that is, a graphic (often in both senses) Japanese comic book. All this is a common sight. You will be surprised, however, to discover that quite a few passengers are reading translated literature in the form of a tiny *bunko* or pocket-size paperback, or an e-book, which are easy to carry and take out in such crowded places.

Let's take a closer look at them. A middle-aged businessman is reading a well-known mystery, *Murder on the Orient Express* by Agatha Christie. A male college student is reading *The Martian Chronicles*, a classic science fiction novel by Ray Bradbury. A young female office worker is reading *Sense and Sensibility* by Jane Austen, which was a big Hollywood hit some years ago. A schoolgirl is reading *Anne of Green Gables* by Lucy Montgomery, the first volume of the popular Canadian *Anne* series, which most Japanese girls come across during their school years. A middle-aged female school-teacher is reading *Camilla*, Sheridan Le Fanu's vampire novel. Finally, a young female musician is reading *Whip Hand*, a prize-winning novel from Dick Francis's horse racing adventure series. These works were all originally written in English, but are from various countries, periods and genres. Think of what is happening to these people on the train. Clearly, they are all going through a literary experience, whether enjoying it or not. Would it not be odd, however, if the readers were receiving some common impressions from such disparate sources? The readers themselves probably do not suspect that these common impressions are providing them with a surprisingly uniform experience as a part – despite all the differences between the works.

This book suggests that this is indeed the case, and that the shared experience can be attributed to distinctive properties found in the language used. These texts belong to a category which exists only in the world of translated literature: in other words, the text-type is available as a strategic device to provide a norm in translating a certain kind of literature from English into Japanese. As Japanese has never been a language of international communications, Japanese readers only have two ways to access material written outside their own linguistic domain. They can experience the material in a foreign language or through translation. In practice, most readers rely on the latter option, so translation has become an integral part of everyday life. The commonly used phrase *hon'yaku ōkoku Nippon* [Japan, the translation kingdom] refers to the long tradition surrounding this activity and reflects the large number of translations that are regularly published in the community, although the quantity of translated publications does fluctuate. In *Hon'yaku to Nihon Bunka* [Translation and Japanese Culture], Haga (2000: 152–153, my translation) emphasises the significance of translation when seeking to understand the cultural development of the country:

> Let us review the history of Japanese culture. Japan first imported Chinese and Indian culture in ancient times, in the form of Chinese writing, poetry and Buddhism, and some kind of translation was always involved during this process. In the Tokugawa period, people were immersed in Dutch studies. Since the Meiji period the Japanese have been absorbing Western culture (its political, economic and philosophical aspects, as well as the expressions used in literature) and this has taken place entirely through the medium of translation. One could even say that in Japan the history of the culture of translation is equivalent to the history of culture itself.

Thus translation into its local language has been the key to Japan's access to overseas culture and its assimilation. This is however hardly unique to Japan, so why should Japan be called "the translation kingdom" in particular? The index of foreign books translated into Japanese gives us a clue. On the UNESCO's "Index Translationum – 'TOP 50' Target language" list (since the 1950s to 2017), Japanese usually ranks around fifth place, after German, French, Spanish and English. Western languages dominate the ranking from first place to twelfth place. Given that Japan is so geographically, linguistically, and culturally remote from the languages of Europe and

America, it is surprising that it should rank so highly in the UNESCO list. Furthermore, while the overall number of publishers that have been actively involved in publishing translated books declined during the recession in the 1990s, there has been a steady flow of new publishers putting more focus on or even launching the publication of translations in Japanese (*Shuppan Geppo* [Publication Monthly Report], 2000: 6). It is these trends that make Japan stand out.

These statistical data indicate the stable, long-term popularity of published translations. In addition, these data hint at a deeper implication that Japanese people traditionally may even welcome the idea of importing foreign cultures via translation. Japan is a model case among Asian countries for the full-scale acceptance of Western culture (Kawakatsu 1991: 245). Witnessing the fusion of Western culture and more traditional Japanese elements in all fields, one cannot help but be bewildered by the endlessly open attitude (even if only on the surface) to different ideas and experiences from overseas – "otherness" from an out group or *soto* of *uchi/soto*, which literally corresponds to inside/outside, traditionally utilised to identify social distance between people. We should not forget the reality that such foreign influences are very often introduced to Japan through encounters with people and publications overseas, and hence via the medium of translation, which allows the Japanese to make adjustments to those elements of otherness to conform to expectations within their community. This seems to be an activity that they particularly relish, and they recast the source text information so that it can comfortably fit into some part of the existing Japanese world. When readers look for a certain established linguistic style, translation can assist by providing the desired flavour. Assigning a specific writing style to the translated text seems to be one way of providing such assistance. As translators have the power to incorporate foreign terms into their own culture, this gives them also power to control this particular cultural interaction.

A translated text and its original source are supposed to be equivalent in their meaning. Learnings from studies on translation made in recent years, however, have made it increasingly clear that static equivalence cannot be simply transferred from a source text to a target text (TT), as the target text needs to be attuned to the contextual requirement. For a translated text to fulfil the desired function – which is to communicate successfully in a given situation – it must be written in an appropriate text-type (Kußmaul 1997: 68). In conforming to text-type norms, a translation will often move away from the form and/or content of the source text. Equivalence between the two texts is constantly reshaped during the adaptation of the target text to the rules of the selected target type. Without question, text-typology is one of the central issues crucial to an understanding of the process and production of translations.

Among the several issues involved, a basic but intriguing question is: which text-types are available in the target language? When one writes, one usually gives an appropriate register or a language variation to the text according to the purpose. Many text-types are commonly found within various genres, such as business reports, academic papers, diaries, poetry and novels. The conventionalised formulations found in non-translational writing are often valid and can also be utilised in translation; the text-type resources available in the source language and target language do not always match, however. Sager (1997b: 39) claims that translation-specific text-types exist:

> Another facet of classification, based on text-types, which influences translation strategies, must differentiate between target language text types which are fully established in the target language culture and those which are specific to translation products and occur only as a result of translation.

This book enquires into the way in which literary translation of certain genres is made from English into Japanese taking a norm-oriented point of view, in order to identify a translation-specific text-type, its properties, and its cultural implications. Here the term "cultural" is used to refer to any kind of knowledge or perception of the world which one is presupposed to have to understand people's behaviour (including use of language) in their society or community. In other words, culture is a totality of elements which make language work in a particular social context. Hatim and Mason (1997: 216) define "cultural code" as "a system of ideas which conceptually enables denotative meanings to take on extra connotative meanings and thus become key terms in the thinking of a certain group of text users, ultimately contributing to the development of discourse".

Chapters 2 and 3 provide background information on translations and research on translation in Japan. They look at some of the major theoretical issues in the field of translation studies and show how they have been treated in the Japanese environment. A brief history of translation, and selected discussions on translation in Japan, are provided. The issues relevant to the main arguments in this book are also presented here, including specific problems identified in contemporary translation between English and Japanese.

Chapters 5 and 6 attempt to undertake a textual analysis of some translation examples. Pieces of source text in English and their Japanese counterparts are presented and analysed, and the translation process is (when necessary) reconstructed. The texts are selected from so-called popular or mass fiction translations aimed at the Japanese general public.

In Chapters 7 and 8, attention is redirected to the systematic description of the stylistic properties found in the translations analysed in the previous chapters. The discussion focuses on the experiences that the readers of Japanese translations of Agatha Christie and Ray Bradbury inevitably share, and on the categories into which such texts are sorted within the whole system of Japanese translated literature. These considerations can highlight and reveal an abundance of cultural backgrounds beyond mere linguistic or literary phenomena, since translation can be understood as a reflection of how the two (or more) communities involved interact with each other.

To rephrase, this book employs close text-to-text contrast to examine the motivations behind the choices made during the transfer from the original sentences to the translated ones, and consequently from the original text-type to the resulting text-type. By investigating which techniques are regularly used, the properties emerging in the target text become clearer. An attempt is made to classify the most frequently used strategies. Certain translations may also be commented upon from various perspectives, such as those of reviewers, my own reading of the texts, and the points of view on texts in "native" Japanese and as found in translations. However, finding fault is certainly not the object of the exercise. Similarly, the intention is not to cast aspersions on the use of the so-called "translationese", but to identify its presence and constitution. In this context, the term "translationese" is usually taken as an English translation of the Japanese word *hon'yakuchō*, which is occasionally linked with a negative connotation and used to highlight its problematic aspects. On the other hand, "translationese" has played an important role in the formation of the Japanese language itself: as commented by Meldrum (2009: 94) "Despite some scholars' arguments against "translationese" as being bad Japanese, many argue that "translationese" has contributed to the development of the Japanese language throughout its history". In this book, to maintain a neutral stance, I will avoid using the term "translationese" due to its sometimes slightly negative overtones in everyday language, except when the term is used in the works of other scholars in the field. Terms like "translational Japanese", "translational discourse" or "translationalese" will be used instead. To express the obvious difference from original Japanese, I use the term "translationalness", as coined by myself.

This book aims to advance the field of translation studies in the following three ways. Firstly, it focuses on Japanese – considered as a language of limited diffusion (LLD) – as a target language. Secondly, the traditional concepts of domestication and foreignisation and their modified adaptations, as reviewed by Venuti (1995), are discussed and utilised as yardsticks for identifying stylistic features of translation-specific language. Since there is a wide linguistic and cultural gap between English and Japanese, it is potentially productive to investigate translations between the two languages from this point of view. Thirdly, the results of this research may lead to further consideration as to whether some of the properties regularly found in translated popular literature go beyond the English-Japanese domain, and whether some kind of uniformity can be detected in a wider context. This study thus generates suggestions concerning both theoretical and strategic studies of how popular fiction can be successfully translated from a target-cultural and norm-oriented point of view. The text-type and its stylistic features which, it is suggested, are features of the translation of popular fiction, indicate what is acceptable for Japanese readers – and this certainly deviates from the principally normative or adequate style exhibited by original Japanese works of popular fiction. The way in which fiction is produced reveals much about a society, and a people – as does translation. This is surely true of the translation of popular fiction as well.

Translation into Japanese naturally draws attention to the peculiarities of the Japanese writing system. The basic functions of each component of this system can be described as follows: the Chinese characters are used for nouns, the stems of verbs, names and other words with fundamental meanings. *Hiragana* is used for grammatically functional words, for example for the ending of a verb indicating tense, and for some native Japanese (not Chinese) words. *Katakana* is the other phonetic syllabary and is used for loanwords and names of foreign origin. For a target language to have a writing tool specifically for representing imported items and names is a unique linguistic feature, although *katakana* was not originally created for that purpose. Finally, *rōmaji* is for writing Japanese using the letters of the Latin alphabet. It appears in information for tourists (for example, names of stations), or in everyday settings for its fashionable effect (for example, in the popular press or in the name of a café or boutique). Some acronym loanwords are conventionally transcribed using the *rōmaji* corresponding to their original wording or their intended market, such as "CD", for compact disc, and "EU", for the European Union.

Following conventional usage, the language from which translation is carried out is called the source language (SL), and the original text to be translated is called the source text (ST). The language into which translation is conducted is called the target language (TL) and the translated text is called the target text (TT). Other technical terms will be introduced as appropriate, together with their definitions and abbreviations. Japanese text examples are all accompanied by a romanised version, transcribed into the Latin alphabet using the modified Hepburn system. Japanese names are presented in Japanese order, surname first. In the case of quotations from secondary literature by Japanese scholars or translators, only my English translations are presented in the text. Back translations (BT) are provided where necessary for the discussion.

CHAPTER 2

The Traditional Discussion of Equivalence and Its Relevance to the Japanese Context

2.1 Defining Translation, Defining Equivalence

This book introduces some new perspectives on Japanese literary translations and their interaction with foreign pieces of information. I believe that it is not only meaningful but also enjoyable for researchers, translators and readers of translated literature to be aware of these perspectives when dealing with literary texts. "Translation" is a very generic term which everyone knows and many people use in daily language and/or in a professional context. Paradoxically, as the definition of translation is rarely questioned, this means that it is difficult to debate or share information on translation with people (especially crossing over from one speciality area to another). Therefore, I would like to first examine, and provide an overview of what translation can refer to, as well as address some related issues which may help us understand the activity better, especially in the Japanese context.

Translation has been defined in various ways throughout the history of its study. It can, for instance, be succinctly described as the act of transferring the meaning of an expression from one language to another. However, the term "meaning" always remains unclear. Accepted definitions include Jakobson's (1959), Catford's (1965) and Lawendowski's (1978), which, as stated by Barnstone (1993: 227), share the following: "Verbal signs in A are interpreted and transferred into verbal signs in B". However, he continues and states that, "Having said this we have said everything and nothing about the activity of translation. [...] The simplest of all definitions of translation reads: *translation is the transposition of messages between tongues*" (ibid. 227). Landa quoted by Viaggio (1999: 125) also defines it without resorting to the term *meaning*:

[A] special way of speaking – speaking in order to re-say "*what has been said*" or written or conveyed through gestures; re-producing in a new act of speech and in a different language what has been said in a previous act of speech.

Given that the act of translation allows the receptor access to "what has been said" or the "message" in the original text by bridging the gap between the SL and the TL, the translation is regarded as a new piece of communication produced from an existing, fixed communication. A message can be passed and be received successfully, or in other words, communicated as intended by the sender, only when it is conveyed in an appropriate narrative, mode or environment. As the main objective of this book is to identify the particular stylistic features used in Japanese translations of literary works, and to discuss the way in which this determines the nature of the messages that are conveyed to the TL community, it is particularly important to understand that the task (or at least one of the tasks) of translation is communication.

The term "translation" corresponds to *hon'yaku* (or *yaku* for short) in the Japanese language, in both the sense of the action and the product. The commonly accepted definition of translation, the act of transferring the meaning of an expression from one language to another is to a large extent shared in Japanese at the present time, although in the Meiji period (1868–1912), the term *hon'yaku* used to refer to a literal rendering and was one of the three terms that referred to three different methods of translation.[1] The *Nihongokokugodaijiten* (2000: 278, my translation), one of the major contemporary reference works for the Japanese language, defines *hon'yaku* as: "the act of converting a piece of language or text from one country to a piece of language or text for another country, which has the same meaning". The use of the word "country" shows that the description does not fully take multilingual societies or countries into consideration, and this

1   The three terms were defined by Sugita Genpaku, who translated scientific texts, as *hon'yaku* [translation into the corresponding Chinese characters], *giyaku* [free translation] and *chokuyaku* [phonetic translation]. Mori Ōgai identified a further four methods in the translations of Western poems, such as those by Byron, Goethe, and Shakespeare: *iyaku* [paraphrasing], *kuyaku* [idiom-for-idiom translation], *in'yaku* [phonetic translation] and *chōyaku* [free translation] (Haga 2000).

represents the rather limited appreciation of the Japanese – as a basically monolingual society – on the issue. Isoya (1980: 2, my translation) states:

> In general terms, translation involves transferring something written in a natural language (such as English, French or Chinese) into another natural language (for example, Japanese). Specifically, we might think of the act of converting foreign literary works or various practical texts into our own language, with the term covering both the operation and the product. The operation must change the means of expression without changing the content. The relationship between the original text and the translation is defined by terms such as correspondence or equivalence.

Let us pick up a few contemporary arguments on how some Japanese authors perceive the process of translation. One argument is that translation is a real-life situation, in which one encounters different cultural information and it involves dealing with difference in terms of one's own cultural norm (Torikai 2013); accordingly, it is a practice which can nurture global perspectives and skills needed for international cooperation. This notion goes beyond the normative domain of interlingual translation, and translation in this case covers what to say and how one behaves in a foreign or trans-cultural setting. Yanabu et al. (2010) give a broad overview of translated texts written from the beginning of the Meiji Era to the wartime period and the translators' attitudes and approaches from a diachronic perspective. A number of scholars of translation studies have selected one or two key figures in the history of Japanese translation and discussed their contributions in terms of domestication and foreignisation. Some argue that the original text can be changed to make it readable and comprehensible for the new readers, taking the perspective of "domestication" which will be fully discussed in later sections of this book. For example, Watanabe On claimed in the nineteenth century that we can change a nominal phrase in the original text into a sentence in the translated version (Mizuno 2010). Also, he asserts that we can change the order of sentences in the texts at the time of translation. Miyajima Harumatsu emphasises that the most important thing is that readers should not be bored when reading a text and should understand it easily, if it is not an academic title (Satō 2010). Although Tsubouchi Shōyō claims in his early twentieth-century essay that we should beware of not losing the content of the original text, his argument is similar to that of Miyajima. For Uchida Roan, the essential point is to deliver the feeling or impression that translators gain after reading through the original text (Cockerill 2010), while Venuti (1995) suggests that domestication also includes the selection of the texts to be translated.

Other authors think that we should avoid changing the text as far as possible even though the TT may become difficult to read. Thus, they would rather work on translation with a "foreignisation" approach. Fujita and Ozaki claimed in 1885 that we should take a risk by impinging on the culture of the SL to remain faithful to the original text (Mizuno 2010). For Takeuchi Kenji, an early Shōwa era writer, when we translate texts in a specific field of expertise, it resembles solving a mathematical problem. He only accepts that a literal translation be made, by emphasising the importance of word-for-word translation and insisting that there is only one meaning for one word, and one word for one meaning (Yamaoka 2010).

According to Naruse (1978), a contemporary technical translator, an English text consists of linguistic elements with some meaning, and the accumulation of the meanings is perceived as the meaning of the whole text. The elements are transferred to Japanese elements with the same meaning and they are accumulated into a text. This is the generally shared perception of translation and this "analysis and unification" method has been widely utilised in the Japanese translation community. However, Naruse (ibid.) questions whether this modern scientific approach is in fact valid for dealing with translation, which is such a human – and thus organic – linguistic activity.

Translation has been the subject of discussions lately, both academically and among practitioners; given this encouragement, the very definition has also been debated. Established Western reference books on translation studies, such as those by Snell-Hornby (1995) and Munday (2008), have been translated into Japanese and this has made for easier access to the field of translation studies. In addition, new introductory works in the field have been published in Japanese (Torikai 2013, Nohara 2014). These developments have encouraged and accelerated thinking on issues related to Japanese translation in the framework of translation studies.

To understand how Japanese generally perceive translation as an activity, it is important to understand that from as early as the Nara (710–794) and Heian (794–1185) periods, they have employed a technique for reading texts written in Chinese known as *kanbun kundoku*, or *kundoku* (Wakabayashi 2009). This system provided the key to Chinese culture, from which the Japanese obtained their first writing system, and accessed Buddhism, Confucianism, laws and much other basic knowledge for the formation of early Japanese society (see section 3.1). This *kundoku* system involves the vocalisation of Chinese idiographic characters as corresponding Japanese words, according to their meaning and function, the addition of particles and other necessary grammatical devices between the characters, and the provision of special aids (such as *kaeriten*) that indicate the order in which the characters should be followed to be able to read the text as Japanese. Some scholars regard the system as involving the reading of a written Chinese text using Japanese pronunciation, or the production of a kind of Sino-Japanese creole, and try to distinguish it from translation proper, because the original Chinese text remains unmodified. It is, however, clear that the *kundoku* system allows people who do not read Chinese to have access to the content of the text through Japanese, and, in this sense, it can be said to fully fulfil the function of translation. Tsukishima (1963: 43), one of the most influential Japanese linguists, analyses the process of *kundoku* and elucidates it in Figure 1.

Process of Understanding (Reading)		➡		Process of Expression (Writing)	
Writing (Chinese characters)	→ (Sound / Image-acoustic)	→ Concept	→ (Image-acoustic)	→	Writing (Japanese characters, aids)

Figure 1: Converting Chinese characters into Japanese: Tsukishima (1963: 43, my translation) version of the *kundoku* method.

In the first part of the process, receptors of the ST determine the concept that the Chinese characters refer to. In the latter part, they select appropriate Japanese expressions and then actually write them down using Japanese syllabaries and auxiliary symbols. Tsukishima compares the above model of the *kundoku* translation process with Tokieda's (1941) model of general linguistic expression and understanding (see Figure 2).

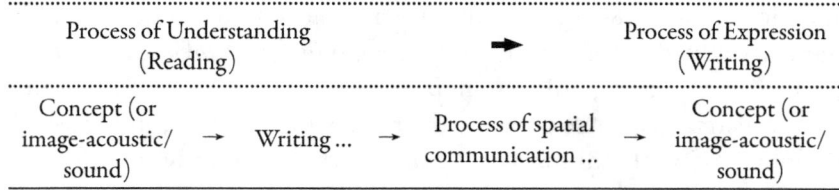

Figure 2: Converting Chinese characters into Japanese: Tokieda
(1941: 91, my translation) version of the *kundoku* method.

Tsukishima's (1963: 43, my translation) *kundoku* emphasises the double process (first reaching the concept and then departing from the concept) of "linguistic expression and understanding", and also states that, "after all, *kundoku* was an extreme word-for-word translation". It is significant that such a drastic linguistically alienating technique has traditionally been authorised and widely used as an official and scholarly method of translation, dealing with Chinese (and later, Western) languages, although a number of different translating methods have also been experimented with (see section 3.1). Tsukishima (ibid.) goes on, stating that:

> The form of Japanese used in *kundoku* has become distant from original pure Japanese, as it was bound to the lexemes and word order of the original Chinese. Surely one can often find the influence of the original vocabulary and grammar in translations in general and, in fact, since the Meiji period translational language has largely developed in Japanese through the translation of Western languages. If we had no *kundoku* system but only ordinary translation for dealing with Chinese texts, Chinese would not have had so much influence upon Japanese.

Kundoku has certainly had a considerable impact on the formation of the Japanese language, literature, people's attitude towards translation and, more importantly, the way the Japanese interact with foreign cultures and assimilate some of their features into their own cultural domain. This point will be considered in more detail in Chapter 8.

As far as terminology is concerned, the term "translation studies" is commonly used to refer to the discipline and seems to emphasise the inter-disciplinary nature of the subject, and to deal with all types of text as research materials, without excluding either literary or non-literary texts (Snell-Hornby 1995: 1–3).

Next, the concept of equivalence has repeatedly been the centre of attention as a unique element in translations of all text-types. Translators typically share the following four presuppositions concerning the process of translation: (1) there is the ST produced in the SL as original material which conveys a certain message; (2) the message is transferred into the TL, which is another, already existing, set of linguistic devices; (3) the TT is produced through this process; (4) the ST and the TT are equivalent to each other in one sense or another. The intricate notion of equivalence has constantly given rise to innumerable questions, starting with its possible definitions and its achievability, particularly when considering the obvious gap between the two languages and contexts. The reality that it is impossible to obtain exact equivalence, and its general acceptance by translators, is mentioned by Biguenet and Schulte (1989: xiii):

> The activity of the translator starts with the reality of the word on the page. It is common knowledge that no language has created enough words to express all the nuances of our emotional and intellectual existence. Some languages are richer than others in their word count; some languages are richer in sound quality than others. The atmosphere that a romance [sic] language creates through the sounds of words might have to be recreated in English through other linguistic possibilities. An exact equivalence from one language to another will never be possible. This could be characterized as both the dilemma and the challenge for the translator.

It is nowadays accepted that there are no exact equivalences, even on the level of individual words, either within the same language or between languages, even if the unlimited creation of new vocabulary by loan were to be allowed. Indeed, structuralism claims that actualisation of particular phonological, grammatical and semantic distinctions in different language systems is completely arbitrary. A certain limit is preset for the act of interlingual translation by emphasising that all language systems are unique, and that since there are no universal properties of human languages, human thoughts are thus fixed and determined by each language (Lyons 1977: 245–250). Nevertheless, equivalence is regarded as a key term for the unique relationship between a ST and its TT, by both translators and theorists. The challenge of defining equivalence is naturally related to the problem of identifying *message* or *meaning*, and various levels of meaning, such as referential, connotative, pragmatic, textual and functional have been recognised. Here, Pym (1992a: 37) points out the circularity inherent in this theoretical concept: equivalence is supposed to define translation, while translation defines equivalence.

It has increasingly become clear that holding on to a static idea of equivalence would, in practice, not take us much further in understanding translation: equivalence is indeed amorphous. Translators seek a way to recreate the ST beyond its semantic equivalence "as appropriately as they can" according to the function of the text, and not simply "as much as they can". Based on the views of functionalism and universalism, that is, that every language system has a universal infrastructure, and that each structure is determined by the particular functions that it has to perform, Katz (1976: 37) states that, "(e)very proposition is the sense of some sentence in each natural language". This makes it possible to achieve pragmatic or textual equivalence between languages.

Here arise the key questions on the issue: what kinds of equivalence are attainable and attained in practice? Equivalence can be defined as the relationship between an ST and a TT that allows the latter to be a translation of the former, with the exact nature of that equivalence varying depending on the case. Toury (1980: 47) argues the importance of a textual equivalence under a particular set of circumstances and states that:

> The question to be asked in the actual study of translations (especially in the comparative analysis of TT and ST) is not whether the two texts are equivalent (from a certain aspect), but *what type* and *degree* of translation equivalence they reveal.

Although his definition of equivalence is rather broad, this standpoint liberates scholars from the endless burden of defining equivalence in translation, and directs them to a more empirical analysis of the texts and the methods used in creating them. This attitude would also make it more productive to look at Japanese-English translations as by their very nature they have wide semantic and stylistic discrepancies, and it is therefore realistic to search more for pragmatic equivalence than semantic equivalence, let alone formal equivalence.

2.2 Evaluating Translations

In talking about translation, people tend to think about which kind of translation is good, right or correct – probably more so than when talking about any other linguistic activity. Arguments about translation can easily become judgemental since people may have different ideas and expectations about translation, so that when they encounter a translation that deviates from their expectation, they find it inappropriate. This gives rise to the idea that equivalence in a translation itself carries some ethical value. The two accepted criteria in many communities of a good, moral translation are faithfulness or fidelity to the original text and readability, that is, smoothness or naturalness in the transformed text. Faithfulness seems to refer to semantic or structural correspondence and readability refers to closeness to the native TL in style or simply to the quality of flow of reading.

Pym (1992) states that some kind of ideal loyalty to a ST, author or sender, exists and has to be pitted against a similar loyalty to a receiving language, culture or receiver. To be seen as adequate, a translation is required to satisfy both demands to some extent, although the required balance differs with time, place and case. A lack of proper attention to the former aspect puts the translator at risk of receiving severe criticism for inaccuracies in the text; neglect of the latter dimension, on the other hand, makes the text seem stylistically immature and unsophisticated, unless this is clearly intended for some experimental purpose. It is also important to be aware that faithfulness and readability can be interpreted in various ways, as translation is not a mere mirroring operation between the SL and the TL but a complex cultural transaction. In any context, the question must be asked: in what sense are "faithful" and "readable" desirable?

As the debate on what equivalence should be, and what can be achieved, has escalated, a number of theorists have fallen into the trap of attempting to find a generally applicable yardstick for good translation. As a consequence, they have made prescriptions about translation activities to try to identify criteria which justify or rationalise their verdicts. Bell (1991: 10) rightly points out that normative prescriptions deriving from the subjective and evaluative description of "good translations" have become ground-rules for the study of translation and criticises that propensity:

Translation theory finds itself today seriously out of step with the mainstream of intellectual endeavour in the human sciences and in particular in the study of human communication; to our mutual impoverishment. The fundamental cause of this state of affairs is, we firmly believe, the normative approach – the setting up of a series of maxims consisting of do's and don'ts – which can be traced back to the orientation quoted above.

Likewise, Toury (1995) argues that too much emphasis has been placed on establishing and achieving norms, and that theorists have consequently tried to formulate preconceived principles which may or may not be relevant to any particular case. He admits the value and use of theoretical work in translation studies as a means to establish explanatory hypotheses – which is a more overarching concept of translation – but warns that the approach taken has to be purged of prescriptive bias:

> The apparatus for describing all types of relationship which may obtain between target and source items, segments, even whole texts, is one of the tools PTS [prescriptive translation studies] should be supplied with by the *theoretical* branch of the discipline. Fortunately, translation theory can offer great help here, due to a long tradition of preoccupation with problems of "equivalence" vs. "formal correspondence". What it must still do, however, is rid itself of vestiges of the *prescriptive* bias, which is only pertinent to the *applied* extensions of the discipline. (ibid. 85)

It should be noted that formal correspondence and other kinds of equivalence have been reanalysed and redefined by a number of scholars, and various other formulations have been suggested. This is reflected in dichotomies such as "formal equivalence" versus "dynamic equivalence", "overt" versus "covert" translation, "primary" versus "secondary" translation, "semantic" versus "communicative" translation, and "translation which preserves the function of the original" versus "translation which changes the function of the original" (Kußmaul 1985: 12). Nida (1964, in Pym 1992b: 221–226) argues that nineteenth-century translation was predominantly "literalist", "mimetic" or oriented towards "formal equivalence", and that the twentieth century has seen the emergence of a less literalist tendency. Pym (ibid. 225) points out that these widely held beliefs are "monolithic periodisations based on numerical majorities" and that the nineteenth century reveals a complex transfer pattern in different translation communities, concluding that Nida's is a superficial perception that is not based on substantial, systematic research. Chino (1983: 21) also states that Nida's portrayal is too simplistic. He argues that the concept of the desirable method of translation has been changing since the seventeenth century, affected by the contact between European and non-European languages, and by the development of linguistics. More issues of formal correspondence will be touched upon in 2.3.

By definition, in translation the original material inevitably contains something linguistically (and often culturally) foreign or unfamiliar to the TL system. Thus, the act of expressing the ST content using the TL immediately challenges the serviceability of the established TL. If faithfulness is judged at the semantic level, and readability or naturalness of the text is judged by the similarity to the native TL, whenever one of the two aspects (faithfulness or readability) starts to increase in a translation, it progressively threatens the other. This kind of trade-off model is remarkably evident in the case of English-Japanese translation, in which a translator often suffers because of (or enjoys) the wide linguistic and cultural gap between the SL and the TL. In this context, Japanese writers and researchers have also been active in the pursuit of identifying criteria for evaluating equivalence, but most of their arguments are often formulated independently of the discussions taking place within translation studies. As the translation studies activity which developed in Europe during the 1970s did not lead to a similarly active movement in Japan (Sato-Rossberg 2012), the debate has thus often ended up in a stalemate argument over whether a literary translation should be literal or whether there should be more allowance for adjustments (see Chapter 3).

2.3 The Formal-to-Dynamic Continuum

Evaluating translations is a universally popular activity. Corresponding to the two criteria of either (a) faithfulness or (b) readability/fluency, we find that two very general methods or attitudes are identified: literal translation and free translation. Nida (1964) formulated formal equivalence and dynamic equivalence on the basis of structural and semantic correspondence (later to be called functional equivalence), as two goals run parallel to literal and free translation. In this section, I shall consider how the classic dichotomies were presented in the original works by Nida (ibid.). His theories remain a landmark in both the Western translation studies communities and the Japanese translation community, although in two rather different ways. The following are the most quoted (and belaboured) passages by Nida (ibid. 159), but are still relevant to the discussion because they have had such significant impact upon some contemporary intellectuals' attitudes towards translation in Japan:

> Formal equivalence focuses attention on the message itself, in both form and content. In such a translation, one is concerned with such correspondences as poetry to poetry, sentence to sentence, and concept to concept. Viewed from this formal orientation, one is concerned that the message in the receptor language should match as closely as possible the different elements in the source language. This means, for example, that the message in the receptor culture is constantly compared with the message in the source culture to determine standards of accuracy and correctness.

Dynamic equivalence is, on the other hand, designed to generate the same effect on receptors as the original text provides to its receptors, without being concerned with formal word-for-word or sentence-to-sentence correspondence:

> In contrast, a translation which attempts to produce a dynamic rather than a formal equivalence is based upon "the principle of equivalent effect" (Rieu and Phillips, 1954). In such a translation, one is not so concerned with matching the receptor-language message with the source-language message, but with the dynamic relationship [...], that the relationship between receptor and message should be substantially the same as that which existed between the original receptors and the message. (ibid.)

This formulation made people aware of the dimension of creating a certain effect on, or response in, the receptor of the text and introduced the notion of dynamic equivalence to the field of translation studies as a valuable goal. Nida and Taber (1969: 1) later summed up the shift they desired, moving attention from the form of the text to its effect, as follows:

> The older focus in translating was the form of the message, and translators took particular delight in being able to reproduce stylistic specialties, e.g., rhythms, rhymes,

plays on words, chiasmus, parallelism, and unusual grammatical structures. The new focus, however, has shifted from the form of the message to the response of the receptor. Therefore, what one must determine is the response of the receptor to the translated message. This response must then be compared with the way in which the original receptors presumably reacted to the message when it was given in its original setting.

Even the old question: "Is this a correct translation?" must be answered in terms of another question, namely: "For whom?"

Nida and Taber (ibid. 173) clearly place more value on dynamic equivalence, subscribing to the view that by focusing too much on the formal features, the ST meaning is lost or distorted. Here, dynamic equivalence is believed to be more faithful to the original meaning in another sense, because it is considered to recreate the effect intended by the original author on the receptor of the TT (although the word faithful has traditionally been used in reference to literal translation). Thus, textual equivalence as an appropriate goal is identified here in the form of the intended effect. It is strongly emphasised nowadays that there is no such thing as perfectly literal or free translations anyway, and thus the two qualities should be perceived as part of a single continuum. As Hervey and Higgins (1992: 21) state, any TT can be located at some point on the continuous line between the most extreme literal quality and the most extreme free quality or between the two polarities of extreme SL bias and extreme TL bias.

Three years after Nida and Taber's original, in 1973, another book also titled *Hon'yaku – Riron to Jissen* [*The Theory and Practice of Translation*] was published in Tokyo. This is to a large extent a Japanese translation of the English version, but not of the entire work. Brannen, who joined Nida and Taber as a co-author in producing this version, emphasises that it addresses several problems specific to English-Japanese translation, and includes some Japanese examples, unlike the original. The groundwork research by Nida and Taber has been translated into a great number of languages and there is no doubt that their arguments have had a significant influence on the development of scientific discussion on translation.

In the preface to the Japanese version, Brannen (Nida et al. 1973: ix) points out that a peculiar style of Japanese, the so-called "translationese", has been developed and largely accepted by translators and receptors in

Japan. "Translationese", or *hon'yakuchō*, can have a profoundly negative connotation as it often refers to a style resulting from the unskilful handling of words. In this book, the kind of language used in the style clearly identified as translation is treated as a social dialect and will henceforth be called "translational language", "translational dialect" or "translationalese" rather than "translationese", to avoid value judgements. Brannen also states that Nida and Taber's advocacy of dynamic equivalence should have a rather special function in the context of the Japanese translation community, and should act as a trigger to push translation in a more effect-oriented direction. Their book offers the following text as a typical example of formal translation and the resulting "translationese" style, materialised in a Japanese text that is stiff and stylistically unattractive:

> Very few letters were written in those hard times that were not touching, especially those which fathers sent home. In this one, little was said of hardships endured, the dangers faced, or the homesickness conquered. (Alcott, *Little Women*, *Gaigokenkyūsha*, 31)

> 今読み聞かされるこの手紙には、よく耐えている艱難、物ともせず戦っている危険、また強いて抑えている郷愁については何にもほとんど言ってありませんでした。

> Ima yomikikasareru kono tegami niwa, yoku taete iru kannan, mono tomo sezu tatakatte iru kiken, mata shiite osaete iru kyōshū ni tsuite wa nannimo hotondo itte arimasendeshita. (Nida et al. 1973: 13)

Also, while discussing connotative meanings and associations of words, a translator needs to be careful to achieve a smooth communication flow. Nida et al. (ibid. 107, my translation) examine some Japanese product names, most of which are either loanwords or Japanese-made English words, and compare how differently Japanese and Americans would react emotionally towards the terms:

> For example, some names of Japanese cars such as *Toyopetto*, *Purinsu*, and *Sedorikku* are given to dogs or horses in America and they impart the impression that the cars could get spoiled and damaged. As for a coffee whitener named *Creap*, or a breakfast cereal called *Crap*, I do not know how to express the possible emotional reaction a native English speaker would have.

Purinsu, Sedorikku are transcribed versions of "Prince", and "Cedric" respectively. *Toyopetto* is the name of the main Toyota dealer chain, produced by combining "Toyota" and the suffix – *petto*, which originally comes from "pet" in English; intended presumably to suggest that their cars are lovable and easy to control. All three names seem to be viewed positively by the majority of people in Japan, and the reverse is found in the USA, as stated in the quotation. Taking into consideration the large-scale linguistic and cultural distance between Japanese and English, as indicated by these examples, the necessity to use the method of dynamic translation becomes immediately obvious, especially for texts whose purpose or intention is not to convey factual information.

The activity of Bible translation, which is Nida's primary concern, is no exception, and translating the Bible into Japanese is doubtless a complex task, often forcing a translator to take a flexible attitude and make decisions on controversial matters. For instance, Andō (1975) points out the multiple possibilities of interpretation in the Bible's text, taking the famous passage from Matthew 5:38 as an example ("an eye for an eye"). Nida et al. (1973) suggest adding a footnote to a translation for any non-Christian society stating that this phrase does not advocate retaliation, but rather the spirit of equal compensation. According to Andō (1975: 25), however, that is not enough, since the note would not refer to the Christian principle of non-resistance, which he believes the phrase implies. He thus asserts that their dynamic interpretation includes an element of cultural misunderstanding.

In literary translation, texts often incorporate particular stylistic effects which are significant in terms of the function of the text itself; hence, there is justification for transferring these effects to the TT. In cases where formally or semantically faithful translation would disturb the realisation of similar effects, translation aiming at functional equivalence does have validity as a method. However, a writing style derived from formally close translation from Western languages – especially English – is often used, and contributes to the formation of "translationese" in Japanese translations. This shows how remarkable the tolerance of "translationese" was (and, as I believe, still is) in the target community. The impact of formal rendering has indeed been immense, particularly in the development of the modern Japanese language, and thus Brannen (Nida et al. 1973) is right in attributing the persistent presence of "translationese" to the convention of seeking lexical and structural correspondence. There are, however, more layers to the phenomenon. The traditional use of strong "translationese" and its function in Japanese culture will be fully discussed in Chapter 8. At this stage, we can point out that Nida's arguments were introduced in the form of a specifically edited and revised version of the translation of one of his co-authored books, in which the necessity of dynamic translation is emphasised due to the extensive use of extreme "translationese" that could be found in practice. Nida and Taber's book has stimulated many scholars to discuss the practice of translation in Japan. Sato-Rossberg (2012) quotes Masukawa and Sawanobori, who translated Nida and Brannen's work, and points out that Japanese translators make strenuous efforts to communicate the exact meaning and style that is found in the ST, which is extremely difficult, and any hope of success is due to the translator's skill or "art". They argue that Nida accepted the concept of translation as "art", yet still advocated his scientific way of analysing it (ibid.).

Nida's impact on defining translation has been immense: he is frequently quoted and the value of his dynamic translation is rarely undermined in contemporary theoretical discussion in Japan, and elsewhere. This is certainly partly due to the value of the work itself, but also to the regrettable fact that only a limited number of books or articles on translation were translated into Japanese up until the 1980s, and therefore little attention was paid to them by practitioners. Since the translated works are in fact dispersed among many fields of research such as philosophy, literary studies and linguistics, they are rarely combined to be used in constructing an argument on translation in a systematically integrated manner. Thus, a peculiar *status quo* exists in Japan, whereby translation conventionally produces what is called "translationese" whenever that is an acceptable norm for the receptors, but coexists with the theoretical argument that dynamic equivalence and consequential readability should be achieved through translation. I will come back to this point in Chapter 8.

CHAPTER 3

Particular Challenges in Dealing with Translation between English and Japanese

When the focus is shifted from theoretical issues associated with Anglo-American translation to problems of translating from English into contemporary Japanese, several aspects are immediately apparent. The first point is that the evaluation standards shared in the particular community, and the extent to which translation meets them in reality, vary significantly according to the target community. Although it is never easy, or even appropriate, to identify a monolithic concept of the dominant values and norms in any culture, it is possible to find a prevailing convention in translating. Japanese has its own translation norms, and many of them are substantially different than those of the USA or European countries. A number of Western scholars, including linguists and Japanologists, have noticed that one frequently observes a wide discrepancy between the Japanese used in translations, and the Japanese normally used in similar situations. The unmistakable presence of a translational language often upsets foreign researchers, such as Brannen (Nida et al. 1973) and Grootaers (1979), since it is usually perceived as a sign of lack of sophistication in the communities they are familiar with – particularly in the case of literary translation.

Secondly, the fact that Japanese obviously has a weaker international profile than English generates a certain kind of tension between the two languages, the two cultures and the two texts. In discussing translation within the context of colonisation and postcolonial theory, Niranjana (1992: 2) states that translation into English tends to help a colonial power construct a rewritten image of the East: "Translation as a practice shapes, and takes shapes within, the asymmetrical relations of power that operate under colonialism". Uchiyama (2009) discusses how Fukuzawa Yukichi, a nineteenth-century scholar and translator, not only contributed to modernising the country through translating and importing Western concepts, but also ideologically framed Japan's relationship with other non-Western cultures. The tension between English and Japanese, together with Japan's constant love-hate relationship with the West (see section 3.1.2), is therefore reflected in the way translation is handled, although the institutionalised translational language is a strong feature of Japanese as TL in translation from stronger profile SLs – first Chinese and then Western languages, and lately English. When the SL and the TL are structurally and culturally remote from each other, as in this case, producing a translation which corresponds to the structural and semantic features of the ST without loss of readability and original pragmatic meaning, is inevitably a very difficult task (Seidensticker 1989). Following Bell (1991: 37), the term "pragmatic meaning" is used here in the sense of a meaning without which a piece of text would only convey a literal meaning and would lack situational or communicative value. In any case, the distance between the two languages and cultures gives a reasonable excuse, or at least an explanation, for having a translational character, as straightforward translation simply yields text that sounds clumsier. Translation can, however, be done in other ways, which means that there is a certain motivation for choosing this specific method. Let us look at the historical context in which this approach to translation developed in Japanese society.

3.1   A Brief History of Translation and Thoughts on Translation in Japan

Considering the special translation challenges that have been introduced above, it is relevant to place the current situation in the context of the long history of translation in Japan starting from the first translation of imported Chinese texts to the modern day.

3.1.1   Early Translations

Japan has a long history of translation dating back to the fifth or sixth centuries, when information started pouring in from China, together with the

Chinese character system. Translation is one of the essential factors which has brought the Japanese language to its current state of development, but identifying the earliest cases of translation with certainty is difficult because Japanese lacked a writing system, so people could not write down what they understood, or what they had possibly translated. Korean scholars, monks and students were the intermediaries who introduced the Chinese script to Japan, and this was one of the very first impacts which the act of translation had on the country. The complex activities of finding the meaning of a foreign word or expression, identifying its Japanese equivalent, and learning how it was written in Chinese (and then how the Japanese equivalent word or expression could be written using Chinese characters), were carried out simultaneously. Chinese characters, which are idiographic signs, were adapted as the writing tool in a careful and complex manner: they were used phonetically to write down Japanese, and they were also sometimes allocated to represent Japanese words with roughly corresponding meanings. By the ninth century, an effective annotation system, *kanbun kundoku*, had been established to enable the conversion of Chinese texts into Japanese, although the Japanese produced using this system was far from fluent. Strong linguistic foreignness (reflecting Chinese structures and lexemes) in translated texts was, however, not regarded as a problem, but as inseparable from the process and thus justified. In fact, Japanese with a heavy Chinese influence later developed into a solid writing style (*gabuntai*), which was regarded as elegant and high-brow, and was thus deployed in the literary and academic context. Although the system was invented specifically to cope with Chinese and was designed to be efficient when the language was read, it was later applied to translation from other languages and the principle of formal translation, which has been dominant in the country, seems to have its earliest roots here. Wakabayashi (1998) claims that the *kanbun kundoku* practice, used from the ninth century through to the nineteenth century, laid the foundations for the acceptance of "translationese" as a distinct variety of Japanese.

Two phonetic *kana* scripts were developed from the Chinese script (*katakana* in the eighth century, and *hiragana* in the tenth century). The Chinese script was, however, never abandoned. Of the two writing systems, *kanbun* (or Chinese) and Japanese, the former was used for scholarly works and conveyed a more formal and prestigious impression (Konishi 1993: 52–53).

During the Heian period (794–1185), *kanbun* was mainly used by male officials, while *hiragana* was used by female clerks, reflecting the distribution
of functions. This is the social and linguistic context in which *The Tale of
Genji*, one of the oldest Japanese classical novels, was written in *hiragana*
by Murasaki Shikibu, an eminent female writer in service at the imperial
court at the time. In the seventeenth century, in the middle of the feudal
Edo period (1603–1868), translation of Chinese literature was encouraged by the Tokugawa shoguns. Chinese literature had attracted virtually
no public interest since the end of the Heian period, but throughout the
Kamakura (1185–1333) and Muromachi periods (1336–1573) it regained
its appeal and had a significant impact on Japanese literature during this
time. Chinese popular literature in particular (the plots for which were
derived from Chinese and Japanese historical and political sources) was
translated, and had a large influence on the development of the Japanese
gesaku [novel] genre, especially *yomihon* (Haga 2000: 34). In these translations, various methods can be observed: Ogyū Sorai, a Confucian phi-
losopher heavily influenced by the way *Oranda tsūji* [Dutch translators]
translated at that time, identified two options for dealing with Chinese
texts (i.e. word-for-word and sense-for-sense), rejected the value of the
kundoku system, and instead urged the use of everyday Japanese (Sugimoto
1996: 143). He emphasised the significance of the context and stated that
the transfer of the intention within the text is more important than sticking to the old *kundoku* method. Similarly, Ogata Kōan, a renowned Edo
period scholar, pointed out that there are many translated texts which are
incomprehensible to most people, and accused the translators of obsessive
literalism (Morioka 1999). Hayashi Razan, an early Edo period scholar of
Confucian studies, frequently included words with no equivalent in the
source Chinese classics of his time. On the other hand, Asai Ryōi, another
renowned priest and novelist, relied on traditional word-for-word render-
ings in translation of literature. Likewise, later scholars such as Yamazaki
Ansai and Gotō Shizan attempted to produce a more literal rendering of
the original, and their technique was used until well into the Meiji period
(1868–1912) (Twine 1991: 40). These individual examples clearly indicate
that a variety of translation approaches were tried out in the early stages of
incorporating foreign materials into Japanese culture, with *kundoku* acting
as a pivotal, default method.

3.1.2 Encounters with the West

In the sixteenth and seventeenth centuries, the need for translation from Western languages arose with the arrival of Portuguese and Dutch merchants. The model of *kanbun kundoku* again allowed foreign texts to be read in the form of distorted Japanese (Shibauchi and Takai 1967: 56–57), and it was some time before people started translating them into more standard Japanese. The first Western materials translated were related to Christianity, such as the Catechism, and language textbooks. Considering the translation of Christian *contemptus mundi* [*Kontemutsusu • Munji*], for example, Matsuoka (1993, in Morioka 1999: 11) points out that translation was handled almost completely in a word-for-word fashion, and that the method was already very much like *kundoku*. Portuguese missionary João Rodriguez produced a Japanese grammar book for missionaries, later translated into Japanese (*Nihondaibunten*, 1604). The first Western work of literature to be translated was *Aesop's Fables* (*Esopo no Fabulas*) in 1593, and this was first translated from Latin into formal *bungo* [classical writing] style using *rōmaji*, then notably retranslated into colloquial Japanese using the Japanese writing systems developed by Fabian, an *Amakusa-ban* or Japanese missionary.

By the close of the seventeenth century, the Tokugawa Shogunate had decided to ban trade, and missionary activities in particular, to protect the country from foreign influence, as Christianity was regarded as a challenge to the feudal system. This political development, however, did not halt the act of translation of Western texts. Government officials and *Oranda tsūji* [Dutch interpreters], who worked for the Dutch merchants and were allowed to reside (as an exception) in the restricted area of Dejima in Nagasaki, continued to produce translations. Maeno Ryōtaku, a famous scholar of Dutch studies (*rangaku*), invented a system by which a Dutch text could be read through an extreme word-for-word method, very similar to the one used for *Kontemutsusu • Munji*, as noted above. He provided semantically corresponding Chinese characters alongside the Dutch text to be translated, after which the text looked like a pseudo-Chinese text (Morioka 1999: 38). This is called the *rankateiyakumonshiki* method and was the beginning of the tradition of translating Western languages using *kundoku*, which led to the formation of modern Japanese *hon'yakuchō* [translationese] (ibid.). Many of the texts translated during this period were of a non-literary nature, such as a Dutch (originally Latin) anatomical work translated by Motoki Shōdayū (later Ryōi) in 1682 (*Pinax Microcosmographicus*). These were subsequently translated into classical Chinese, because of their scientific and academic importance (Sugimoto 1959, in Tsujimura 1991: 358–390). It is worth mentioning that an *oranda tsūji*, Motoki Yoshinaga, who introduced Copernican theory to Japan by translating astronomical works, wrote one of the first theoretical essays on translation methods, *Wage Reigon* in *Taiyōkyūriryōkaisetsu*, which was published in 1798 (Sugimoto 1959, in Yamamoto 1965: 62). Ban Kōkei's *Yakumon no Jō* [Article on Translation] in *Kunitsufumi Yoyo no Ato* also appeared in this period. One of Ban's (1777) arguments was that translation should identify the sense [*omomuki*] of the text, "using (one's) heart (*kokoro o mochii*)" (Sugimoto 1996: 69–75). Although Ban did not advocate dynamic translation as such in his article, he encouraged flexibility in choosing words, and also promoted the writing of *wabun* (texts in *hiragana*, or combining more than one system) rather than *kanbun* (texts in *kanji*). These writings are among the earliest theoretical works on translation in the country.

As research on grammar developed during the late eighteenth and nineteenth centuries, translation was often done using a new method, and the classification of each word was clearly recognised in the TT. Specific expressions were established in the process, for example, for relative pronouns which do not exist in Japanese (e.g. for the English term "which", the Japanese formula of *suru tokoro no* was used as a modifier instead). Obara Tōru's *Sōyaku Garamachika* emerged during this time, as a guide book for translating Dutch using the classic *kundoku* method (Morioka 1999: 25). A Dutch-Japanese dictionary, *Dōyaku Haruma* or the *Doeff Halma*, by Hendrik Doeff, in which a rare colloquial style is observed, was also completed in 1833. Then, in the nineteenth century, during the last phase of the Edo period, yet another translation method emerged. When Dutch grammar textbooks were translated, explanatory parts were roughly translated using Japanese classical style, while example sentences were strictly and literally translated like *kundoku*. This method of compromise continued to be used for dealing with texts written in English, which supplanted Dutch as the dominant SL, as the study of English (*yōgaku*) developed (Morioka 1999: 25). A change in the official Shogunate attitude towards translation took place during the closing decade of Tokugawa rule: the authority promoted translation more eagerly after the first encounters with the Western powers and subsequent pressures from them (Clements 2015: 6).

3.1.3 The Meiji Period (1868–1912) and Afterwards

Following the Meiji Restoration, which brought back imperial rule in Japan, the Meiji period saw an abundance of translations from Western languages, such as English (which replaced Dutch after Japan was fully opened up), German, Russian and French. Their influence on society was immense and has attracted much attention from scholars in the field. Translation and Japanese modernity are discussed in Levy (2010), in a collection of essays by various scholars and in a wide range of perspectives and relevant topics focusing on translation in the post-1860s Japan. The translation of political texts began to flourish early in this period. Western thought was introduced during the wave of modernisation through the medium of translation by intellectuals such as Nakae Chōmin (who translated *Du Contrat Social* by Jean-Jacques Rousseau, *Min'yakuyakukai*, 1882) and Nakamura Masanao (who translated *On Liberty* by John Stuart Mill, *Jiyū no Ri*, 1872). They generally reproduced both the content and form of the original texts using a structurally and semantically faithful method, also used in the translations of language textbooks. This thereby produced stiff Japanese, although a more fluent version was sometimes appended (Bekku 1979: 38–39). Previously unknown concepts found in the original texts inevitably forced translators either to invent new words or compounds (often consisting of morphemes of Chinese origin) or borrow existing Chinese words (Seeley 1991: 136). Their efforts to recreate not only lexical items but also grammatical features of foreign languages also affected written Japanese beyond translation, playing a significant role in the formation of modern Japanese, and the products are nowadays regarded as non-translational, native Japanese (Kamei et al. 1966: 175–179). An exception was Fukuzawa: he represented the few translators who doubted the blind advocacy of linguistic foreignisation. In *Fukuzawa Zenshūshogen* (1897), he questions why people use *shikakubatta moji* [square, stiff-sounding words] in translating Western materials, and insists on using *odayakanaru nihongo* [(gently) flowing Japanese]. It is ironic that when translating Western political texts, he coined or imported some extraordinary words, such as *dokuitsukojin* (独一個人) for "individual", and revealed the strict limitations of "gently flowing Japanese" in the act of translating between Japanese and Western thought at that time (Yanabu 1982: 34–41). As Nae (1999) argues while quoting Yanabu (1982), translation during the period of the Meiji Restoration created the intellectual background against which Japan became acquainted with new concepts such as society and the individual.

3.1.4 Literary Waves from the West

Beginning with *Robinson Crusoe's Record of Wanderings* (Usami 1989), numerous Western literary works, including poetry, were translated into Japanese during the Meiji period. Translators were often writers themselves. In the early years, the translation method employed in literary translation tended to lean to freer adaptation, but the principle of literalness gradually began to be adopted by the writer-translators. Examples include Futabatei Shimei (Ivan S. Turgenev's *The Rendezvous*), Mori Ōgai (Hans Christian Andersen's *Improvisatoren*) and Morita Shiken (Jules Verne's *Deux Ans de Vacances*). Morita was known as *Hon'yaku ō* [the king of translators], especially after he advocated a more literal approach in his preface to *Keishidan*, a translation of Edward Bulwer-Lytton's *Kenelm Chillingly*. In the preface to *Hon'yaku no Kokoroe*, Morita emphasised the significance of the influence of foreign literary styles on Japanese literature and strongly supported *seimitsu yaku* [precise translation] (Akiyama 1998: 107–108). Their attitudes towards the strategies used in translation are covered in great detail in various works in the field of Japanese studies and translation studies, including Cockerill (2003), Kawamura (1981) and Mizuno (2007).

In the Taishō period (1912–1926), Iwano Hōmei also supported word-for-word translation, which introduced a new word order into Japanese (Kawamura 1981, Inoue 1994). In the preface to his translation of Arthur

Symons's *The Symbolist Movement in Literature* (1913, in Kawamura 1981), he decries both lazy free translation and the peculiar literal form of translation that had formerly been in vogue. The translation of certain Western literary writings using a uniform style to give them a common image was a method used beyond the translation of contemporary popular fiction (see Chapters 7 and 8).

It was out of these formal or literal translation methods, which writers propounded or actually practised, that a new writing style grew, and by the 1890s seemed to have been developed from a fusion of foreign styles and existing Japanese (Shibauchi and Takai 1967, Sugimoto 1960). Writers began to find it inappropriate to translate Western literature written in colloquial style into the old literary-style Japanese. At the same time, it changed the writing style, which had up until that time been classical Japanese or Chinese (Twine 1991: 47). The new colloquial style which they formulated was not only used in translations, but also in all kinds of original Japanese literature which were influenced by European works (Keene 1979: 27–28). The writer-translators were stimulated by Western literary works, and this led to the development of revolutionary literary movements in Japanese *bundan* or literary circles. Among the recognisable modes which influenced style are: Realism, introduced by Tsubouchi Shōyō (*Shōsetsushinzui*); Romanticism (strongly coloured by Christianity, *The New Testament* having been translated into Japanese in the 1880s), introduced by Mori Ōgai and Kitamura Tōkoku; and Naturalism, introduced by Shimazaki Tōson (*Hakai*) and Tayama Katai (*Futon*) (Konishi 1993: 192–200). Writers concerned with new issues, such as personal identity and social problems, often required and developed a new writing style. A series of phenomena, such as the advocacy of *shintaishi* or new-style poetry, the movement for writing with *kana* syllabaries and the *genbun'icchi undō* [movement for the unification of written and spoken languages], which were in many ways triggered by the spread of translations of Western texts, could be regarded as a kind of enlightenment movement in the form of literature (Konishi 1993: 192–193). Tsubouchi (1928, in Bekku 1983: 71, my translation) initially translated from an extreme literalist position, but then gradually came to believe that one needed to be more flexible, especially when dealing with idioms and metaphors:

> A characteristic of Shakespearean works is the quality of the word usage and style, and they make the readers or audiences instinctively feel the characters' disposition, mood or emotions ... So the factor requiring most attention in translation is the transfer of the connotations of the words, such as the flavour of noble/humble, elegant/vulgar, wise/silly, decent/indecent or relaxed/panicky.

According to Twine (1991), the rise of the *genbun'icchi* movement was probably the most significant outcome in this period, although it should not be forgotten that there was opposition to this movement, and a number of heated debates were held about the reforms, as exemplified by Ozaki Kōyō's advocacy of a return to the traditional use of classical style in literary writing.

Particularly noteworthy was the theory on untranslatability presented by Uchimura (1899, in Kamei 1988: 77, my translation), a Christian propagandist famous for his non-church movement:

> European languages and Japanese are completely different in their forms, language structure, and organisation of words. The difficulties of transferring their beauty to us and our beauty to them, bridging the gap between people who have different cultures, different religions, and a different view of life, are too great for people who are not involved in the act.

The influence of Western theories of translation was scarcely visible in Japanese writing for a long time, particularly outside the theoretical field of translation, but there were in fact many potential interfaces. In his *Kaichō-on written in 1905*, Ueda Bin (in Kawamura 1981: 29, my translation), known for initiating symbolism in poetry, criticises the word-for-word method which was fashionable at the time:

> I confess that I have an identical view on translating poetry to Dante Gabriel Rosetti, as expressed in the preface to his translation of ancient Italian poems. Anyone who tries to transplant the beauty of a foreign country should not sacrifice concepts unknown to the target culture for the sake of the techniques of poetry in the target language, which is already full of established expressions. On top of that, word-for-word translation is not necessarily faithful.

Thus, Ueda was aware of, and interacting with, Rosetti's (1861) thoughts on translation: one of the strong motivations for translating poetry into a new language is to acquaint people with different conceptions of beauty.

Since writing poetry is not a strict science, translating it literally is not important. He calls it literalness, but not fidelity. The terms used, and the original and the translation are, needless to say, not identical (Rosetti 1861, in Kawamura 1981: 29), and there are other possibilities for seeking one of the goals of translation, namely being faithful to the original (Kawamura 1981: 28–29). In 1895, in an article published in *Teikokubungaku*, the most academically respected literary journal of the time, Ueda (1895: 98–99), a supporter of government-directed language standardisation and of the use of colloquial style in writing, criticised the explanatory method and free rendering used by the German scholar Karl Florenz in his translation of a collection of *waka* [thirty-one-syllable Japanese poems] into German. In his response to this attack, Florenz (1895a: 12–16, my translation) introduced Goethe's theories about the tasks and methods of translation, which were regarded as rather revolutionary by the Japanese world of literary criticism:

> The essential mission of translation is not in deciding on the choice of words (a matter of secondary importance) but in precisely transplanting the thoughts, emotions and poetic impression of the original. [...]

> Translation of poetry which is too literal is rather dangerous. It is not only ineffective but actually tends to damage the spirit of the original.

Florenz (1895b: 78) tries to validate this argument by stressing some literary peculiarities of Japanese poetry and states that the internal soul and spirit interpreted from the text must be given priority over the form which carries them. This exchange of comments between the two scholars developed into an intense dispute over attitudes towards literary translation, known as *the Ueda-Florenz hon'yaku ronsō* [The Ueda-Florenz translation dispute]. Thus, one of the traditional core issues in translation – that of formal versus interpretive translation – temporarily attracted attention, but the focus soon shifted to the assumed uniqueness of Japanese poetry. Unfortunately, these arguments did not evolve into a constructive debate. Translation has since been discussed from the viewpoint of literary criticism (Kimura 1975), linguistics (Andō 1975, Imai 1975, Kunihiro 1981) and semiotics (Isoya 1980) among others, but literature in the field of literary criticism has often focused on a particular author, translator or literary work, and not found a comfortable venue for a continuing debate.

Numerous foreign literature works were translated during the Taishō and Meiji periods. Almost every work of so-called "world masterpieces" had been translated by the beginning of the Shōwa Era (1926–1989). People often preferred reading foreign mystery and detective novels and children's literature in the translated version, not the original. As Japanese novelists were inspired by those translated works, they started to produce detective and horror novels of their own.

From the Meiji Era to the beginning of the Shōwa Era, diplomatic negotiation was executed solely by the elite, and professional translators and interpreters did not yet exist. As officially appointed interpreters spoke Japanese fluently, they worked as interpreters in Japanese foreign consulates. Professional military interpreters were needed during the war period, and some people were forced to work as military interpreters; others became interpreters voluntarily. Some found themselves torn between two cultures, for example, Watanabe Kiyoshi in *Small Man of Nanataki* (1972) and Tokizane Hiroshi in *Gen'ei no Tairen* (1978).

During the Second World War, socialist translations were censored by the militarist Japanese government. In addition, many writers were employed as journalists by the government to report on military movements. These factors created an abnormally complicated situation for both translators and writers, and little high-quality literature was produced. Dazai Osamu, a successful early post-war writer, was fully aware that Western lifestyle had rapidly become established in a material or superficial sense, but that Western thought and morals had been neither fully understood nor accepted. The social tensions created by the coexistence of two value systems – old and new, Japanese and Western – is accurately described in a colloquial style, using many Western words written in *katakana*, in Dazai's novel *Shayō*, which was published shortly after the Second World War. As can be seen from Kawabata Yasunari's *Yukiguni* and *Senbazuru*, which appeared during the late 1940s and 1950s, Japanese fiction gradually pulled itself together and got into its stride in the continuing post-war confusion (Keene 1979: 123–124). The shift from importing and translating European literature to importing and translating American literature was a major feature of the post-war period.

After Japan's defeat in the Second World War, Europeanism was still visible in Japan. Although German culture was in the mainstream during the Taishō period, American and French culture came into fashion after 1945. As French and English were languages of Japan's opposing countries during the Second World War, a large number of American and French literature works were translated on the rebound. Famous French novelists of the nineteenth and twentieth centuries, such as Stendhal, Balzac, Proust and Gide were translated in this period. Also, the philosophical books of Camus and Sartre became popular, with Camus's translated version of *L'Étranger* [*The Stranger*] becoming a best-seller in Japan (Hara and Nishinaga 2000). French literature was popular between the late 1960s and the early 1970s and, during this period, many Japanese people seemed to be more attracted to translated works, including novels and movies by European and American writers and directors, than by Japanese works (ibid.).

It is impossible to attempt to sum up in a generic manner how Japanese intellectuals continued to handle foreign texts in translation. A variety of methods have been invented and adopted throughout the history of interaction with foreign cultures. It has to be pointed out that the Japanese have always maintained the *kundoku* (or modified *kundoku*) system, through which foreign text is transformed into a classical narrative style remote from standard Japanese, as a default translation method. More natural methods have continued to challenge the traditional principle, producing a new writing style and a literary mode represented by *genbun'icchi*. At first sight, contemporary literary translations certainly appear free of the effects of the old approach, yet many of the translated texts in different literary genres reflect the ongoing battle between the deeply rooted word-for-word principle and a more dynamic approach. The following section examines the thoughts that contemporary scholars and translators have on translation.

3.2 Some Contemporary Writings on Translation in Japan

In this section, I will roughly classify contemporary literature on translation into four categories: (1) theoretical, prescriptive writings by translators or researchers on how translation should be carried out; (2) descriptive analysis by researchers, which does not exclude writings on their own experiences in translation; (3) practical manuals on how to translate, mostly by experienced professional translators; (4) commentaries and criticism on individual works of translation. Some overlap is inevitable – for instance, works which belong to the first category often include tips and ideas about practical problems. To give an idea of current writing on translation in Japan, some examples are included from each category. As mentioned earlier, despite the high interest in translation as a key cultural activity, there has not been a huge amount of theoretical discussion and many of the arguments are submitted independently of the development of translation studies in the West. The noteworthy feature found in earlier research on translation is the interaction between Japanese researchers and a limited number of Western scholars, such as Dryden (in Biguenet and Schulte 1989), Nida (1964) and Savory (1957), whose works were translated into Japanese relatively early and were widely read by academics involved in writing on translation. On the other hand, a vast number of publications on issues concerning translation, intended for general reading, are regularly published in Japan. Books offering secret tips revealed by experienced translators, and comments or criticism of individual translation works make up the bulk of these. The lack of descriptive, statistical or analytical perspective, and an endless stream of individual examples and anecdotes are common features of this type of publication. Books of this kind attract a large readership and are indicative of the high level of interest people have in translations and the act of translating.

Among a number of experienced translators who are aware of the various problems involved in transforming meanings between English and Japanese, Bekku (1979: 162–163, my translation), while basically approving of Nida's theory of equivalent effects, gives the following general guidelines:

> Japan and Western countries are extremely different with regard to their cultural environment. [...] Nowadays, mutual understanding is fairly widespread, but even so there are bound to be many discrepancies. Translators have to be fully aware of them. What they need to do is, having grasped what a word or gesture signifies, to transform it into a Japanese word or gesture if that is possible, or when that would be going too far, to convey the meaning clearly by some method or other. They should not be satisfied with achieving only a surface resemblance.

When looking at other translators' work, Bekku noticed many problems in texts translated from English, including common mistakes and awkward discourse (see also Yanabu 1979, Grootaers 1979, Satō 2007). He often blames "big-name professors" who translate foreign academic books into obscure Japanese, claiming that although they might be specialists in their field, they are unaware of the complexity of translation. According to his argument, academic translations – as well as literary translations – should be in a natural, easy-to-read style (Bekku 1979, 1983). This claim is rather interesting, because such a smooth style does not necessarily match the current norm for Japanese original writings in the corresponding genre. Japanese academic or informational texts typically contain stiff, difficult-to-read sentences inherited from language used in translations originally from Chinese. People actually complain about the difficulty of reading such texts, and criticise them when the stiffness exceeds an acceptable level. Still, in fields of study such as law, science and economics, people (both from within and outside the fields) regard academic writing as not for a broad readership, but aimed strictly at specialists, and accordingly accept the peculiar writing style as mysteriously respectable and untouchable. When translators, commentators or researchers, including Bekku, take a prescriptive attitude towards translating into a natural style, the criterion of naturalness does not seem to depend on the norms for the original style in the genre. It often refers to a style which does not require people of average intellect to make an exceptional effort, or possess technical literacy, in order to read and understand the text. Thus, their goal is set beyond the norm of the native writings, although they paradoxically tend to claim that language in translation should not be special.

I will now introduce a dispute which took place in the 1970s and has parallels with the Ueda-Florenz dispute in the Meiji period. In the Hara-Kitamikado dispute in *The Asahi Journal*, Hara Takuya and Kitamikado Jirō exchanged opinions over the value of formal equivalence. Hara (1979: 65, my translation) compared Kitamikado's translation of Tolstoy's short stories with translations published earlier by Yonekawa and with his own, which had been criticised in Yonekawa's:

> [I]t is clear to anybody who reads it that Kitamikado's version is the easiest to understand [...] Here I cannot help posing the question of whether it is enough for a literary translation to be obvious at first sight. To my regret, I cannot quote the ST here, but I do not understand where one can find (for example) words such as "*tsuka no ma*

no" or "*akkenai*" in the sentence which Tolstoy wrote. In the first place, the original is written using a negative construction [...] Mr. Kitamikado has carried out a free and radical translation, which deserves the title of linguistic mistranslation, and has ignored the style and rhythm that are unique to Tolstoy.

In his refutation, Kitamikado (ibid., my translation) calls the word-for-word translation or "the principle of sticking to the original", which Hara favours, a *tenuki* [lazy] construction:

> [H]owever tedious Tolstoy's style may be, he never wrote incomprehensible text. We should not spare any effort to come as close as possible to what he would have written if he had been Japanese. What unskilful Japanese writer would write such mysterious language as is found in translations by Yonekawa or Hara? Only by extracting "x" from Tolstoy's text, and transferring the "x" into Japanese, can one produce a translation which essentially grasps the spirit of the original literature, even if the form is linguistically changed.

Clearly the dispute took place without reference to any theoretical backbone available in translation studies or other fields. Just like Ueda-Florenz in 1878, it follows the pattern into which a literalist and a non-literalist can easily fall when discussing ideal translation in the context of literary criticism of Japanese translation. The presence of "x" in their debate is intriguing. It seems to refer to the literary essence that many Western theorists value in propagating the naturalisation of translation, so as to discourage the production of translations with a veil of exotic oddness.

Subsequently, Itagaki (1995) advocated the establishment of studies on translation as an academic discipline in Japan, for the practical and theoretical understanding of translation. It should, he claimed, present norms and standards, particularly for commercial translation which is always in substantial demand. Industrial translation covers various fields, such as law, patents, business, management, finance, advertising and journalistic articles. He clarifies the nine maxims of respectable translation conventionally accepted by the community as: (1) one should understand and translate the ST author's intention, (2) one should make no addition/omission with respect to the ST author's intention, (3) the TT should be in correct Japanese, (4) one should transfer the style of the ST to the TT, (5) one should give an appropriate title to the TT, (6) the TT should be readable, (7) one should give adequate consideration to cultural differences between the SL and the TL, (8) the TT should look tidy and solid as a piece of text, (9) one should target specific readers (Itagaki 1995: 25–64). He also presents another five (rather ambiguous) axioms of translation ability that are traditionally respected in the community, saying that translation ability is proportional to: (1) the number of words the translator has learned, (2) the idioms the translator has learned, (3) the range of grammar the translator has learned, (4) the reading and writing ability in the first and second languages which the translator has acquired, (5) the width and depth of the translator's knowledge of extralinguistic matters (ibid. 74–90). Itagaki's work being one of the few efforts in Japan at that time to employ Western theories to generate rules for translation by the Japanese, he utilises these maxims and axioms, together with Dryden's Theory of Translation, as a yardstick to measure the quality of translations. He demonstrates practical methods for satisfying the criteria in practice (for example, how to deal with antecedents, pronouns and colons in English) and attempts to establish translation-teaching methods based on theoretical criteria. The work is relevant, although its scope is restricted to industrial translation.

Let us turn to some commentators who take a more descriptive and linguistic approach to the field. In *Hikakunihongoron*, Yanabu (1979: 221, my translation) sums up his observations on the general tendency in the Japanese translation community to value formally corresponding equivalence over more paraphrastic translation:

> It is generally believed that a direct translation is faithful to the original, although not skilful, compared to a paraphrastic one. By "faithful," people mean that it communicates the original meaning correctly.

> When ordinary Japanese readers look at a piece of literal translation, on the other hand, they immediately realise that it is a translation. It is difficult to read and understand. People who are responsible for translation, however, think that when a text faithful to the original is hard to comprehend, it is primarily because the level of difficulty of the original meaning is too high. It is preferable to translate in such a way that the receptor will understand the text without difficulties, but it is not necessary, because it is done only for the sake of convenience, taking into account the level of the reader's ability to understand. Generally speaking, this is the way people think.

Yanabu maintains that literal translation is, in the main, historically pre-ferred in Japan due to the uncritical appreciation of foreign cultures among the people. He uses the term *chokuyaku* [direct translation] following the everyday Japanese usage to refer to a method of translation in which there is a word-for-word correspondence between units of the ST and units of the TT. However, the term is also used in a wider sense to refer to a seman-tically faithful translation, as in Gutt's (1991: 122) terminology. However, Yanabu's usage of the term does not encompass translation without an intermediate translation, or translation within the Japanese community into the translator's native language. Because of this ambiguity, the term is avoided in this book, except for when it occurs in quotations. Yanabu also clarifies common properties of the so-called *hon'yakuchō* or "translationese" of Japanese from a linguistic point of view (see section 3.1).

In the 1970s, the theoretical analysis of the process from the decom-position of a ST to the restructuring of the TT was introduced to Japan through Nida's works. Nevertheless, little systematic research was seen on the question of how productively, and to what extent, Japanese transla-tion materials can be processed using his classical models. Naruse (1978) presents the Three-Layer Analysis method, a combination of the analytical techniques of Nida's back-transformation and Savory's (1957) three points of reference (what is said, what is meant and how it is said), and attempts to analyse the correspondences found between a ST and its TT. The three layers referred to are: (1) expression, (2) information and (3) presupposi-tion, which correspond to style of expression, cognitive act and cultural aspect respectively. Naruse claims that the method helps us identify the content from the expressions, observe typical ways of thinking specific to the language and culture, and realise the necessity or possibility of using certain expressions in the language.

Isoya (1980) is one of the researchers who seems to have been fully aware of the developments of translation studies outside his own country during the 1980s, and of the importance of adding to the discussion by offer-ing descriptive analysis of Japanese translation. In particular, he discusses translation from the points of view of the fields of semiotics, linguistics and literary studies. In presenting his summary of the structure of the field of translation studies, he roughly divides the theoretical issues into three categories: (1) issues of contrastive linguistics; (2) issues of correspondence based on the arguments in comparative culture; and (3) issues of evaluation, which is the contrastive assessment of the ST and the TT, and which involves comparisons between different TTs and different translators (ibid. 23). He advocates active discussion on translation theory, claiming that:

> A translation theorist is expected to try not only to construct a formal structure of translation theories and a model of the translation process, but also to describe a certain correspondence between a foreign language and his/her mother tongue and to generalise it from the points of view of contrastive linguistics and comparative cultural studies. [...] in order to activate discussion on translation theories, I encourage the readers to work on these. (ibid., my translation)

He also mentions the productivity of structurally or lexically straightforward translation and argues that the consequence of the introduction of fresh and unfamiliar linguistic devices – which inevitably takes place in the case of literal translation – can be recognised as progress or evolution in the TL culture. The value of the word-for-word method is not only in the formal equivalence in the TT; a further benefit is gained by the transference of the forms in the ST which should not be neglected. Isoya's (ibid. 44, my translation) ambition for transference of the form is built on Nida's classic argument for the transference of the meaning:

> Nida asserts that communicating the meaning is more important than the form. It certainly is. In the translation of literature, however, this is a matter of course, and in addition we should tackle the transference of the forms. Only when we have succeeded in this task are new words born.

According to Isoya, translating the meaning, that is, the content of the literary work as a whole, is the primary task in literary translation. However, mirroring the form in the TT is an even higher goal, since it not only upgrades equivalence to the level of linguistic features and their effects, but also enriches the TL as a means of expression. The TT receptor can have a new linguistic and cultural experience created through the interaction of the SL and the TL within the framework of the TL. The unquestioning acceptance of the canon which values fluency, and as a consequence, domestication of the ST, easily denies the potential for creativity. He recognises foreignisation as key to progress for the Japanese language, who experienced a stormy and stimulating encounter with Western languages in the Meiji period after a long isolation and engaged in a subsequent, and rather radical, transformation of their own language. The descriptive or analytical approach taken by researchers such as Isoya provides a useful contrast with the large number of writers engaged in providing "How-to" books, which are not discussed in this work. Nakamura (1989: 46, my translation), who is an influential contemporary literary translator mainly in the field of science fiction and popular literature, claims that:

> One [a translator] is supposed to "follow the original", being neither too direct, nor too paraphrastic. Once I translated *The Floating Admiral*, a relay novel by Chesterton, Agatha Christie, Dorothy Sayers and others. One reader pointed out, "Mr. Nakamura, you have changed the style of the original author." I was surprised as I was completely unaware of this. This is a good example of being successful in "following the original". If you follow the original, the translation naturally changes.

The shortage of descriptive translation analysis in Japan has not yet been addressed. To understand how the Japanese treat alien elements within their culture, we need to face reality and come up with a prescriptive approach based on the true nature of translation.

3.3 Significance of the Investigations: Japanese as a Target Language

Investigating problems in Japanese translation is useful for two main reasons: firstly, as mentioned at the beginning of this chapter, relatively little systematic research has been conducted on translation between English and minoritised languages, including Japanese, compared to the amount of research published on translation between the major Western languages. Baker (1992) attempts to identify potential sources of difficulties in translation between English and non-European languages, such as Arabic, Chinese and Japanese, and offers possible strategies for resolving them. She elaborates on the importance of the investigation of the translation process from or into non-European languages, stating that:

> The emphasis on non-European languages may seem unusual, but it is meant to counterbalance the current preoccupation with European languages in translation studies. It is high time the European translation community realised that there is life – and indeed translation – outside Europe and that professional non-European translators use a range of strategies that are at least as interesting and as useful as those used by European translators. Moreover, it is particularly instructive for translators of any linguistic background to explore difficulties of translation in non-European languages because the structure of those languages and their cultural settings raise important issues that could otherwise be easily overlooked in discussions of language and translation. (ibid. 7)

From a linguistic point of view, Radó (1987: 12–13) likewise emphasises the importance of focusing on translation from a major, widely spread and widely spoken *world language* into a *language of limited diffusion* (LLD) and vice versa:

> Literatures written in LLDs also have their place in that world-wide complex, and their role can be made effective only by translation from LLDs. [...]

> Translations from an LLD are a decisive factor in the history of the cultural relations of the country in question. The methods by which literature written in an LLD is and has been translated cannot be a matter of indifference.

Although LLD is a term used for small or minoritised languages by the Fédération Internationale des Traducteurs, Radó (1987: 6) additionally defines it as a language whose diffusion is "intensive, centripetal, limited", whereas a world language has, by contrast, "extensive, centrifugal, universal" diffusion. Translation between an LLD like Japanese and a world language is, according to Radó (ibid.), not only problematic in itself because of their distance (physical, cultural and linguistic), but also because it causes secondary problems, such as the necessity for indirect translation through a third, intermediate language or rough translation. For Radó (ibid. 8), a so-called rough translation is used mostly for translating poetry, and it consists of "a rendering of the original work in TL prose – it is a literal translation. As an instrument for producing an artistic TL, rough translation can be compared to attempting to paint a copy of a picture without ever having seen the original, simply by reading a verbal description of it". The effects and influences of major languages on LLD TL culture are immense and complex, especially in literary translation, and much remains to be revealed concerning how these languages act in translation.

The situation has improved slightly since 1987, but not considerably. In recent years, more attempts to take up less common languages have been made in studies of literary translation, but for now the level is still far from substantial. In particular, more research needs to be undertaken from a descriptive point of view. One issue which has been ignored in discussing Japanese translations is how norms differ according to the genre or the linguistic makeup of the ST. In his 1995 book, Toury proposes the importance of establishing laws of translational behaviour but researchers have not yet come up with adequately substantiated answers to the question: which behavioural patterns are witnessed in the Japanese translations of English texts? Toury (ibid. 259) states:

> Granted, in translation studies, very little conscious effort has so far been invested in attempts to establish such laws. However, as soon as the applicability of science to the complex of problems clustered around translation has been accepted as such, there is no reason why the formulation of laws should not mark the horizon here too. Moreover, any quest for laws would seem desirable not only in terms of the discipline itself, but from the point of view of its applied extensions as well, to the extent that the underlying rationale favours basing them on *reality* rather than on some kind of wishful thinking.

In his attempt to exemplify laws of translational behaviour, Toury (ibid. 278) discusses the law of interference, among others, in the following terms:

> Tolerance of interference – and hence the endurance of its manifestations – tends to increase when translation is carried out from a "major" or highly prestigious language/culture, especially if the target language/culture is "minor" or "weak" in any other sense.

Identifying tendencies and regularities in translation between English and Japanese would provide some useful guidelines for grasping exactly into what kind of language the English texts are translated, and for ascertaining what function is collectively given to it in the TL cultural settings. It could potentially generate more laws eventually applicable to other pairs of languages that fall into the category of major-minor language translation.

The historical background of translation into Japanese adds to the importance of studying it. As mapped out in section 3.1, translation has played a significant role in a number of crucial moments throughout Japan's history. Japan's writing system was developed based on Chinese, and Japanese has also been considerably influenced by it in its structural and lexical facets; the impact beyond language on Japan of this advanced neighbouring country was enormous, ranging from law to literature. Later, by interacting with Western languages, including Dutch, Portuguese, German, French and English, the country went through a similar process of adapting itself to various sources and degrees of "otherness". Otherness may be expressed by a group of people, or by their language or culture, show differences from "our group", and when present in an out-group, it can mark the identity of the in-group to which one belongs, since it does not share the same characteristics (Lévi-Strauss 1966, Anderson 1983, Chanlat et al. 2013).

Japanese is a language remote from Western languages in the structural, lexical and cultural sense, and translation of those languages into Japanese has historically created repeated pressure to modify and modernise the country. The activity of translation is no less significant in contemporary Japan, because, for Japanese monolinguals, it is still the key to other cultures. In discussing the development of modern Japanese and how it relates to translation from Western languages, Yanabu (1982) touches upon vocabulary imported through translation from Western literature since the Meiji period. He cites as examples several words in current Japanese, such as *shakai* [society], and *sonzai* [existence], and discusses the process by which these words were invented with only vague meanings (without users understanding the precise ST meaning), and hence how new Japanese words with abstract concepts emerged. Some vocabulary from Western languages was absorbed into modern Japanese with modifications, and this in turn catalysed changes in its new host. Yanabu (1979: 12) turns to the structural aspect and states that:

> Translation changes and recreates the native language. It alters each word and produces idioms. Moreover, it even changes the whole sentence structure. Or rather, I think that it is more appropriate to say that what we nowadays understand by "a

sentence" is a product of translation from the Meiji period on and was created by translational thinking.

He argues that structural units, such as the sentence, emerged in Japanese in the early nineteenth century, when the translation of Western languages started to flourish. The Japanese language originally had a unit which contained one or more *kakarijoshi* [propositional particles], such as *wa* and *koso*, and a *musubi* [corresponding end]. It was not necessarily independent of other parts of a bigger unit, such as a paragraph or text, and thus did not require a full-stop marker at the end. Translating English, for instance, has inevitably introduced the stricter, more solid concept of the sentence, and officially authorised Japanese grammar accordingly came to recognise the *bun*, a unit equivalent to the sentence. The ambiguity of sentence boundaries, however, remains a characteristic of Japanese today. Yanabu (ibid. 19) quotes the following example of such a unit from Kawabata's *Izu no Odoriko* and its English translation, *The Izu Dancer* (1964), by Seidensticker.

Original text	Translation
"Te wa itaku nai kai" *Odoriko wa taiko o utsu toki no utsukushii* *temane o shite mita.* *"Itaku nai (ryaku)"*	"Your hands aren't sore?" The girl went through the graceful motions of beating a drum. "They're not sore ..."

The point is the "They" in the last line in the English version. In the original text, the subject is not present because *Te* [hands] in the very first line is effectively functioning as one, crossing over the two formal sentence boundaries marked by full-stops. This example shows the tension between the heavy influence from outsiders and the resistance to change of the Japanese language of the time. While modern Japanese may have adopted certain structural features of Western languages on the surface, it retains its original mechanisms.

These anecdotes are rather symbolic. As Venuti (1995) argues, every translation can be interpreted as domestication in terms of incorporating foreign information into the TL system, and foreignisation does not necessarily change the fundamental system of the TL. The Japanese community has developed the continuing tradition of radical foreignisation of its language and culture at the surface level, while maintaining its original values by assimilating the incoming information into established Japanese culture at a deeper level. Haga (2000) analyses the Japanese case, discussing the active translation of Chinese literature and the use of the linguistically foreignised style in the Edo period. From the seventeenth century, Chinese popular literature written in *hakuwa* [spoken language] had been imported to Japan (*Tsūzoku Sangokushi* [1689] by Konan Bunzan, *Shōsetsu Sōeigen* [1743], *Shōsetsu Kigen* [1753] and *Shōsetsu Suigen* [1758] by Oka Hakku) and had had a strong impact on the native literary scene, as exemplified by the development of *yomihon* novels, a genre of popular Japanese literature in the Edo period, books that were usually fully illustrated and with plots taken from Chinese and Japanese historical and political sources. Adopting the *kundoku* method in the translation of these works was not easy because most Japanese intellectuals had no idea about spoken Chinese as earlier Chinese literary works, including poetry, were in *bungen* or the written language. Translators nevertheless persistently transformed the novels into the classic narrative style which they had always used in *kundoku* translation:

> From the time of the *Kaifūsō* and the *Man'yōshū* until the Edo period, Japanese cul-
> ture continued to accept Chinese culture with great enthusiasm. The acceptance was,
> however, never unlimited but always with manipulations, such as selecting and modi-
> fying, according to its own intention. The experience of constant interaction with
> otherness in the form of Chinese culture helped when it faced another otherness in
> the form of "Western culture" after the Meiji period. (Haga 2000: 37, my translation)

Thus, by persistently translating Chinese using the rigid *kundoku* method, Japan developed a rich experience of modifying the original text using an existing technique. Coping with the pressure from new idiosyncratic languages from the West again involved the application of this technique. However, the *kundoku* utilised in translating Western languages has merged with other techniques and produced a variety of translating dialects distinct from the old narrative style. This has taken place in the context of the development of, for example, various literary styles and criticism in support of dynamic translation. Creating such dialects, or special vessels for translated texts to be shaped into, was certainly a handy approach when facing Western otherness. When we, the Japanese, recognise the West as a vague but vivid image, we may sense a feeling of substantial otherness. This book analyses this sense of otherness in translation and describes some of its linguistic properties.

I would like to present and examine the hypothesis that creating a particular kind of otherness is the approach taken by many translators, and that the resulting emergence of a peculiar discourse is particularly remarkable in translated Western popular fiction (see Chapter 7). At this stage, I would simply like to emphasise the significance of the investigation of Japanese as a TL fully equipped with a translation-specific writing style that functions as an existing matrix capable of receiving Western otherness by virtue of its historical background.

CHAPTER 4

Methodology of the Investigation and the Importance of a Systematic Text Comparison in Popular Fiction

In the subsequent chapters, published texts translated by professional translators, from English into Japanese (and vice versa when necessary), will be examined to identify the presence of a translation-specific text-type in Japanese and the features which distinguish it. In this chapter, the method of investigation and relevant issues will be discussed.

4.1 Finding Japanese Norms for Text-Types

Prose fiction has a wide range of sub-genres, such as detective stories, thrillers, historical romances and science fiction (Hervey and Higgins 1992: 139). The sub-genres which this book focuses on such as detective stories, mysteries, adventure stories, romance stories, horror stories and science fiction, are usually described collectively as popular fiction, or as entertainment literature in the USA. It is conventional to divide fictional literature into two groups: high-brow and low-brow or popular. Doing so is never simple, however, and generates increasing scepticism. While high-brow literature is generally intended by its providers to require an intellectual grasp and knowledge in order to understand the cultural codification or suggested meanings and values, popular literature requires transparency of code and simplicity, for easy appreciation by the masses. Although the demarcation line separating the two is increasingly blurred in many communities (including Japan), this does not negate the simple fact that some works function as easy entertainment for a wider, less specific range of readers. Several internationally recognised Japanese novelists, such as Murakami Haruki, Murakami Ryū and Yoshimoto Banana, are understood to create *chūkanshōsetsu* [in-between literature]. The distinction between the two prestigeous literary prizes in Japan (the Akutagawa Prize for high-brow works and the Naoki Prize for popular works) is also becoming increasingly blurred. An interesting point here is that high-brow literature is supposed to be more ambitious in terms of stretching the literary frontier by creating something new, while entertainment literature appears to stay within an existing literary polysystem.

In the polysystem theory an individual work is analysed as part of a literary system, not in isolation, and literature is seen as embedded in the social, cultural, literary and historical framework. The function of translated works for a literature as a whole, or its position within that literature, needs to be recognised (Even-Zohar 1978); it is therefore important to appreciate where popular literature stands in the Japanese literary framework in order to understand translated popular literature and its functions. In a public lecture given on 12 July 1998 at Osaka Municipal Library, Takamura Kaoru, a popular contemporary novelist, suggested that mass literature is something that is written based on ordinary sensibilities, and which can be understood by any reader – just like enjoying a Rodin sculpture (in artistic terms). Pure literature, on the other hand, is something that requires particular skill or understanding in order to appreciate it – in the same way that modern sculpture embodies more complex abstraction. She emphasised that popular literature is, after all, for the unidentified masses to read, and this probably represents the reality of the Japanese publishing market.

More significantly, when translated into Japanese, with intricate codifications based on the ST culture and ST knowledge embedded in the text, pure literature tends to be treated differently from popular, light reading. The text-type of the ST is one issue and that of the TT is surely another. Not surprisingly, the two do not always match. There are cases in which the ST is regarded as a piece of high art but in translation is instilled with the stylistic features of popular fiction. Milton (2000: 174) discusses the reduction of higher literature to mass fiction in Brazil, referring to Macdonald's (1960) argument regarding midcult, and states:

> *Wuthering Heights* and *Pride and Prejudice* become no more than the "love stories" of Catherine and Heathcliff and Elizabeth and Darcy; *Huckleberry Finn* loses all socio-political and ethical commentaries to become an adventure story for children. *Moby Dick* loses all mythical elements to become merely the fight between Captain Ahab and the whale. Stylistic complexity is lost. Only emotions are foregrounded: love, excitement, fulfillment, or struggle. The classic becomes a soap opera.

These examples sharply illustrate the privilege of text-type manipulation exercised by translators by means of adjusting the stylistic mode. Returning to the issue of Japanese translation of popular fiction, Meldrum (2010: 91–98) discusses the characteristic features of Japanese "translationese" and readers' attitudes towards it within the framework of descriptive translation studies (Toury 1995). In the text analysis, Meldrum focuses on the following items: (1) overt personal pronouns, (2) more frequent loanwords, (3) female-specific language, (4) abstract nouns as grammatical subjects of transitive verbs, and (5) longer paragraphs. Two of these features (third-person pronouns and longer paragraphs) are presented as characteristic of "translationese", while others are proven otherwise or deemed questionable. Readers' attitudes towards "translationese" and "non-translationese" are also investigated by means of a survey and the results indicate that readers do not regard "translationese" in an overtly negative light. Meldrum's study shows that producing more domesticated translations of popular fiction is becoming the major translation norm, thereby making translations easier for the readers. Regarding Japanese "translationese", Wakabayashi (2009: 20) states:

> The main hypothesis to be examined is that Japanese have (in fact a set of) text-types with certain linguistic properties whose use is more or less limited to translation and one of them is specifically used for translating Western popular fiction. The existence of translationese means that translation in Japan cannot be regarded in clear-cut terms of source and target languages and that the notion of target language in Japan is not monolithic, but differentiated.

She goes on to say:

> I conclude the article with a discussion of the putative "betweenness" that is often problematically ascribed to translational language. The question is whether translational language in the Japanese context lies between the source language(s) and Japanese (that is, external to both) or whether it is a part of the Japanese language.

> I suggest that translational language does not constitute a language "between" the
> source and target languages; rather, it is an integral part of the Japanese language
> and an innovative force that has contributed to the modernization of the Japanese
> language, literature and thinking, while translation as a whole elides the boundaries
> that artificially demarcate source and target languages. (ibid.)

Wakabayashi thus sees translational language as an integral part of the
Japanese language and, taking this position, I attempt to shed light on the
ways in which foreign information is incorporated into the TL system
and how it fits its cultural values within the existing Japanese language.
In this, the notions of domestication and foreignisation (see section 4.4)
will be used as a yardstick to see if it is possible to identify how accepted
normative styles deviate from the original style and change in form. Let
us examine some more of the relevant theoretical issues.

4.2 Arguments on Style and Text-Types

Assuming that translated popular fiction is in a mode of language that
differs somewhat from that of Japanese original literature, or that it does
not exist in the SL culture, it is reasonable to suggest that the generation
of the TT text-type has something to do with the way in which the text
has gone through the translation process. A text-type, which conforms to
"specific linguistic regularities and rules" (Kußmaul 1997: 68), is often the
result of intentional, motivated choices of linguistic devices by the writer
or translator. In the case of a translation, a text-type can be a reflection of
attitudes towards the material imported from outside the TL community. During the 1970s, Reiß (1977) correlated text-types and translation
methods, offering practical aids for translators and triggering a theoretical
debate on the activity.

Taking a functional approach, Reiß (ibid.) and Nord (1991) have presented a set of text-types that help to achieve and analyse equivalence at text
level. This realises communication at the whole rather than at the word or
sentence level. The *skopos* or purpose of the translation and the function

of the TT determine what text-type the TT needs to have, and thus the translation method that needs to be employed: "A *translatum* (or TT) is determined by its *skopos*" (Reiß and Vermeer 1984: 119). Nord (1991) goes on to suggest functional models of ST elements to provide models for text-linguistic analysis. When the functions and the text-type of the ST and the TT match, this is called function-preserving translation. Whether the text-type can be truly identified or not is a major question – especially when it comes down to smaller strata such as divisions within a literary category. It is most likely to be subtle. One cannot merely measure the number or frequency of the use of certain words or sentence structures, but the presence of those features can give a sense of the text-type, and the purpose or significance of the text, and accordingly aid the reader.

Let us revisit the concept of *norms* – a major and frequently discussed theoretical notion which is highly relevant to the attempt to find consistencies in Japanese translations. It is regarded as a key concept in the recent development of descriptive translation studies. When we regard translation as a decision-making process, as Levý (1963) suggests, our concern becomes the question of what are the factors inside and outside the original text that affect and constrain it. Like most kinds of human linguistic and social activity, the act of translation seems to be a norm-regulated behaviour. In identifying and categorising norms in translation to explain the translator's decisions and behaviour, Toury (1995: 5455) describes the concept as follows:

> Sociologists and social psychologists have long regarded norms as the translation of general values or ideas shared by a community – as to what is right and wrong, adequate and inadequate – into performance instructions appropriate for, and applicable to, particular situations, specifying what is prescribed and forbidden as well as what is tolerated and permitted in a certain behavioural dimension ... Norms are acquired by the individual during his/her socialisation and always imply *sanctions* – actual or potential, negative as well as positive.

Also, as an explanatory device, norms have been utilised in analysing various human social behaviours: "It has an interdisciplinary aspect to it, in that norm concepts are widely used in the social sciences, from law and ethics to social psychology and international relations" (Hermans 1988: 80). Although Hermans (ibid. 82) distinguishes norms from conventions, there is no clear agreement among researchers on the definition of norms, or, in fact, of other related concepts such as conventions, rules, and constraints:

> Norms can then be understood as stronger, prescriptive versions of social conventions. Like conventions, norms derive their legitimacy from shared knowledge, mutual expectation and acceptance, and the fact that, on the individual level, they are largely internalised [...]

> Unlike conventions, norms have a directive character. They tell members of a community not just how everyone else expects them to behave in a given situation, but how they *ought* to behave. They imply that there is, among the array of possible opinions, a particular course of action which is more or less strongly preferred because the community has agreed to accept it as "proper" or "correct" or "appropriate".

Since norms function as reliable standards to follow in practice and do not simply show what is conventional, they are believed to be useful as an explanatory tool for recurring behaviour or decisions made by translators. Any linguistic or extra-linguistic phenomenon found in a translation is subject to judgement, for example, whether it is common, acceptable, adequate or correct. As translators probably ask themselves whether the selection of a word, expression, style, or tone employed is adequate according to norms, we are in the position to judge whether the selected decisions satisfy the norms or not. At the next stage, the type and extent of equivalence produced by the translator's decisions is also judged according to norms:

> The notion of norms is closely related to how we can recognize the concept of equivalence which is assumed to be perceived between the ST and the TT. [...] The study of norms thus constitutes a vital step towards establishing just how the functional-relational postulate of equivalence [...] has seen realized – whether in one translated text, in the work of a single translator or "school" of translators, in a given historical period, or in any other justifiable selection. (Toury 1995: 61)

The study of norms thus helps scholars identify what is defined as accepted functional equivalence in a specific translational context. Toury (ibid. 56–59) presents various kinds of norms identified in the process of translation and translation analysis. In particular, it is fruitful to divide the options the translator can choose from into two: source norms, which would lead to adequate translation, and target culture norms, which would lead to acceptable translation. Satō (2009) investigates various critiques of translations of the same literary works from the Meiji to contemporary periods by different translators (such as *Le Rouge et le noir* by Stendhal and *Catcher in the Rye* by J. D. Salinger) in terms of translation norms. She finds that while a normative translation method which values loyalty and precision is accepted as a standard method for translation, this is not exclusively so: other ways of translating literature exist, including some which are less semantically precise.

Returning to the focus of this book, the task can be re-described as assessing the kind of equivalence desired as normative, as well as the stylistic norms specific to the text-type. Using Toury's terminology, I intend to highlight the stylistic features found in the Japanese TTs and the linguistic and cultural norms identified in some works of popular fiction. Discussing "translationese" in Japan, Furuno (2005: 147) says: "This acceptance of foreignness on the part of Japanese readers seems to have existed throughout Japan's history". This scholar suggests that this norm, once accepted, somehow merged into the general Japanese style of original writing. I will consider another angle, which is possibly part of the same phenomenon. The style employed can be linguistically identified, and not necessarily simply accepted but rather aggressively desired, to be noticeably foreign. It is my contention, therefore, that even if some of the features are shared with the original writing, the overall impression that the reader receives from the text is fundamentally idiosyncratic.

The various text-types are not generally recognised by the Japanese community, while the obscure presence of *hon'yakuchō* [translationese] – particularly in non-literary genres – is commonly acknowledged and attributed to the heavy linguistic influence of the ST as discussed in section 3.2. The tolerance of the stiff writing style in translated texts seems to blur the clear recognition of the presence of the text-type, which consists of a variety of linguistic features that go beyond being a mere reflection of the SL. Acceptance or tolerance of the style somehow degrades the style itself into one which has resulted accidentally from the translator's lack of ability. The characteristic of *hon'yakuchō* which distinguishes it from other registers, such as journalese or legalese, is in fact the widely recognised negative connotation attached to the term: any sign of it is ascribed to

incompetence or negligence on the part of the translator. While the community generously allows Japanese that is clearly identifiable as translation
to be used in published translations, they do make theoretical criticisms in
this regard (see Chapter 8).

There are two important questions in terms of the text-type specific
to translations: firstly, does it exist beyond individual cases? The question
can be rephrased as the query of whether stylistic norms can be identified
at a linguistically describable level. In her attempt to describe Finnish
translational language, Tirkkoen-Condit (2002: 207) states: "[I]t is one
of the challenges of translation studies to find out by empirical research if
translations are indeed systematically different from originally produced
texts". In the case of Japanese, there is no doubt that they are different, and
the real question is whether the features of the dialect are beyond simple
linguistic foreignness. The second question is trickier: "If it turns out that
they are different, we must try to find out why" (ibid.).

The reason why a translated text seems to be in such a different style is
that this is the result of an accumulation of the translator's choice of strategies. Thus, the mode or the particular way of arranging words is something
that has been adopted, out of all the choices available, and this selection is
always part of the translator's long-term decision-making process. Creating
an appropriate text-type involves the appropriate selection of translation
strategies. Thus, determining the text-type is the first step in producing a
piece of communication which functions as intended or expected. Kußmaul
(1997: 68) states that:

> Conventions imply conformity and expectation (cf. Lewis 1985: 78), and when people
> use words, they can normally be expected to use them in the same sense as other
> people do, i.e. to conform to generally agreed-on regularities. In the same way, when
> people produce specific text-types, such as business letters, they can be expected to
> conform to specific regularities and rules. If they do not, communication may turn
> out to be difficult or even break down.

Similarly, Sager (1997b: 30) discusses the performability of the appropriate
text-type in translation in the following terms:

> The most visible means of expressing intention is through the choice of conventional
> text-types. Text-types have evolved as patterns of messages for specific communicative

situations. When we write a message, we first think of the text-type that is suitable for the occasion and the content, and formulate our text accordingly. Regular repetitions of messages in particular circumstances have created expectations of recognisable structural and rhetorical features which condition our modes of reading a message.

In his attempt to identify a group of text-types only found in translations in English, Sager (ibid. 39) thus understands a text-type to be "a pattern of messages" equipped with "recognisable structural and rhetorical features", and these prepare the readers for a particular mode of reading. Different cultures may have different text-types "because they have evolved different patterns of communication" (ibid.) and it is indeed intriguing to identify a translation-specific text-type and relevant cultural factors which encourage translators to generate a specific pattern in a given communication context.

There are obviously other notions relevant to the issue of text-type, such as *genre*, *register* and *style*. Trosborg (1997: 10) explains the term *genre* as follows:

> [T]he text categories readily distinguished by mature speakers of a language, and we may even talk about a "folk typology" of genres. Texts used in a particular situation for a particular purpose may be classified using everyday labels such as a guidebook, a nursery rhyme, a poem, a business letter, a newspaper article, a radio play, an advertisement, etc.

This effectively sums up the two notions:

> Genres and text types are clearly to be distinguished, as linguistically distinct texts within a genre may represent different text-types, while linguistically similar texts from different genres may represent a single text-type (cf. Biber 1989: 6). (ibid. 12)

Style is studied not just in the field of stylistics, but also widely in linguistics, literary studies, translation studies and other fields. The precise meaning of the term varies: Leech and Short (1981: 10) concisely define it as "the linguistic characteristics of a particular text". Malmkjaer (2002: 591) explains it in a little more detail: "By style is meant a consistent occurrence in the text of certain items and structures, or types of items and structures, among those offered by the language as a whole". Style is obviously found in the text, and as such it can be seen as a form of usage of language, though is not language itself. Whether the use of a certain item or a structure is consistent or not needs to be interpreted by the reader. Lecercle (1993: 17) states that:

> The trouble with stylistics is that no-one has ever known exactly what the term meant, and that nowadays hardly anyone seems to care. And yet, paradoxically, the object, style, seems to be as fascinating as ever, and the subject, stylistics, like the phoenix, is forever reborn.

Looking at the social context of a particular style is intriguing, and the aim of this book is deeply interlinked with it: if the Japanese translation of popular fiction makes up a certain style, it must then account for something within the literary and social stylistic system, just as Bourdieu (1980) regards style as distinctiveness within a lived and social-semiotic system. Boase-Beier (2006: 5), in thinking translation and style, finds it important to consider style from the following points: (1) choices of the ST author, (2) impact of the style on the ST reader, (3) choices of the translator, and (4) impact of the style on the TT reader. Stylistic equivalence between the ST and the TT is important but translational style can also indicate or symbolise the position of the translation work in society. A reader who is reasonably receptive of linguistic nuances can sense fluency or stiffness in translation in comparison with the original language.

Register, on the other hand, is not so clearly distinguished from genre. Gregory and Carroll (1978: 4) define it as "contextual category correlating groupings of linguistic features with recurrent situational features" and genre is usually supposed to underlie register. I employ certain technical terms in this book based on the following understanding: I consistently regard translated popular fiction as a literary *genre*, in the sense understood by the general public, and the set of linguistic properties regularly found in and attached to it as a *style, discourse* or *(social) dialect* (see section 3.1). When this kind of communicative pattern is found to a clearly recognisable extent in a certain message, that message can be regarded as a text-type, although the text-type categories do not necessarily match its genres. Thus, translational Japanese used in the genre of translated Western popular fiction can – in light of its social, communicative function – be an independent text-type, if the structural, lexical or rhetorical features are systematically identified. This issue of translation-specific text-types is also discussed in section 7.1, after detailed textual analysis.

4.3 Methods of Text Comparison

The methodology used in this TT-oriented investigation is close to that suggested by Hatim and Mason (1990), among others. They emphasise the importance of systematic comparisons and analysis of the ST and TT when considering regularities found in the translation process in a certain genre, and the translator's motivations or attitude that can be deduced from them:

> Critiques of individual translations abound. But from the perspective of translation studies, what is needed is systematic study of problems and solutions by close comparison of ST and TT *procedures*. Which techniques produce which effects? What are the regularities of the translation process in particular genres, in particular cultures and in particular historical periods?
>
> [...] In other words, the resulting translated text is to be seen as evidence of a transaction, a means of retracing the pathways of the translator's decision-making procedures. [...]
>
> In this sense, texts can be seen as the result of *motivated choice*: producers of texts have their own communicative aims and select lexical items and grammatical arrangement to serve those aims. Naturally, in translating, there are potentially two sets of motivations: those of the producer of the source text and those of the translator. (ibid. 3, 4)

Following their approach, this book employs the method of close text-to-text contrast in examining which motivated choices are made during the transfer from the original sentences to the resulting sentences, and consequently from the original text-type to the resulting text-type. By investigating which techniques are regularly used, the mechanism by which certain properties emerge in the TT will become clearer. An attempt will be made to classify some frequently used strategies, whenever necessary. Translations selected as examples will occasionally be commented on to reconstruct the possible translation process and context, but finding fault is never the objective of the exercise. Similarly, the task is not to cast aspersions on the use of "translationese", but to identify its presence and constitution.

We can determine the presence of translationalness by breaking it down into the set of concrete strategies employed. For instance, in considering the compromises and compensations that recur in translations between English and French, and which the translator inevitably makes when transferring one cultural mode of expression to another, Hervey and Higgins (1992) categorise four aspects of compensation strategies for methodological purposes: compensation in kind, in place, by merging and by splitting. Likewise, Baker (1992: 26–42) suggests eight strategies of translation at the word level, and supplies accompanying examples: (a) translation by a more general word (superordinate), (b) translation by a more neutral/less expressive word, (c) translation by cultural substitution, (d) translation using a loan word or loan word plus explanation, (e) translation by paraphrase using related words, (f) translation by paraphrase using unrelated words, (g) translation by omission, (h) translation by illustration. She makes it clear that the examples do not provide an exhaustive account of the strategies available, and encourages readers to discover more and learn "to assess the advantages and disadvantages of using each strategy in various contexts" (ibid. 42). Just as these writers do, I regard the TT as the product of actual strategies: not correct or incorrect, good or bad, desirable or undesirable. The examples are discussed – sometimes at length – to illustrate the translation approach, method and techniques which have been employed to shape the text into a particular form of language.

Taking the context into consideration, as would the general ST readers, helps to achieve a more precise reconstruction of the translation process. Snell-Hornby (1995: 69) points out the importance of this kind of macro level text analysis in translation:

> With the development of text-linguistics and the gradual emergence of translation studies as an independent discipline in its own right, there has been an increasing awareness of the text, not as a chain of separate sentences, these themselves a string of grammatical and lexical items [...], but as a complex, multi-dimensional structure consisting of more than the mere sum of its parts – a gestalt, [...] whereby an analysis of its parts cannot provide an understanding of the whole. Thus textual analysis, which is an essential preliminary to translation, should proceed from the "top down," from the macro to the micro level, from text to sign.

The sentences selected will not be treated as isolated pieces of language, but as part of a complex network of recognition, whose written and unwritten contexts constantly constrain the translator's decision-making as he/she deals with them. In this work, the term "context" is used to refer to both specific parts of a text near or adjacent to a translation unit which is the focus of attention (Fibras 1986), and to the wider linguistic and cultural environment around the text. The former is also known as co-text but I do not differentiate between the two. When the term is used to discuss some situational or cultural contexts that are features of the non-linguistic world in relation to which linguistic units are systematically used (Halliday 1985), this will be indicated.

The term "unit" in this book refers to pieces into which a translator breaks the original sentence – either consciously or subconsciously – during the process of translation. In discussing the development of translation studies as an independent academic discipline and the approaches taken, Snell-Hornby (1995: 16) sums up the notion of a "translation unit" as follows:

> In the earlier stages of the discussion opinions varied as to what was to be equivalent, whether words or even segments of words or longer units. Gradually the concept of translation unit emerged, which was generally understood as a cohesive segment lying between the level of the word and the sentence.

Such a unit is a grammatically undefinable concept. More relevant, however, is its functional definition. A translator can deal with language only in segments of a manageable size, such as a morpheme, a word, a sentence or an idiom. Identifying an idiomatic or phrasal item as a controllable translation unit, for instance, requires a fair amount of practical knowledge and experience, and the ways in which it is identified will probably vary according to the text-type. Any linguistic segment which gives the translator a solid piece of information and can be handled in one go can be considered a translation unit. Thus, theoretically a text can be divided into any number of translation units. In fact, finding translation units according to the TL characteristics – or indeed the text-type – is the starting point of translation: it clearly distinguishes the act of translation from reading a text for the sake of reading it. In the following, I present some relatively simple examples of translation units, identified in English and Japanese.

In this example, the ST question pretty much corresponds to the TT question. "You" can be considered as one translation unit and can be analysed as being allocated to two TL items: *kimi* and *wa*. The grammatical function of

In a café	
ST (English)	TT (Japanese)
Q: What will you have? A: I will have a cake.	Q: 君は何を食べる？ Kimi wa nani o taberu? A: 私は ケーキ。 Watashi wa kēki.

"you" in the ST demands the insertion of the particle *wa* (which functions as a topic marker), although it can be omitted (the omission increases the informality of the utterance). Similarly, the unit *nani* is given as "what" in the TT. "Will" and "have" in the ST question can be regarded as one unit for the purpose of the translation process, because they are squeezed into one component, *taberu* [to eat], which functions in the same way as "will (expressing intention or decision, or a future action) + have". The ST answer, *Watashi wa kēki* does not mean "I am a cake" (unless the sentence is rather unusually contextualised). *Watashi wa ... (desu)* is a common expression which in this kind of casual dialogue means "I would like ...". "As far as I am concerned, (what to have) is a cake" is a semantically close translation. Thus, in this case, the whole sentence in the ST, "I will have a cake", can be interpreted and treated as one unit and its semantic and pragmatic meanings are nicely transferred into a more conventional TT sentence.

It is possible to say "I'm the cake" or "I'm the hamburger" in English when the waitress arrives with the food, to indicate who ordered what. These, however, do not precisely correspond at the semantic level to sentences such as *Watashi wa kēki* in the above example. As for the TT answer, it is also possible to assume that *o* (a particle acting as an object marker) + *taberu* is left out in the sentence after *kēki*. In this case, *Watashi wa* and *kēki* are considered to be counterparts of "I" and "a cake" respectively, and it is reasonable to think that the unit "will have" has simply been omitted during the process. The term "translation unit" will be used frequently in text analysis for convenience, but it should be noted that the manner in which a sentence or a piece of text is divided into smaller translation units is often open to each individual translator's or researcher's interpretation.

Another technical concept useful for text comparison is *back-translation* – translating the TT as literally as possible into the SL to contrast it with the ST or other TT versions. Baker (1992: 8) summarises the theoretical problems associated with the notion and its usefulness as an analytical technique:

> *Back-translation*, as used in this book, involves taking a text (original or translated) which is written in a language with which the reader is assumed to be unfamiliar and translating it as literally as possible into English – how literally depends on the point being illustrated, whether it is morphological, syntactic, or lexical for instance. I use the term back-translation because, since the source language is often English, this involves translating the target text back into the source language from which it was originally translated. A back-translation can give some insight into aspects of the structure, if not the meaning of the original, but it is never the same as the original. The use of the back-translation is a necessary compromise; it is theoretically unsound and far from ideal, but then we do not live in an ideal world – very few of us speak eight or nine languages – and theoretical criteria cease to be relevant when they become an obstacle to fruitful discussion.

Sentences that correspond semantically between the English ST and the Japanese TT tend to be structurally distant. Back-translation is a particularly useful tool for demonstrating the adjustments involved in the process of translation between them. At the same time, back-translations will give readers of the book who are not familiar with Japanese or Japanese culture some idea of the TT.

4.4 Domestication and Foreignisation as Analytical Tools

Another set of notions, domestication/assimilation and foreignisation/discomfort, have been deployed as an analytical tool in this work. In developing a picture of the style or dialect used in the TT, an examination of how each unit is treated linguistically and culturally in the TT will reveal a variety of patterns in the process. The way words are handled is always related to the overall picture of the product the translator desires – or is supposed to obtain – as the result. In other words, the kind of equivalence targeted by the translator immediately impacts the way texts are treated. Even when the intended effect fails to emerge for some reason, the translator's motivation is frequently visible in the language resulting from the translation.

Nida's (1964) dynamic equivalence gives a translator more flexibility and a larger pool of TL vocabulary from which to choose linguistic tools. The desired qualities are similar effect and readability. Any expression whose meaning or prominence in the text is characteristic of the cultural patterns (such as common behaviours, manners, traditions), of the SL context and not of the TL, should either be adjusted to the TL norm or simply omitted – dynamic translation aims to relate receptors to modes of behaviour that are relevant within the context of their own culture. According to Nida (1964: 160), Phillips (1953) has, in *Some Personal Reflections on New Testament Translation*, managed to allow the receptors to read the TT without being momentarily disconcerted at the foreignness injected by the expression "a holy kiss", by transforming it into "a hearty handshake", which fits more naturally into the context of modern English society. What Nida is advocating here is shifting the semantic content of an expression in the ST to a different semantic content which is less culture-specific to the SL. This amounts to domestication, one of the two fundamental strategic options suggested by Schleiermacher (1813: 205–245), the other one being foreignisation, to which all other methods can be reduced:

> But now the translator, who really wants to bring together these two entirely separate persons, his author and his reader, and to assist the latter in obtaining the most correct and complete understanding and enjoyment possible of the former without, however, forcing him out of the sphere of his mother tongue – what paths are open to the translator for that purpose? In my opinion, there are only two. Either the translator leaves the writer alone as much as possible and moves the reader toward the writer, or he leaves the reader alone as much as possible and moves the writer toward the reader.

The first approach means that the translator will take a more literalist attitude, while the second one leads to more sense-to-sense transfer. Accordingly, domestication minimises the otherness of the TT for the readers, while foreignisation maintains elements of the ST in the TT, breaking with TL conventions. For Pym (1995: 5), Schleiermacher obviously prefers the latter: "His ideal translation should retain something of the source-text's foreignness. Most of those who have since used or referred to Schleiermacher have expressed the same basic choice; preferring relative foreignising to relative naturalisation". Venuti counts as a translator or researcher who puts more value in discomforting translation, although he clearly distances his concepts of domestication and foreignisation from Schleiermacher's classic dichotomies – foreignising translation employs less familiar domestic language and discourse and rewrites the foreign text, while Venuti's (1995: 20) foreignness can be viewed most decisively in domestic terms, and domestication is "an ethnocentric reduction of the foreign text to target-language cultural values". He presents his own translation of a poem by Milo De Angelis, *L'idea centrale* (1976), in his anthology selection *Somiglianze*, using radical foreignisation as an example in which he has put this theoretical advocacy into practice. It demonstrates that foreignisation is achieved by applying a particular translation strategy, or through the mere choice of a foreign text for translation – in effect a choice that deviates from the current canon of foreign literature in translation. Looking at English, he considers strategies that cultivate a linguistic and cultural heterogeneity that deviates from standard English and from canonical literary styles in the target community. He views domestication as dominant, and at the same time considers this a sign of growing narcissism in Anglo-American culture because of the monolingual, unreceptive connotation that this attitude exemplifies (1995: 19–20). He calls for a reconsideration of the current canon and advocates foreignisation. Thus, Venuti establishes the criterion for domestication or foreignisation as being the way in which the ST is treated in terms of the existing TL conventions and values. It is important to recognise that all translation is domestication according to his notion, because it inevitably involves taking a text and rewriting it to meet domestic intelligibilities and interests. Thus, a TT will deviate from the cultural norms of the TL community in one way or another due to foreignisation, while it will be at the same time constrained by domestication.

Venuti attempts to explain the traditional popularity of domestication in terms of TL (American English in this case) values by referring to Nida and de Waard's (1986: 14) emphasis on the importance of the naturalness of the TT to reproduce the original effect:

> The phrase "naturalness of expression" signals the importance of a fluent strategy to this theory of translation, and in Nida's work it is obvious that fluency involves domestication. As he has recently put it, "the translator must be a person who can

draw aside the curtains of linguistic and cultural differences so that people may see
clearly the relevance of the original message.

And Venuti (1995: 21) also points out that:

> This is of course a relevance to the target-language culture, something with which
> foreign writers are usually not concerned when they write their texts, so that relevance
> can be established in the translation process only by replacing source-language fea-
> tures that are not recognizable with target-language ones that are. [...], he is in fact
> imposing the English-language valorization of transparent discourse on every foreign
> culture, masking a basic disjunction between the source- and target-language texts
> which puts into question the possibility of eliciting a "similar" response.

While foreignisation of the TT has been preferred as a theory and practised
in certain European countries at certain historical times, there is, in the
current translation world of the UK and the USA, an established canon
that translation should be invisible and transparent: "Anglo-American
culture, in contrast, has long been dominated by domesticating theories
that recommend fluent translating" (ibid. 21).

Most of the dichotomies suggested along the line of a literal-to-free
continuum, such as formal and dynamic equivalence, or semantic and
communicative translation, can be more generally reformulated into
ST-oriented or TT-oriented translation, linguistically and/or culturally,
and then be reduced to the question of domestication and foreignisation.
Any method or strategy situates itself somewhere on the line between the
two polarities of moving the reader towards the writer in the SL world
(more SL-oriented), or moving the writer towards the reader in the TL
world (more TL-oriented). However, as is highlighted in Venuti's claim
above, there is another dimension of domestication and foreignisation
to consider – that of dominant values in the TL translation culture. It is
often the case that the TL writing and translating norms do not match,
but attempts may be made to bring them closer to each other, and the
picture can then become rather complicated: "'Dominant cultural values'
shift, overlap and contradict each other" (Harker 1999: 30). Berman (1985)
speaks of "textual deformation" when it comes to the prevailing negation
of foreignness in translation. This naturalisation is carried out through
systematic textual deformation and "[t]he negative analytic is primarily

concerned with ethnocentric, annexationist translations and hypertextual translations (pastiche, imitation, adaptation, free writing), where the play of deforming forces is freshly exercised" (ibid. 286). He lists twelve ways of deforming text: (1) rationalisation, (2) clarification, (3) expansion, (4) ennoblement, (5) qualitative impoverishment, (6) quantative impoverishment, (7) destruction of rhythms, (8) destruction of underlying signification, (9) destruction of linguistic patternings, (10) destruction of vernacular networks or their exoticisation, (11) destruction of expression and idioms, and (12) effacement of the superimposition of languages.

Textual deformation can of course occur in a different cultural setting as well. Whether the above patterns (submitted as universal) prevail in naturalised or domesticated parts of the Japanese translation of popular fiction will be examined in this book. By shifting the focus to contemporary Japanese translation from English, I aim to examine the translationalness of the genre by checking whether the style exhibits some of the features of deformed text that Berman itemises above.

As pointed out earlier, foreignising translation (in the sense of Schleiermacher's word-for-word or literalist foreignisation) has traditionally been part of the prevailing norm in literary translations in Japanese (Yanabu 1979). The essential hypothesis is that the language used in some literary translations is not stiff simply because of linguistic awkwardness, which mirrors the original formal or semantic features, but more because of its multi-dimensional structural uniqueness. So, the dialect used in popular fiction translated from English to Japanese exhibits particular linguistic regularities, which are generated through certain patterns of Western foreignness which non-literary translations, or other groups of literary translations, do not share. This hypothesis will be tested throughout this book. The use of a style that clearly encompasses translational features is, according to my observations, so normative in the community that imparting it to a certain range of literary translations is very culturally domesticating in Venuti's sense – that is, in conformity with TL cultural normative values. However, the claim that this translational style is the result of the use of solely foreignisation techniques in Schleiermacher's sense is ungrounded. Translating English into Japanese in a TT-oriented direction would often conform to the TL cultural norm. Translationalness, a kind of quality which makes us realise the text is a translation, is not always perceived as unfamiliar to a culture. Within any language, one can find some translation in "the third language" (Duff 1989), although its status as a dialect, style or register, varies and is rarely precisely identified. In the process of producing Japanese translations, translationalness seems to be carefully measured and left there in acceptable proportions of naturalness and foreignness. The habitual allocation of a certain set of linguistic features to the text achieves the above effect. Since the translationalness established in this way consists of many contradictory factors, it is never simple to find out which process on the text actually functions as a deconventionalising agent in the TL context. Chapters 5 and 6 look at translated texts in terms of how the two fundamental ways of handling texts – domestication and foreignisation (in Schleiermacher's sense) – are conducted. Then in Chapters 7 and 8, the discussion will be extended to explore how the selection of domestication and/or foreignisation is made in practice, and to ascertain whether the norms of the TL translation culture are, in fact, satisfactory or deconventionalising, thus focusing more on Venuti's notions and their overall cultural implications.

CHAPTER 5

Textual Analysis (I): Linguistic Domestication and Foreignisation

5.1 Linguistic Domestication

As I start this examination of translations between English and Japanese, I intend to focus on one of the four major strategic options, that is, linguistic domestication, which has a significant impact on language used in translation. In essence, I look into how an ST is domesticated or naturalised through the translation process.

5.1.1 Linguistic-Oriented Japanisation

The yardstick for measuring this is not the Japanese translation discourse, but the way a native speaker writes or speaks in a literary setting. This approach is domestication and is divisible into two types: linguistic domestication of the ST and cultural domestication of the content. The two are obviously interlocked – that is, when the text is linguistically domesticated to the TL, the receptor can remain within the TL's social and cultural setting and think in accordance with the logic of the TL (the normative order and connection of the TL reader's thoughts and arguments). Hence, the TL's cultural setting and logic are, strictly speaking, inseparable in most cases. Nevertheless, it is often convenient to consider these two aspects separately when analysing examples of domestication, because in some translations, cultural elements are more clearly adjusted to fit the values and norms of the TL's culture. This results in a large, (supposedly) intentionally created semantic gap between the ST and the TT; called *cultural domestication*

(CD) here. *Linguistic domestication* (LD) is, on the other hand, relatively language-oriented and a certain alteration is made to produce a more reader-friendly TT to express the ST's semantic meaning – however foreign the content of the TT may be for the receptors. It is a method which a translator constantly needs to employ to avoid a formal translation, which would make the TT sound awkwardly remote.

While it is often possible to transfer the ST's literal meaning to the TL in one way or another, more common lexical items which have a meaning close to the original, or more natural sentence structures from which a similar situational result can be deduced, may be selected – what is known by Toury (1995: 268) as the Law of Growing Standardisation. Such LD can be carried out only partially, without covering the whole text. When it is performed on a phrase or a sentence only, domesticness (i.e. the features of the text created through domestication) is limited to that small unit. Such fragmentation of domesticness imparts an impression which is unique to a certain kind of translation; this may make the translation appear half-baked or unsophisticated, but that is, in fact, one of the core qualities of the translating style. This book looks closely at LD and its results, as it is one of the major components of the translational discourse of the genre.

5.1.2 Frequent Use of Attitude-Marking Adverbs (AMAs) in Non-Translational Japanese

In looking at linguistic domestication, some practical strategies that are frequently found can be used as examples. First, one linguistic feature is particularly characteristic of oral Japanese and tends to be problematic to translate. Among the various Japanese attitudinal markers, there is a group of adverbs which not only modify a (often the succeeding) part of the sentence but also add some subtle nuance expressing the speaker's attitude towards, or evaluation of, the addressee, referent, or state of affairs. Adverbs of this type will be called attitude-marking adverbs (AMAs) in this book. Ujiie (1987: 652) suggests that such adverbs in Japanese convey the speaker's mental processes, and only very rough equivalents can usually be found in English:

I originally selected some adverbs such as "dohnimo, yappari, sasuga (ni), semete, isso, ittai" etc. as well as conjunctions and some particles, on the basis of their particular character of showing "the enfolding of the speaker's mental processes". I created the term of "gan-katei kohzoh [sic]"; the structure of a word which enfolds the speaker's mental processes (SEMP) in 1973.

Example 1 shows their use in conversation in a well-known Japanese novel written by Ariyoshi Sawako in the 1980s.

Example 1: Ariyoshi Sawako, *Akujo ni tsuite* [*Regarding an Evil Woman*], 1983: 112–113

主人は宝石から料理屋から、手広くやっていましたけれど、私は宝石には関心がありませんでした。何しろ(1)子供を育てるのに精一杯でしたし、台所をして荒れた指に、宝石なんて似合いませんからね。高いお金を出して宝石を買う女の気が知れませんよ。まあ(2)綺麗と言えば綺麗ですけど、硝子で作っても同じものが出来るんですからねえ。

ともかく(3)、私たちの夫婦喧嘩から、ふっつり彼女が家に姿を見せなくなったのも、私は別段怪訝にも思わなかったんです。

だって(4)、まさか(5)、あんなことが起るとは思いませんもの。

あるとき、あの人が、そうですね、半年もたっていたかしら、もっとたっていたかしら。ともかく(6)、一人でやって来たんです。こんな大きなお腹で、ですよ。もちろん私は三人子供を産んでますから臨月間近だということは分りましたわ。

「あらま、君子さん、あなた結婚していたの? 知らなかったわ。私は主人に頼まれていいお婿さんを探しかけていたんだけど、そんな必要なかったのね」

軽い気持で、その次は、おめでとうと続けるつもりでした。

ところが、どうでしょう。あの女は、そのソファに坐ったまま、あの眼に涙を浮かべて、私の顔を黙って見ているんです。

「どうしたの? 何か、困ったことでもあるの?」

「いいえ、困ってはいないんです。覚悟はしていたんですから。ただ、私は、やっぱり(7)奥さまには本当のこと知っておいて頂きたかったんです」

私は首から下の血が一瞬で凍ったように思いました。いつかの予感が当ったんだと思うと、喉が渇いて、なかなか(8)言いたい言葉が口から出ないのです。

「まさか(9)、あなた、それは主人の」

「はい、そうなんです」

Shujin wa hōseki kara ryōriya kara, tebiroku yatteimashita keredo, watashi wa hōseki ni wa kanshin ga arimasendeshita. Nanishiro(1) kodomo o sodateru no ni seiippai deshita shi, daidokoro o shite areta yubi ni, hōseki nante niaimasen kara ne. Takai okane o dashite hōseki o kau onna no ki ga shiremasen yo. Mā(2) kirei to ieba kirei desu kedo, garasu de tsukuttemo onaji mono ga dekirundesu kara nē.

Tomokaku(3), watashitachi no fūfugenka kara, futtsuri kanojo ga ie ni sugata o misenakunatta no mo, watashi wa betsudan kegenni mo omowanakattandesu.

Datte(4), masaka(5), anna koto ga okoru to wa omoimasen mono.

Aru toki, ano hito ga, sō desu ne, hantoshi mo tatteita kashira, motto tatteita kashira. Tomokaku(6), hitori de yatte kitandesu. Konna ōkina onaka de, desu yo. Mochiron watashi wa sannin kodomo o undemasu kara ringetsu majika da to yū koto wa wakarimashita wa.

"Arama, Kimikosan, anata kekkonshiteita no? Shiranakatta wa. Watashi wa shujin ni tanomarete ii omukosan o sagashikaketeitanda kedo, sonna hitsuyō nakatta no ne."

Karui kimochi de, sono tsugi wa, omedetō to tsuzukeru tsumori deshita.

Tokoroga, dō deshō. Ano onna wa, sono sofa ni suwatta mama, ano me ni namida o ukabete, watashi no kao o damatte miteirundesu.

"Dō shita no? Nanika, komatta koto demo aru no?"

My husband was running an extensive range of businesses, from jewellery shops to restaurants, but I was not interested in jewellery. I had my hands full bringing up my children anyway(1), and jewellery doesn't suit fingers made rough by kitchen chores, does it? I don't understand women who spend lots of money on jewellery. Well(2), it's pretty if you like, but the same things can be made with glass.

Anyway(3), I didn't find it particularly suspicious that she suddenly stopped showing up at our home just after our husband-and-wife quarrel.

Because, as you can understand(4), I could not possibly(5) imagine such a thing could happen.

One day, she, let me see, half a year later, or even later, anyway(6), she came on her own. With a huge belly like this. Since I have had three kids as a matter of fact, I could see the baby was almost due.

"My, Kimiko, did you get married? I didn't know. I was about to look for a good husband for you because my husband asked, but there was no need."

I was going to carry on congratulating her light-heartedly.

But what do you think? That woman just sat on that sofa there looking at me wordlessly with her eyes brimming with tears.

"What's the matter? Is there any problem?"

"No, there is no problem. I've accepted the situation. I just wanted you to know the truth, after all(7)."

"Iie, komatte wa inaindesu. Kakugo wa shiteitandesu kara. Tada, watashi wa, yappari$_{(7)}$ okusama ni wa hontō no koto shitteoiteitadakitakattandesu."	I was numb with shock. Thinking my earlier presentiment had come true, <u>my throat got so dry that the words I felt like saying did not come out easily</u>$_{(8)}$.
Watashi wa kubi kara shita no chi ga isshun de kōtta yōni omoimashita. Itsuka no yokan ga atattanda to omou to, nodo ga kawaite, <u>nakanaka</u>$_{(8)}$ iitai kotoba ga kuchi kara denainodesu.	<u>"You, you don't say</u>$_{(9)}$ that it's my husband's."
"<u>Masaka</u>$_{(9)}$, anata, sore wa shujin no."	"Yes, it is." (my translation)
"Hai, sō nandesu."	

This passage contains as many as nine AMAs, listed below with some indication of how they can be semantically translated into English: *nanishiro* [anyway, you know], *mō* [well, if you like, I should say], two instances of *tomokaku* [anyway], two instances of *masaka* [you don't say, incredibly], *yappari* [as expected, after all], *datte* [because, you must understand], and *nakanaka* [(not) easily].

In the novel, a lady is telling an old story about her husband and his mistress to a journalist. The whole text is supposed to be a direct quotation and is written in a flawless colloquial style. In addition to their respective semantic contributions, the presence of the adverbs makes the text flow smoothly and sound realistic. Adverbs with these functions appear frequently and play an important role in native colloquial Japanese (Bekku 1979, Morimoto 1994) especially in informal situations. Nakau (1980, in Kunihiro and Tamamura 1983) shows the frequent prominence of adverbs in colloquial Japanese by means of a statistical survey. On the other hand, it is unusual to find words in English which correspond formally and semantically to them. Table 1 lists adverbs which can be used as AMAs, with rough English translations. The list is not exhaustive and some of these adverbs are traditionally classified into diverse categories within Japanese grammar.

Since the Meiji period, a number of researchers in the field of *kokugogaku* [Japanese linguistics], including Yamada (1936), Tokieda (1941), and Sakuma (1940) have been interested in the semantic and structural functions of Japanese adverbs. One of the most noteworthy contributions

Table 1: List of Japanese attitude-marking adverbs (AMAs)

	Attitude-marking adverbs (AMAs) Japanese	English
1	あくまで *akumade*	completely, stubbornly, to the last
2	だいたい *daitai*	generally, on the whole
3	だって *datte*	because, rightly enough
4	どうも *dōmo*	somehow
5	どうせ *dōse*	after all, anyway
6	どうやら *dōyara*	it seems, it looks like
7	いっそ *isso*	had better, would better
8	まあ *mā*	well, if you like, I should say
9	まさか *masaka*	surely [not], incredibly, you don't say
10	なかなか *nakanaka*	[not] easily
11	なまじ *namaji* / なまじっか *namajikka*	thoughtlessly, half-heartedly
12	なにしろ *nanishiro*	anyway, you know
13	さすが（に) *sasuga (ni)*	as expected, naturally
14	せっかく *sekkaku*	especially, in spite of all the trouble
15	てっきり *tekkiri*	surely, certainly
16	とかく *tokaku*	frequently, it tends to, generally
17	ともかく *tomokaku* / とにかく *tonikaku*	Anyway
18	とても *totemo*	hardly, it can't possibly
19	わざわざ *wazawaza*	taking the trouble to, on purpose
20	やはり *yahari* / やっぱり *yappari*	as expected, still
21	よもや *yomoya*	surely not, it is not very likely

has been that of Watanabe, which was published during the 1980s. In the article *Fukuyōgensōron* (1983), he presents a major work on *fukuyōgen*, or adverbial words and phrases, and points out that, while they are regarded as one of the key issues in Japanese grammar, their semantic and structural functions are still unexplored and thus need to be elucidated. Watanabe attempts to define and classify adverbials, and to describe each group's function, in order to establish a more solid system of Japanese syntax. Similarly themed work has been undertaken by other scholars such as Sawada (1978), Kudō (1982), Morimoto (1994), and Sugimura (2009), and the group of adverbs named attitude-marking adverbs here have been allocated various names and functions in these researchers' own original grammatical systems, such as *yūdō fukushi* [leading adverbs] or *chinjutsu fukushi* [modal adverbs].

5.1.3 AMA as a Potential Japaniser in Translation

These adverbs open up complex issues and cause disagreement among scholars over their grammatical classification within the framework of Japanese syntax and semantics, as shown above. In a Japanese ST, they sometimes become one of the thornier problems for a translator, as straightforward counterparts are rarely found in English. On the other hand, because their usage is often peculiar to Japanese, they can be introduced into a Japanese TT as effective naturalisers (in this case, Japanisers) and their appropriate prominence can be used to enhance the Japaneseness of the TT. When analysing their usage in a TT, they can be divided into two categories: those conveying a certain attitude in conjunction with a clearly recognisable complementary unit in a sentence; and those not requiring any particular complementary unit and being used to express an attitude by themselves.

5.1.4 Transforming the Speaker's Attitude into an AMA

A. THE AMA *MASAKA* IN THE TT

Some passages from translated texts in which attitude-marking adverbs are effectively used in the TT as a naturaliser will be presented and examined here. AMAs are underlined in the translated texts. The corresponding sentences are underlined in the English texts, and especially relevant parts are also indicated by a double-underline:

Example 2: Agatha Christie, *The Mousetrap*, 1993/1954: 317

Trotter: Superintendent Hogben doesn't think it is a coincidence, sir. [...] He'd have come himself if it had been in any way possible. Under the weather conditions, and as I can ski, he sent me with instructions to get full particulars of everyone in the house, to report back to him by phone, and to take what measures I thought fit to ensure the safety of the household.

Giles: Safety? What danger does he think we're in? <u>Good Lord, he's not suggesting that somebody is going to be killed here.</u>

Trotter: I don't want to frighten any of the ladies – but frankly, yes, that is the idea.

Giles: But why?

Trotter: That's what I'm here to find out.

Gile: But the whole thing's crazy!

Japanese TT: translated by Narumi Shirō, *Nezumitori*, 1980: 85–86

トロッター署長は偶然とは考えてないんですがね。[...]	Torottā: Shochō wa gūzen to wa kangaetenaindesu ga ne. [...]
できるなら署長みずから出向きたいと言ったんだが、なにしろこんな状態だ、スキーができる私が派遣されてきたってわけです。私の受けた指令は、現在この家にいる人全員の実状を調査して電話で報告すること、それからその人々の安全を確保するための適切な処置を講じること...	Dekiru nara shochō mizukara demukitai to ittanda ga, nanishiro konna jōtai da, sukii ga dekiru watashi ga hakensaretekitatte wake desu. Watashi no uketa shirei wa, genzai kono ie ni iru hito zen'in no jitsujō o chōsashite denwa de hōkokusuru koto, sorekara sono hitobito no anzen o kakuhosuru tame no tekisetsuna shochi o kōjiru koto ...
ジャイルズ　安全? いったい、どんな危険があるっていうんですか? <u>まさか、</u> <u>ここでまさか殺人が行なわれるとでも。</u>	Jairuzu: Anzen? Ittai, donna kiken ga arutte yūndesu ka? <u>Masaka, koko de masaka satsujin ga okonawareru to demo.</u>
トロッター　ご婦人方もいることだし、おどかしたくはないけど―正直にいえば、そういうことですな。	Torottā: Gofujingata mo iru koto da shi, odokashitaku wa nai kedo – shōjikini ieba, sō yū koto desu na.
ジャイルズ　だって―なぜ?	Jairuzu: Datte – naze?
トロッター　それを調べにやってきたんですよ。	Torottā: Sore o shirabe ni yattekitandesu yo.
ジャイルズ　気ちがいじみてますよ、そんな。	Jairuzu: Kichigaijimitemasu yo, sonna.

This is an example of translation in which *masaka*, one of the very common AMAs, is used twice in the TT. The ST is taken from *The Mousetrap*, the classic theatre script by Agatha Christie, which holds the record for the longest running West End show in London. The play has never been performed in Japan, so the translation targets Agatha Christie readers, rather than people who have viewed or will view the play in a theatre. First, let us focus on the second *masaka* in the sentence, *Masaka, koko de masaka satsujin ga okonawareru to demo*. There is no doubt that the original, "Good Lord, he's not suggesting that somebody is going to be killed here" is not a simple negative statement. Instead, it is supposed to have a rising intonation and indicates that the speaker, Giles, the owner of the small hotel, has realised that Superintendent Hogben may in fact have made such a suggestion and is asking Trotter if his idea is correct. Giles knows that there has been a murder in the area and this suggestion means that the murderer might be in the hotel, and about to commit another crime. This line is also an answer, which he has worked out for himself, to the question he raised in the previous line "What danger does he think we're in?". The line in question starts with "Good Lord", to show how great his surprise at his own idea is, and smoothly leads to the use of *masaka* in Japanese, which expresses disbelief or scepticism about a proposition. Giles's general scepticism towards the possibility of murder in the house is expressed by "But why?", and then more strongly by "But the whole thing is crazy!" *Masaka* has a slight tinge of disapproval at the idea that "somebody is going to be killed" as well as surprise and disbelief.

B. RECONSTRUCTION OF THE PROCESS

A back-translation (BT) of the sentence in question in Example 2 could be as follows:

> BT: Incredibly, (is [he] suggesting that) a murder will incredibly be conducted here?

In discussing examples, I provide a back-translation or literal rendering of the meaning. I do not claim they should be taken as a standard translation but rather as a sample. Taking into consideration the assumed intonation (almost like an interrogative sentence), a literal translation of the TT (marked LT) could be as follows, garnished with a combination of an auxiliary *deshō* (conjecture) and a suffix *ne* (confirmation).

LT (2) my translation	彼はここで誰かが殺されると は考えてい<u>ない</u>でしょうね。	Kare wa koko de dareka ga korosareru to wa kangaetei<u>nai</u>deshō ne.
BT [LT (2)]	He's <u>not</u> suggesting that somebody is going to be killed here, is he?	

Narumi, the translator, has selected *masaka* from among various linguistic options because Giles's strong feelings – a mixture of surprise, disbelief and disapproval sensed from the ST sentence and the rest of the text – can be effectively conveyed by it.

C. COMPLEMENTARY UNIT TO AMA

It is worth noting that something is omitted after *koko de satsujin ga oko-nawareru to demo*, as indicated by the particles *to* (quotation) and *demo* (suggesting that the foregoing is an example). Because *masaka* requires negation or an implied negative answer within the same sentence, we can assume that there is an omitted unit containing one of them. *Masaka ... nai* (negation) or *masaka ... ka* (interrogative particle) are the two conventional patterns in which this adverb is used. Many AMAs require a certain corresponding complementary linguistic unit – such as negation, interrogation or conjecture – later in the sentence, although the forms are not necessarily fixed. This type of correspondence is termed *fukushi no koō* or adverbial complementation in Japanese grammar. Kudō (1983: 216, my translation) defines it as "use of modal adverbs in cooperation with a certain form that has modal meaning". In colloquial speech, the interrogative or negative element is often omitted and such an omission in a translation adds to the smoothness, and hence the authenticity, of the text.

D. CONDENSATION

In Example 2, the complementation of *masaka* should be, for instance, *kangaeteinaideshō ne* [(he) is not suggesting (or thinking) ..., is (he)?], which matches the LT (2). *Masaka* cannot be analysed as semantically equivalent to "he's not suggesting", but *masaka*, together with a complementary unit such as the one indicated above, can be. In other words, the meaning of the unit "he is not suggesting" in the TT appears to split into two units: *masaka*, and the omitted part. This reminds us of compensation by splitting, one of the four types of compensation in translation suggested by Hervey and Higgins (1992: 39):

> *Compensation by splitting* may be resorted to, if the context allows, in cases where there is no single TL word that covers the same range of meaning as a given ST word. A simple example is furnished by the title of an article on lepidoptera, "Les papillons", which has been to [sic] translated as "Moths and butterflies" (or "Butterflies and moths").

As *masaka* takes a heavier role in carrying the attitudinal meaning than the complementary part, the strategy used here is not a simple splitting, but, more precisely, *condensation* of the meaning, which was spread over the whole ST sentence, into a single word assisted by the (omitted) complementary unit in the TT. *Condensation* can be described as a strategy by which the meaning expressed in the ST by more than one word – often by the whole sentence – is translated into one word or a shorter phrase in the TT. Malone (1986: 13) refers to this strategy as repackaging whereas Hervey and Higgins (1992: 38–40) call it compensation by splitting and compensation by merging.

E. DRAGGING

The first *masaka* in the ST sentence (beginning "Good Lord") will now be analysed. "Good Lord" expresses Giles's surprise at his own idea that Superintendent Hogben is suggesting that somebody is going to be killed. This exclamation of surprise is followed by the rest of the sentence "he's not suggesting" which carries a tone of disbelief, as we have seen. Although the two feelings – surprise and disbelief – are closely linked to one other, "Good Lord" is an expression which is uttered when one comes across an unexpected situation or idea. This means that the first *masaka* in the TT is expressing an additional attitude of the speaker, beyond that in the original – *Masaka*, which expresses disbelief more specifically than "Good Lord" in English, replaces it in what Hervey and Higgins (1992: 35–37) call compensation in kind and Malone (1986: 13) substitution. The translation procedure is obviously affected by the context that follows. It is semantically justifiable to translate "He is not suggesting" as *masaka*, and the "Good Lord" at the beginning of the sentence is given an extra nuance of disbelief too. This nuance, which "Good Lord" is meant to carry, is pulled, or dragged, towards the meaning of the latter part of the sentence. Thus, the first *masaka* is the result of translation using a strategy which can be specifically called *dragging*, that is, a strategy by which the meaning of an ST expression is affected by another part of the ST during the translation process and becomes closer to the meaning of that part.

F. TWO TYPES OF CONDENSATION STRATEGY

Let us examine more examples of the term *masaka* found in another translation to attempt to find the specific strategies used (see Example 3).

Example 3: Dick Francis, *Banker*, 1982: 197

"What does teratogenic mean?" I asked.
"It means," Pen said, "that it produces deformed offspring."
"*What*?" I exclaimed. "<u>You don't mean ...</u>"
Pen was shaking her head. "It couldn't affect Sandcastle. It's impossible. It would simply poison his system. Teratogens have nothing to do with males."

Japanese TT: translated by Kikuchi Mitsu, *Mēmon* 1988: 361	
「テラトジェニックというのは、どういう意味ですか？」私がきいた。	"Teratojenikku to yū no wa, dōyū imi desu ka?" Watashi ga kiita.
「奇形生成性がある、つまり、奇形の子供をつくる性質がある、ということ」	"Kikeiseiseisei ga aru, tsumari, kikei no kodomo o tsukuru seishitu ga aru, to yū koto."
「なにっ？」私は思わず叫んだ。「<u>まさか</u>...」	"Nani (geminate consonant)?" Watashi wa omowazu sakenda. "<u>Masaka</u> ..."
ペンが首を振った。「サンドキャッスルには影響しないのよ。それは不可能。体に害を及ぼすだけ。奇形生成性というのは、牡には関係ないの」	Pen ga kubi o futta. "Sandokyasuru ni wa eikyōshinai no yo. Sore wa fukanō. Karada ni gai o oyobosu dake. Kikeiseiseisei to yū no wa, osu ni wa kankei nai no."

In this adventure story, taken from the popular series by Dick Francis, Sandcastle, an ex-racing stallion in which people have invested heavily, has somehow produced many deformed foals. "I", a private detective, and Pen are trying to work out whether there is something sinister behind this. Here Pen tells "I" that selenium was found in a bottle of horse shampoo, suggesting that someone might have given poison to the mares. "You don't mean" expresses how shocking, unexpected and unbelievable "I" finds this theory. His feeling is not simply reflecting the context – he hopes that Pen is not serious in suggesting such a cruel possibility, but at the same time he is happy to see the mystery solved. This subtle nuance of both positive and negative surprise is concisely conveyed by *masaka* in the TT. The omitted complementation of the adverb is possibly *dareka ga Sandokyasuru ni sereniumu o yatteita to yūnjanaideshō ne* [(you) are <u>not</u> suggesting that somebody has been giving selenium to Sandcastle, are (you)?]. The whole unit which *masaka* modifies is swallowed by the speaker, making the reader guess. "You don't mean" is, strictly speaking, not a complete sentence either, since the content of the thought he does not wish to believe is omitted. Hence, the two utterances, "You don't mean" and *masaka* correspond well, both in meaning and in style. Example 2 notwithstanding, when the ST does not spell out the object of disbelief, it is often translated as a single *masaka* without any complementary term (the core part of the complementation is omitted from Example 2, although the content of disbelief is indicated). The type of translation found in Example 2, in which an AMA is accompanied by its complementation, will be called *condensation A*, and the type of translation found in Example 3, in which an adverb is used on its own, will be called *condensation B*.

G. MORE EXAMPLES OF CONDENSATION A

Some examples of other common AMAs used in TTs will now be used to examine the strategies that produce them in the process of translation.

The adverb in question here is *nanimo*. The word can be analysed as a compound of *nani* [what] and *mo* [particle] and requires negation within the same sentence. It is an adverb which requires great skill to translate into English in a semantically faithful way. "Whatever the situation is like"

Example 4: Lucy M. Montgomery, *Anne of Windy Willows*, 1994/1936: 170–171

> "I dunno why you should worry as to her having a dog or not. I didn't know you were such friends. She hasn't *any* friends. I never had such an unsociable boarder."
>
> "I think that's why she wants a dog, Mrs Dennis. None of us can live without some kind of companionship."
>
> "Well, it's the first human thing I've noticed about her," said Mrs Dennis. "<u>I dunno's I have any awful objection to a dog</u>, but she sort of vexed me with her sarcastic way of asking. 'I s'pose you wouldn't consent if I asked you if I might have a dog, Mrs Dennis?' she sez, haughty-like. Set her up with it!"

Japanese TT: translated by Muraoka Hanako, *An no Kōfuku*, 1981/1958: 221

「それだからこそ、犬を飼いたいと思うんですよ、おばさん。あたしたちはだれでも、なにかしら友達のようなものがなければ生きていかれませんもの」	"Sore dakara koso, inu o kaitai to omoundesu yo, obasan. Atashitachi wa dare demo, nanikashira tomodachi no yōna mono ga nakereba, ikite ikaremasen mono."
「そうですね、あの人にも人間らしさがあると思ったのはこれが初めてですよ。<u>なにもわたしだって犬がひどくいやだというわけではないけれど、</u>あの人の言い方が皮肉なもんで、わたしも腹が立ったんですよ。『犬を飼っていいかと訊いてみたところで、承知してくれそうもないわね、おばさん？』と、こう尊大ぶって言うんですからね。」	"Sō desu ne, ano hito ni mo ningen rashisa ga aru to omotta no wa kore ga hajimete desu yo. <u>Nanimo watashi datte inu ga hidoku iyada to yū wake dewanai keredo,</u> ano hito no iikata ga hinikuna mon de, watashi mo hara ga tattandesu yo. 'Inu o katte ii ka to kiitemita tokoro de, shōchishitekure sō mo nai wa ne, obasan?' to, kō sondaibutte yūndesu kara ne."

or "whatever you might think" might be appropriate as a literal translation. In the ST of Example 4, Mrs Dennis tries to make it clear that she is not particularly against the idea of having a dog in the house by saying, "I dunno's I have any awful objection to a dog". "I dunno's" is often used to express a compromising attitude. Her state of mind can also be gathered from the context in the conversation before, where Anne, the other speaker, explains why Mrs Dennis's lodger wanted to have a dog. This has obviously softened Mrs Dennis's hard feelings towards her lodger and she has become a little defensive about her refusal to give her permission. Her character has been described as "in spite of fat shoulders and a meddle-some tongue, [...] not unkind at heart" (1994/1936: 170). The meaning of the clause unit "I dunno's" and the defensive tone sensed from the ST are efficiently condensed into *nanimo* and the text that follows, including the complementation *inu ga hidoku iya da to yū wake dewanai*, which is the result of *condensation A*. Some AMAs are produced using the *condensation* strategy.

Dōyara, like "seemingly", means "it only looks" or "one is only guessing". Since the adverb conveys the impression that the speaker is not coming to any firm conclusion or taking responsibility, it is also used ironically when stating something unfavourable that is unmistakably a fact, as in Example 5, taken from a classic science fiction novel by Ray Bradbury.

The context helps us understand the usage of *dōyara*, resulting from *condensation A*. The complementation is *korekara ofu shiizun ni hairisō* ne [it seems to be entering the off-season]. Sam and Elma have just watched Earth explode from Mars, where Sam was going to open a hot-dog stand

Example 5: Ray Bradbury, *The Martian Chronicles*, 1977/1950: 188

Sam did not move.
"What a swell spot for a hot-dog stand," she said. She reached over and picked a toothpick out of a jar and put it between her front teeth. "Let you in on a little secret, Sam," she whispered, leaning towards him. "<u>This looks like it's going to be an off-season.</u>"

Japanese TT: translated by Ogasawara Toyoki, *Kaseinendaiki*, 1976: 247	
サムは身動きもしなかった。 「ホットドッグ・スタンドに、なんて打ってつけの場所だこと」エルマは、手をのばして、壷から楊枝を取り出すと、前歯の間にはさんだ。 「ちょっとした秘密を教えてあげるわ、サム」エルマは、サムのほうに身を寄せると、<u>ささや</u>いた。 「<u>どうやら</u>、これからオフ・シーズンに入りそうね」	Samu wa miugoki mo shinakatta. "Hottodoggu • sutando ni, nante uttetsuke no basho da koto." Eruma wa, te o nobashite, tsubo kara yōji o toridasu to, maeba no aida ni hasanda. "Chottoshita himitsu o oshieteageru wa, Samu" Eruma wa, Samu no hō ni mi o yoseru to, sasayaita. "<u>Dōyara</u>, korekara ofu • shiizun ni hairisō ne."

for immigrants from Earth. Sam is devastated, but Elma, who has been inwardly critical of people's arrogance towards the Martians and their attempts to bring Earth culture to Mars – including Sam's business scheme – is relieved. In spite of the harsh reality that they will never get customers, she begins the sentence with "This looks like", deliberately softening the tone of "it's going to be an off season". The ironical nuance is condensed into *dōyara*. We can see that both the ST and TT expressions successfully represent her sense of humour in this disastrous situation.

Yappari (or *yahari*) is one of the most common AMAs in native spoken Japanese. It means "as expected" or "still" (the situation is the same despite the passage of time), but is also often interjected in conversations without any substantial meaning. In the storyline for Example 6, from yet another short story by Christie, Mary has received a mysterious letter, which says that her diamond, *The Star of the West*, will be taken from her. Poirot, the detective, warns her not to wear it when she goes to Yardley Chase. In this

Example 6: Agatha Christie, *The Adventure of The Western Star*, 1991/1924: 14

"Hoax or no hoax, Mr Rolf," he said dryly, "I have advised Madame your wife not to take the jewel with her to Yardley Chase on Friday." "I'm with you there, sir. I've already said so to Mary. But there! <u>She's a woman through and through</u>, and I guess she can't bear to think of another woman outshining her in the jewel line."	
Japanese TT: translated by Ogura Takashi, *"Seibu no Hoshi" Tōnanjiken*, 1978: 19	
「わるふざけかどうかはともかくとしてですな、ロルフさん」と彼はそっけなく言った。「わたしは奥さんに宝石を金曜日にヤードリー猟場へ持っていかないようにおすすめしました」	"Warufuzake ka dōka wa tomokaku to shitedesu na, Rorufusan" to kare wa sokkenaku itta. "Watashi wa okusan ni hōseki o kin'yōbi ni Yādoriiryōjō e motteikanai yōni osusumeshimashita."
「その点はぼくも同感ですな。メアリーにもそう言ったんですよ。しかしそこがですなあ！...<u>やっぱり女です</u>...こと宝石に関してはほかの女に水をあけられるのが我慢ならんのでしょう」	"Sono ten wa boku mo dōkan desu na. Mearii ni mo sō ittandesu yo. Shikashi soko ga desu naa! ... <u>Yappari onna desu</u> ... koto hōseki ni kanshite wa hoka no onna ni mizu o akerareru no ga gaman narannodeshō."

scene, her husband explains to Poirot why she insists on wearing it: because "she can't bear to think of another woman outshining her in the jewel line". The remark, "She's a woman through and through", suggests that he has a fixed idea about women and that his wife's wish to wear the diamond – despite all the warning letters – confirms this idea. In the TT, the meaning "as expected" or "as I have always believed" is extracted from "through and through" in the sentence and condensed into *yappari*. This example can also be categorised as *substitutive insertion*, which will be discussed later.

The various AMAs seen in the TTs in the above examples all express semantic meaning, often aligned with the subtle nuance of the ST. The decision to introduce an AMA tends to succeed in achieving a smooth, locally readable TT.

H. INSERTION

I will now turn to larger-scale domestication, as represented by more drastic strategies employing AMAs. In the next few translation examples, no actual ST linguistic expression corresponds to the adverb used in the TT. Nevertheless, the adverbs are inserted into the TTs for various reasons, mainly pragmatic or situational. The ST is usually a situation in which a Japanese speaker would use an AMA in a non-translational, colloquial setting. The translator not only transforms the ST but also adds what the speaker would say in the TL in the given context, to achieve more communicative equivalence. This strategy is called insertion, whereby a TL expression is used in translation, without any semantically corresponding expression in the ST.

As can be understood from the ST and the BT of the sentence in question, there is no particular expression which can be identified as the source of *dōmo*. The word literally means "in any way" or "whatever way it is", indicating that the speaker suspects something in an unspecified manner. The butler's inevitable conclusion is that "her ladyship is apt to be a little hasty in her judgments". He has come to this position from his past experiences with his mistress, though the reasons for his suspicion remain unspecified in his remark. *Dōmo* often functions as a softener of tone since it carries the nuance that the speaker does not know any details

Example 7: Agatha Christie, *The Under Dog*, 1994/1960: 118

"What is your opinion – I beg your pardon – the opinion of the servants' hall of the secretary?"   "He is a very quiet, patient gentleman, sir. Anxious to give no trouble."   "*Vraiment*," said Poirot.   The butler coughed.   "<u>Her ladyship, sir</u>," he murmured, "<u>is apt to be a little hasty in her judgments</u>."

Japanese TT: translated by Ogasawara Toyoki, *Makeinu*, 1985: 176	
「ルーベン卿の秘書についての、あなたの―いや、失礼―使用人一同の意見は？」	"Rūbenkyō no hisho ni tsuite no, anata no – iya, shitsurei – shiyōnin ichidō no iken wa?"
「あの方は、とてもおとなしい、我慢強い紳士でいらっしゃいます。いつもトラブルを恐れていらっしゃるような」 「なるほど」と、ポアロ。	"Ano kata wa, totemo otonashii, gamanzuyoi shinshi de irasshaimasu. Itsumo toraburu o osoreteirassharu yōna."
執事は咳ばらいをした。	"Naruhodo (vureman)" to, Poaro. Shitsuji wa sekibarai o shita.
「<u>奥様は</u>」と、執事はつぶやいた。「<u>どうも、すこし、判断を急がれるところがおありになります</u>」	"<u>Okusama wa</u>" to, shitsuji wa tsubuyaita. "<u>Dōmo, sukoshi, handan o isogareru tokoro ga oari ni narimasu</u>."
BT	
Her ladyship has, [...] somehow an aspect of hastening a little in her judgment.	

of the issue under discussion or does not want to admit that he/she does (cf. *dōyara* in Example 5). When the content of the statement is unfavourable to the addressee, for instance, *dōmo* can skilfully transfer the responsibility from the speaker to other unspecified factors, such as experiences, rumours, inspiration or appearances. In the ST, the butler is hesitant to comment unfavourably about his mistress to an outsider like Poirot, as shown by the fact that "he murmured". Although there is no tone-softener in the butler's words in the ST indicating hesitation arising from the situation, *dōmo* is inserted in the TT ("is apt to" and "a little" can be regarded as hesitation-markers, but they are respectively translated as *tokoro ga oari ni*

Example 8: Ray Bradbury, *The Martian Chronicles*, 1977/1950: 91–92

"Will any of those men under you ever really understand all this? They're professional cynics, and it's too late for them. Why do you want to go back with them? So you can keep up with the Joneses? To buy a gyro just like Smith has? To listen to music with your pocket-book instead of your glands? There's a little patio down here with a reel of Martian music in it at least fifty thousand years old. It still plays. Music you'll never hear in your life. You could hear it. There are books. I've gotten on well in reading them already. You could sit and read."

"It all sounds quite wonderful, Spender."

"<u>But you won't stay?</u>"

"No. Thank you, anyway."

Japanese TT: translated by Ogasawara Toyoki, *Kaseinendaiki*, 1976: 116

「あなたの部下のなかで、こういうことを理解してくれる人がいるでしょうか。みんな、骨の髄までのひねくれ者で、もう手おくれです。あなたはなぜあんな連中の所へ帰るのですか。ジョーンズ一家に遅れをとらぬためですか。スミスのと同じヘリコプターを買うためですか。内分泌腺ではなく解説書によって音楽を聴くためですか。あそこの四阿あずまやにはすくなくとも５万年前の火星の音楽のリールがあります。いまでも聴けます。滅多に聴けないような、すばらしい音楽ですよ。お聴きになりませんか。本もあります。解読はだいぶ進みました。ゆっくり本でもお読みになったらいかがですか」 「すばらしい本だね、スペンダー」 「<u>でも、やはり帰るのですか</u>」 「帰る。とにかく、お礼を言うよ」	"Anata no buka no naka de, kō yū koto o rikaishitekureru hito ga irudeshō ka. Minna, hone no zui made no hinekuremono de, mō teokure desu. Anata wa naze anna renchū no tokoro e kaerunodesu ka. Jōnzuikka ni okure o toranu tame desu ka. Sumisu no to onaji herikoputā o kau tame desu ka. Naibunpitsusen de wa naku kaisetsusho ni yotte ongaku o kiku tame desu ka. Asoko no azumaya ni wa sukunakutomo gomannen mae no kasei no ongaku no riiru ga arimasu. Ima demo kikemasu. Mettani kikenai yōna, subarashii ongaku desu yo. Okiki ni narimasen ka. Hon mo arimasu. Kaidoku wa daibu susumimashita. Yukkuri hon demo oyomi ni nattara ikaga desu ka." "Subarashii hon da ne, Supendā." "<u>Demo, yahari kaeru no desu ka</u>," "Kaeru. Tonikaku, orei o yū yo."

narimasu and *sukoshi* and there are no other general tone-softeners). The insertion of "sir" seems necessary here as a matter of course; it is therefore not regarded as a hesitation marker. Through the translation process, the assessment made by the translator that a tone-softener should be inserted in the TT has been achieved with a linguistic item.

Yahari, the adverb inserted here, means that the content of a proposition is common knowledge or is expected, as already discussed. It is one of the most frequently used AMAs and hence an effective domesticator. In Example 8, Spender, an archaeologist captivated by the Martian environment and lifestyle, tries to persuade the captain of the expedition to stay on Mars, and not to report the results of its research to the American government, explaining how wonderful the Martian cultural heritage is. Invited to share Spender's residence, the captain says, "You ask *me* that?" (Bradbury 1977: 91) implying that he is the last person to whom Spender should make such a suggestion, since he is responsible for the expedition and the spaceship. From the beginning, Spender expects the captain to go back to Earth, because of the captain's duty and social status. "It all sounds quite wonderful, Spender" does not answer Spender's suggestion directly, but the very fact that the captain avoids answering makes him realise that his attempt at persuasion has been unsuccessful.[1] *Yahari* is his interpretation, or rather his evaluation, of the captain's decision. The point is that no original words corresponding to *yahari* are found in the ST. The context of the ST produces *yahari* in the TT, which consequently emphasises the tone of resignation by stating clearly that, retrospectively speaking, the captain's decision is not surprising. It also naturalises the TT language. Such insertion aims to bring out equivalence in the ST sentence, whose meaning and tone would require the use of an AMA in Japanese. The semantic equivalence is, however, disturbed when this strategy is adopted (often because some extra meaning not present in the ST is added). The next example is also from the same source:

1   *Subarashii hon da ne, Supendā* in the TT is semantically a mismatch with the ST because the captain is referring not only to the book but also to all the advanced and refined Martian cultural items that Spender has listed. This mistake is not relevant to the discussion here, however.

Example 9: Ray Bradbury, *The Martian Chronicles*, 1977/1950: 31

The man gazed at her in surprise. "We're from *Earth*!"
"I haven't time," she said. "I've a lot of cooking today and there's cleaning and sewing and all. You evidently wish to see Mr Ttt; he's upstairs in his study."
"Yes," said the Earth Man confusedly, blinking. "By all means, let us see Mr Ttt."
"He's busy." She slammed the door again.
This time the knock on the door was most impertinently loud.
"See here!" cried the man when the door was thrust open again. He jumped in as if to surprise her. "<u>This is no way to treat visitors!</u>"

Japanese TT: translated by Ogasawara Toyoki, *Kaseinendaiki*, 1976: 38–39

男はびっくりして夫人を見つめた。「われわれは地球から来たのです！」	Otoko wa bikkurishite fujin o mitsumeta. "Wareware wa chikyū kara kitanodesu!"
「わたし忙しいのよ」と、夫人は言った。「今日はお料理をたくさん作らなくちゃならないし、お洗濯もあるし、縫いものもありますからね。主人にお逢いになりたいんでしょう。主人でしたら、二階の書斎にいますけど」	"Watashi isogashii no yo" to, fujin wa itta. "Kyō wa oryōri o takusan tsukuranakucha naranai shi, osentaku mo aru shi, nuimono mo arimasu kara ne. Shujin ni oai ni naritaindeshō. Shujin deshitara, nikai no shosai ni imasu kedo."
「ええ」と、地球人はうろたえて、目をぱちぱちさせた。「ぜひ御主人に逢わせて下さい」	"Ē" to, chikyūjin wa urotaete, me o pachipachi saseta. "Zehi goshujin ni awasetekudasai."
「主人も忙しいのよ」夫人はまたピシャリとドアをしめた。	"Shujin mo isogashii no yo" Fujin wa mata pishari to doa o shimeta.
今度のノックの音は、一段とあつかましく、やかましかった。	Kondo no nokku no oto wa, ichidanto atsukamashiku, yakamashikatta.
「冗談じゃない！」と、ふたたびドアがあくや、男は叫んだ。そして夫人をおどかすように、中へ跳びこんだ。「<u>せっかく訪ねてきたのに、そんな扱い方をしていいんですか！</u>」	"Jōdan ja nai!" to, futatabi doa ga aku ya, otoko wa sakenda. Soshite fujin o odokasu yōni, naka e tobikonda. "<u>Sekkaku</u> tazunete kita no ni, sonna <u>atsukaikata o shite iindesu ka!</u>"

BT

After all the trouble of visiting, is it ok to treat us that way?

Sekkaku is an AMA which is difficult to translate literally into English, since it seems less important to vocalise the sentiment in English. Thus, the word's semantic meaning does not usually fit into the context in English. It indicates a rather complex state of mind: the speaker thinks highly of something, such as the trouble someone has taken or a present someone has bought, and believes it deserves a decent show of appreciation – often better than it has actually received. In Example 9, the Earth Man has just arrived safely on Mars for the first time (they are in fact on the second expedition, but do not know what has happened to the first one) and he is annoyed with the Martian Woman because she is not excited about their arrival or is not treating them kindly, even though they have come all the way from Earth.

The point about Ogasawara's decision to insert *sekkaku* is that the Earth Man takes it for granted that they are worth more attention and respect because of their long and difficult journey. The passage starts from the scene in which the man tries to talk to the Martian Woman again, after she has slammed the door on him. The Woman is still uninterested in what he says and maintains her blunt manner throughout the dialogue. At first the Earth Man is puzzled by this unexpected unkindness, but then his accumulated dissatisfaction turns into anger. His emotional explosion takes the form of the sentence in question, opening with "See here!" which conveys the Earth Man's indignation. In this case, the Earth Man is convinced that the Martian Woman should start treating Earthlings better. The expression has been given *Jōdan ja nai!* [You must be kidding!] in the TT, but "See here!" and "This is no way to treat visitors!" should be taken as one sequence in the conversation. Therefore, the angry tone aroused by the injustice which he has experienced (as sensed from "See here!") continues later in the speech with "This is no way to treat visitors!". Analysis suggests that Ogasawara added *sekkaku* to verbalise the sense of anger and frustration which the sentence carries over from the previous line. Thus, *sekkaku* is used in the TT, as the word is required in Japanese in this kind of situation.

1. SUBSTITUTIVE INSERTION

Sometimes an AMA in the TT replaces another translation item: the source item can be found in the ST but does not have the same semantic meaning as the adverb used in the TT. An AMA is often selected and inserted to compensate for this. I call this *substitutive insertion* and distinguishes it from the simple insertion (called "substitution" by Malone (1986: 13)) which has been observed and analysed above. *Substitutive insertion* is a strategy by which a TL expression without a ST semantic counterpart is introduced as compensation for another expression. Example 10 demonstrates this strategy.

Example 10: Dick Francis, *Banker*, 1982: 48

I seemed to be continually in his thoughts. He gave me truly vicious looks across the room and took every opportunity to sneer and denigrate. Messages never got passed on, and clients were given the impression that I was incompetent and only employed out of family charity. Occasionally on the telephone people refused to do business with me, saying they wanted John, and once a caller said straight out, "Are you that playboy they're shoving ahead over better men's heads?"   John's gripe was basically understandable: <u>in his place I'd have been cynical myself.</u>

Japanese TT: translated by Kikuchi Mitsu, *Mēmon*, 1988: 84

私のことが頭にこびりついている ようだった。部屋の向こうから 敵意にみちた目で私を見、機会あ るごとに冷笑し軽蔑の表情を見せ ていた。私への伝言は絶対に伝え ず、顧客は、私が無能力で、同族 の憐れみで雇われているにすぎな い、という印象を植えつけられて いた。時折、私に用はない、ジョ ンと話したい、と電話で言う客が おり、一度は、「おまえが、もっ と有能な人間を無視して銀行が登 用しようとしているあのプレイボ ーイか？」とはっきり言った者が いた。 ジョンの妬みは理解できなくはな い―<u>私が彼の立場にあったら、や はりひがむだろう。</u>	Watashi no koto ga atama ni kobiritsuite iru yōdatta. Heya no mukō kara tekii ni michita me de watashi o mi, kikai aru goto ni reishōshi keibetsu no hyōjō o miseteita. Watashi e no dengon wa zettaini tsutaezu, kokyaku wa, watashi ga munōryoku de, dōzoku no awaremi de yatowareteiru ni suginai, to yū inshō o uetsukerareteita. Tokiori, watashi ni yō wa nai, Jon to hanashitai, to denwa de yū kyaku ga ori, ichido wa, "omae ga, motto yūnōna ningen o mushishite ginkō ga tōyō shiyō to shiteiru ano pureibōi ka?" to hakkiri itta mono ga ita. Jon no netami wa rikaidekinaku wa nai – <u>watashi ga kare no tachiba ni attara, yahari higamudarō.</u>

BT

John's jealousy is not incomprehensible – if I were in his place, I would be cynical, as anybody would.

Note the presence in the ST of "myself". "I" is the bank manager's nephew, who has recently been promoted to director. In spite of "I"'s talent and devotion, his colleague John is bitter because "he was older and had worked much longer in the bank" and "I" should not be "jumping the queue" (Francis 1983: 47). He analyses John's psychology: "I'd have been cynical myself" in his position. "Myself" has been transformed into *yahari* in the TT, which amplifies the cynicism in the situation as *yahari* implies the general validity of being "cynical" in such a situation. The ST imposes no semantic pressure to emphasise the meaning of "anybody" in the TT, but the translator smoothes the TT by substituting *yahari* for "myself", utilising the frequent prominence of *yahari* in Japanese. When choices exist between a counterpart of the ST expression (including a semantically closer equivalent), and a potential substitution which would make that part of the text more domestic (or original), many translators select the latter – even if the original meaning is significantly lost or distorted. This suggests that there is a tendency towards partial Japanisation despite the danger of semantic loss, corroborating to some extent the Law of Growing Standardisation proposed by Toury (1995: 267). Example 11 is another example of *substitutive insertion*.

Dōse literally means "however I do (something)", "anyhow" or "regardless of how things turn out", and is used like "at any rate" or "at best". It often carries the nuance that something would not go well in any case and that an unfavourable result is inevitable, so it is pointless to make much effort to improve the situation. *Dōse* also implies that the speaker has entered a pessimistic, cynical state of mind after receiving some information or going through a process of thought. In Example 11, Mollie tries to confess her personal problems to her husband Giles: the fact that one of her students died through her negligence when she was a schoolteacher, her current state of confusion and her guilty conscience. When Giles reacts by saying: "you're crazy" she admits that she is crazy, rather than trying to make him understand her. This hysterical attitude is a reaction to her long process of agony and, finally, her husband's insensitive remark. Her mood of resignation and aggressiveness, as sensed in the ST, matches the nuance of *dōse*, and justifies the replacement of the unit "then" with *dōse* in the TT.

Example 11: Agatha Christie, *The Mousetrap*, 1993/1954: 345

Gilles: (*Moving to left of* Mollie) Mollie, what's come over you? You're different all of a sudden. I feel as though I don't know you any more.
Mollie: Perhaps you never did know me. We've been married how long – a year? But you don't really know anything about me. What I'd done or thought or felt or suffered before you knew me.
Gilles: Mollie, you're crazy …
Mollie: <u>All right then</u>, I'm crazy! Why not? Perhaps it's fun to be crazy!

Japanese TT: translated by Narumi Shirō, *Nezumitori*, 1980: 154

ジャイルズ：モリーの右手に行き）モリー、どうしたんだい、きみは？急に人が変ってしまったようだ。まるで知らない人のような気がする。	Jairuzu: (Morii no migite ni iki) Morii, dō shitandai, kimi wa? Kyūni hito ga kawatte shimatta yōda. Marude shiranai hito no yōna ki ga suru.
モリー：きっと知らない人だからよ。私たち結婚してどれだけ－一年ね？だけど私のこと、ほんとうはなんにも知ってないでしょ。つきあうまえに私が何をしたか、何を考えたか、私の心の悩みも苦しみも。	Morii: Kitto shiranai hito dakara yo. Watashitachi kekkonshite dore dake – ichinen ne? Dakedo watashi no koto, hontō wa nannimo shittenaidesho. Tsukiau mae ni watashi ga nani o shita ka, nani o kangaeta ka, watashi no kokoro no nayami mo kurushimi mo.
ジャイルズ：モリー、気が違ったのか…	Jairuzu: Morii, ki ga chigatta no ka …
モリー：<u>いいわよ、どうせ私は気違いよ！</u> いいじゃない！ 楽しいわよ、気違いになるのも！	Morii: <u>Ii wa yo, dōse watashi wa kichigai yo!</u> Iijanai! Tanoshii wa yo, kichigai ni naru no mo!

BT
OK, anyhow I am mad!

To summarise these observations on the use of AMAs, often the ST unit as a whole and the TT with an AMA share semantic meaning. An AMA sometimes brings an extra nuance to the text. The emergence of the adverb in the TT is frequently the result of the *condensation* of a longer expression in the ST (*condensation A* or *B*). AMAs are, however, inserted in the TT even where no linguistic counterparts are found in the ST (*insertion*). The translator deduces a certain situation or a certain state of mind in the speaker from the information gathered from the sentence in context and expresses it as an adverb. As a result, the receptor of the translation would not suffer any feeling of loss if the adverb was absent in the TT. Rarely, in fact, does a receptor notice the absence of such an adverb. However, a receptor might well sense some stiffness – a lack of flow – in the absence of the marker. AMAs are also inserted as a replacement for an ST expression which has a semantically different meaning (*substitutive insertion*).

AMAs are undoubtedly effective in domesticating the TT by their mere presence in a sentence. Their appropriate use functions as an amplifier of the domesticness of the TT (although the effect of domestication achieved is usually limited to the sentence) because their use is characteristic of Japanese – as distinct from English. These potential Japanisers are beneficially deployed in translated popular fiction. It is noteworthy that when an AMA would make a particular part of the text more domestic, it is usually selected and used, even if the original meaning is significantly lost or distorted. When the use goes beyond the domestic norm, it fails as an attempt at domestication. This is in fact not limited to AMAs, but is also true of other potential Japanisers, such as male/female dialects and idiomatic phrases. This will be discussed later in the presentation of the major normative properties of the text-type in Chapter 7.

5.2   Linguistic Foreignisation

This section considers the second of the two translation options, that is, foreignisation. This is a different approach to unavoidable structural differences between the SL and the TL, which create obstacles in the process of translation.

5.2.1   *Traces of Englishness in the TT*

The idea of foreignisation here is simply to allow some of the SL features to remain in the TT, even if the resulting text becomes idiosyncratic when compared with the normative TL. Such potential obstacles are naturally found in abundance in the case of translations between English and Japanese. Stiff Japanese which retains features of English is conventionally recognised as *hon'yakuchō* and linguistic foreignisation is regarded as a major trigger. Although foreign-sounding Japanese is immediately apparent, the fact that the cause of the strangeness found in translational Japanese is domestication often goes unnoticed.

5.2.2 Frequently Observed Englishness

In what follows, the extensive use of linguistic foreignisation is detectable in the Japanese translation of a text by Sara Paretsky, from her *V. I. Warshawski* series:

Example 12: Sara Paretsky, *Indemnity Only*, 1982: 29

"Morning, Bobby. <u>What a nice surprise.</u>"	
"Good morning, Vicky. Sorry to drag you out of bed," Mallory said with heavy humor.	
Japanese TT: translated by Yamamoto Yayoi, *Samātaimu-Burūsu*, 1985: 46–47	
「いらっしゃい、ボビー、<u>なんてすてきな驚きだこと</u>」	"Irasshai, Bobii, nante sutekina odoroki da koto."
「おはよう、ヴィッキー。ベッドから引きずり出しちまって悪かったな」	"Ohayō, Vikkii. Beddo kara hikizuridashichimatte warukatta na."

Two simple facts explain why the underlined unit is understood as being linguistic foreignisation. First, there is no linguistic custom in Japanese of using the semantic form "what a nice surprise" – even when one genuinely regards somebody's visit as a nice surprise. Second, the adjective *sutekina* [nice] and the noun *odoroki* [surprise] do not suit one another well as modifier and modified noun. The TT unit exhibits a clear stiffness due to the word-for-word translation approach. An interesting point is that Yamamoto translated the sentence beginning "Morning" using *irasshai*, adding domesticness by employing a normative greeting word for a visitor, while leaving the rest of the unit completely foreignised. Even in a sentence as short as this, mixed use of linguistic domestication and

Example 13: Lucy M. Montgomery, *Anne of Windy Willows*, 1994/1936: 306

"Are you feeling better, darling?" said Miss Shirley.
"Have I been sick?"
"<u>You were knocked down by a team of runaway horses on the mainland road</u>," said Miss Shirley. "<u>I, I wasn't quick enough.</u> I, I thought you were killed. I brought you right back here in the flat and your ..., this gentleman telephoned for a doctor and nurse."

Japanese TT: translated by Muraoka Hanako, *An no Kōfuku*, 1981/1958: 392	
「気分がよくなったこと、エリザ ベスちゃん？」	"Kibun ga yoku natta koto, Erizabesuchan?"
シャーリー先生は訊ねた。	Shāriisensei wa tazuneta.
「あたしは病気だったの？」	"Atashi wa byōki datta no?"
「<u>あなたは街道を逃げて走ってき た馬に打ち倒されたのよ。あたし がーあたしがすばやくしなかった ものだから。</u>あたしはーあたしは あなたが死んだと思ったのよ。す ぐに小舟であなたをここに連れ戻 して、あなたのーこの方が電話で お医者さまと看護婦さんをお呼び になったの」	"<u>Anata wa kaidō o nigete hashittekita uma ni uchitaosareta no yo. Atashi ga – atashi ga subayaku shinakatta mono dakara.</u> Atashi wa – atashi wa anata ga shinda to omotta no yo. Suguni kobune de anata o koko ni tsuremodoshite, anata no – kono kata ga denwa de oishasama to kangofusan o oyobi ni natta no."

foreignisation can be observed (see Chapter 7). The next example is from *Anne of Windy Willows*.

In this popular translation of a novel for older children, colloquial expressions are used – especially for the dialogues – and it is evident that Muraoka has made a great effort to domesticate the text. Nevertheless, the TT still contains clear signs of the original foreign elements in the storyline. In Example 13, *uma ni uchitaosareta* [were knocked down by a horse/horses] is not semantically normative: the verb does not go with *uma* because it is an action that is supposed to be performed by a fist or an arm, not by the hoof or body of a horse. In the text, Elizabeth has survived the accident without any major injuries. This leads to the conclusion that the collision cannot have been too violent. Considering this, *kerareta* [were kicked] or *butsukatta* [bumped into] would be a more semantically straightforward equivalent

Example 14: Agatha Christie, *The Mystery of the Spanish Chest*, 1994/1960: 69–70

"I know who you are. Your husband was killed – stabbed, and a Major Rich has been arrested and charged with his murder." The flush heightened. "<u>Major Rich did *not* kill my husband.</u>" Quick as a flash Poirot said: "Why not?"	

Japanese TT: translated by Fukushima Masami, *Supeinhitsu no Himitsu*, 1985: 102	
「存じ上げております。あなたの ご主人は殺害された―刺し殺さ れた。そしてリッチ少佐が逮捕さ れ、殺人罪で起訴されました」 赤みがますます色を増した。 「<u>リッチ少佐は、主人を殺さなか ったのです</u>」 電光石火にポアロがきいた。 「なぜです？」	"Zonjiagete orimasu. Anata no goshujin wa satsugaisareta – sashikorosareta. Soshite Ricchishōsa ga taihosare, satsujinzai de kisosaremashita." Akami ga masumasu iro o mashita. "<u>Ricchishōsa wa, shujin o korosanakattanodesu.</u>" Denkōsekka ni Poaro ga kiita. "Naze desu?"

BT	
Major Rich did not kill (my) husband.	

(both *uchitaosareta* and *keritaosareta* imply a serious consequence). The ST unit got Muraoka to select a structurally closer verb *uchitaosareta* (*utsu* [to knock] + *taosu* [to pull down] + – *reta* [passive, past]).

Example 14, taken from Agatha Christie's *The Mystery of the Spanish Chest*, contains an instance of one of the most characteristic examples of stiffness in translational Japanese, which is caused by an unusual usage of particles.

"She" in the text is asking Poirot, the detective, for help in proving Major Rich's innocence. Her husband has been killed by somebody, and Major Rich, who has always cared for her, is suspected as the murderer. The particle of topicalisation *wa*, underlined in the TT, gives the impression that the speaker deliberately makes Major Rich the topic of the sentence. This sentence emphasises the fact that somebody *did* kill her husband but

Major Rich did not, or the fact that Major Rich did something else. It is obviously not the point she wanted to make and, since her intention is simply to say that Major Rich is innocent, something else should have been topicalised in the sentence. Thus, the part of the TT (14) in question has a tenuous connection with the sentences before and after. The reader can surely guess the intended meaning, but the fact remains that it is conveyed using peculiar language.

5.3 Summary

Some examples have been randomly selected from translation works in the popular fiction genre produced between the 1960s and the present day, and clearly share some common distinct stylistic features. How the features are shared by the works will be discussed and partially quantified in 6.2. The strategies are sorted into two options: domestication and foreignisation, both of which can be either linguistic or cultural. The strategies identified here include ones that are commonly witnessed in Japanese translation of various genres, and in fact in all translation. Nevertheless, the examples selected on these pages represent the types of translations which contain peculiar translational stylistic features of popular fiction.

In looking at linguistic domestication, I have examined Japanese attitude-marking adverbs, such as *masaka*, *dōmo* and *yappari*, as examples of Japanese-characteristic devices, and reconstructed the translation process from which they emerged. They effectively express the speaker's (or the character's) attitude, stance or viewpoint on the state of affairs, to make the TT sound domestic. It is rare, however, that an adverb with the same or similar function can be traced back to a counterpart in the English: the same attitude is expressed by means of other linguistic devices, such as a deletable verb clause (for example "I guess" or "it seems"). The ST translation unit and the adverb in the TT tend not to be lexically semantic counterparts, but they perform the same function at the sentence level. *Condensation* is a strategy which often transforms the ST expression into an AMA. On occasions, there are no counterparts to such adverbs in any recognisable linguistic form in the ST. This poses the question of whether a word without a counterpart in the original can justifiably be called a piece of translation or not. In most cases, there is a counterpart in the form of a situation which potentially requires an AMA (*insertion*); it is not required by the original text itself, but by the necessity imposed by the TL norms, and when its usage and frequency are appropriate, it can successfully domesticate the text.

Secondly, cases of linguistic foreignisation – which are not difficult to find in Japanese translations in general – have been discussed. Some linguistic adjustments are necessary to erase obvious English features, and if they are not made, the TT can exhibit all kinds of linguistic stiffness (there is an inexhaustible supply of expressions and structures which can produce this). Specific kinds of foreignness have been pointed out and recognised by scholars as principal features of Japanese translational language. It is also important to identify particular types of stiffness as properties of the style specifically used in translated popular literature. This will be attempted in Chapter 7. Now the attention turns to domestication and foreignisation at the cultural level.

CHAPTER 6

Textual Analysis (II): Cultural Domestication and Foreignisation

6.1 Cultural Domestication

Here the focus of transformation will be redirected from the linguistic (formal and/or semantic) distance between the ST and the TT attributable to their syntactical and lexical features, to more obviously cultural factors. The term "cultural" is employed here because the shift arises out of extralinguistic discrepancies between life in the SL and TL communities.

6.1.1 Factors beyond Linguistic Phenomena

An entirely new semantic item emerges between the ST unit and the final translation: cultural transposition (Hervey and Higgins 1992: 28) or shifts (Popovič 1970: 79) appear to be required, and are indeed common in any translation situation. Popovič (ibid. 78–81) argues that losses, gains, and changes are a necessary part of the process because of differing cultural values and literary norms.

It is, however, especially noticeable when the cultural gap between the ST and the TT is considerable, and, although the substance of such separation is never easy to identify, is symbolic of distance between the West and the East. A cultural shift from a Christianity-related item to a Buddhist-related item, for instance, might not be confined to a simple resetting of the character's religion in the TT setting but might also demand changes of certain traits in his/her psychology or behaviour, which might disturb internal literary consonance. The issue of such delicate conformity is often bluntly ignored in translated popular fiction. The following are some examples illustrating how cultural disagreement between the SL and TL cultures is treated.

6.1.2 From Neutral to TL Culture-Specific

First of all, I will focus on cases in which a culturally loaded item is used in place of a neutral item in the ST. Baker (1992: 31) cites cultural substitution – known as "cultural transposition" and "cultural transplantation" by Hervey and Higgins (1992: 28–30) – as one of the strategies used to achieve equivalence at the word level:

> This strategy involves replacing a culture-specific item or expression with a target-language item which does not have the same propositional meaning but is likely to have a similar impact on the target reader. The main advantage of using this strategy is that it gives the reader a concept with which s/he can identify, something familiar and appealing.

In Example 15, a culturally neutral term in the ST is replaced by a term that is culturally specific to the TL. Two different metaphors are used to refer to (almost) the same colour in the ST and the TT:

Example 15: Lucy M. Montgomery, *Anne of Windy Willows*, 1994/1936: 201

Certainly Cousin Ernestine was not beautiful, and it was extremely doubtful if she ever had been. She had a dry, pinched little face, faded, pale blue eyes, several badly placed moles, and a whining voice. She [sic] wore a <u>rusty black</u> dress and a decrepit neckpiece of Hudson seal, which she would not remove even at the table, because she was afraid of draughts.	
Japanese TT: translated by Muraoka Hanako, *An no Kōfuku*, 1981/1958: 258	
たしかに従妹アーネスティンは美人ではなく、かつて美しいときがあったかどうかもはなはだ心もとなかった。かさかさやせた小さな顔、色あせた水色の目、配置のわるい数個のほくろ、哀れっぽい声の持主だった。<ruby>羊羹色<rt>ようかんいろ</rt></ruby>の服を着込み、古ぼけたハドソン湾のあざらしの<ruby>襟巻<rt>えりまき</rt></ruby>をしており、隙間風が心配だからといって食卓でもその襟巻をとらなかった。	Tashikani itoko Ānesutin wa bijin de wa naku, katsute utsukushii toki ga atta ka dōka mo hanahada kokoromoto nakatta. Kasakasa yaseta chiisana kao, iroaseta mizuiro no me, haichi no warui sūko no hokuro, awareppoi koe no mochinushi datta. <u>Yōkan'iro no</u> fuku o kikomi, furuboketa Hadosonwan no azarashi no erimaki o shiteori, sukimakaze ga shinpai dakara to itte shokutaku de mo sono erimaki o toranakatta.

Yōkan'iro no is employed in the TT for "rusty black". *Yōkan* is a particular kind of Japanese confectionary made from crushed red beans and has a dark, blackish-purple colour. The colour that "rusty black" refers to is conveyed by the TT replacement: the two phrases refer to the same (or very similar) colours, but use different rhetorical expressions. What is more, the TT version takes the form of a direct metaphor – unlike the source. Leaving aside the possibility of a more straightforward and culturally neutral translation, as for example 錆びたような黒い服 / *sabita yōna kuroi fuku* [an-as-if-it-had-rusted black dress], the unit has potential for Japanisation, which Muraoka obviously noticed and exploited.

In the next example, taken from a short story by Agatha Christie, an idiomatic expression in the ST is replaced by an idiomatic expression in the TT, in which the cultural item "gallows" appears:

Example 16: Agatha Christie, *The Adventure of the Italian Nobleman*, 1991/1924: 178

"I did nothing of the sort. I have sworn in court –" "*Précisément* – and I have a little idea that you have sworn falsely." "You threaten me? Bah! I have nothing to fear from you. I have been acquitted." "Exactly; and as I am not an imbecile, <u>it is not with the gallows I threaten you</u> – but with publicity."

Japanese TT: translated by Ogura Takashi, *Itariakizoku Satsujin Jiken*, 1978: 255

「そんなことしませんよ。裁判所で宣誓したように...」	"Sonna koto shimasen yo. Saibansho de sensēshita yōni ..."
「なるほど...いや、わたしは、あなたが偽証した、という気がちょっとしたもんですからね」	"Naruhodo ... iya, watashi wa, anata ga gishōshita, to yū ki ga chotto shita mon desu kara ne"
「脅迫するんですか？ばかばかしい！あなたを怖れるようなことをしたおぼえはありません。わたしは無罪釈放されたんですからね」	"Kyōhakusurundesu ka? Bakabakashii! Anata o osoreru yōna koto o shita oboe wa arimasen. Watashi wa muzaishakuhōsaretandesu kara ne."
「そうでしたな。ところで、わたしは共犯者でもなんでもないから、あなたを脅すといったって、<u>三尺高い木にかけるぞ、などというのではありません</u>...公表するというのです。」	"Sō deshita na. Tokorode, watashi wa kyōhansha de mo nan de mo nai kara, anata o odosu to ittate, <u>sanshaku takai ki ni kakeru zo, nado to yū no de wa arimasen</u> ... kōhyōsuru to yū no desu."

Poirot, who is investigating a murder, threatens a suspect by saying that he will tell what he knows. In the ST he says, "it is not with the gallows I threaten you" – that is, he is not threatening to take him to court. On the other hand, the TT uses *sanshaku* (or *sanjaku*) *takai ki ni kakeru* [hang somebody on a three-*shaku*-high tree], which is an idiomatic expression referring to the execution of a criminal in a lawful manner. *Shaku* is an old Japanese unit of measurement, equivalent to approximately one foot, and hanging a criminal this way was a lawful method of capital punishment during the Edo period (1603–1867). So, the ST and TT expressions share the content of the threat Poirot issued and the same idiomatic quality, but the TT unit adds a strong nuance of Japaneseness to the TT. Since the characters' names remain Western and the setting is still London, the domesticity of the expression is particularly prominent.

6.1.3 *From TL Culture-Specific to Neutral*

Consider the function and significance of "French mustard" in the ST: it is part of the description of the lunch that Janie made for Tom, and of how capable and kind to Tom she is. "With French mustard" hints that a

Example 17: Dick Francis, *Flying Finish*, 1966: 59

"Sandwich?"   "Thanks." I took one. Ham, with <u>French mustard</u>, made in their bungalow by Tom's capable wife Janie, not from the airport canteen. The ham was thick and juicy, home cooked in beer.
Japanese TT: translated by Kikuchi Mitsu, *Hietsu*, 1976: 79–80

「サンドウィッチ？」 「ありがとう」一つとった。辛子を つけたハム・サンドウィッチは食堂 のものでなく、働き者のトムの妻、 ジェイニイが家で作ったものであ る。ハムは厚く、水々しく、ビール を使った自家製である。	"Sandowicchi?" "Arigatō" Hitotsu totta. <u>Karashi</u> o tsuketa hamu • sandowicchi wa shokudō no mono de naku, hatarakimono no Tomu no tsuma, Jeinii ga ie de tsukutta mono dearu. Hamu wa atsuku, biiru o tsukatta jikasei dearu.

sandwich from the airport canteen would not have had French mustard, but only the ordinary English kind. Tom will be shot later in the story – to the main character's great anger and sadness. This detailed description of his wife builds up the reality of Tom as a character and will have a certain effect when the readers realise that he is dead (Tom miraculously survives but this is only revealed at the end of the story). Interestingly, every detail of the text is transferred to the TT except for "French". In the TT, only *karashi* [mustard] appears: the cultural significance of the particular mustard is discarded by the translator as either difficult to convey or irrelevant.

In the next ST Arch, the young boy exclaims "Brother!" It is noteworthy that the woman, who does not have an answering machine, cable, remote control or any video games, is devoted to local church activities and believes that an answering machine is one of "those infernal things" (1995: 178). "Brother!" sounds like a witty choice of word. It is an interjection to express one's surprise but has a double meaning as the resident of the house, whom Arch visited, was known to be a devout Christian. This cultural joke is completely lost in the TT unit *Gegē da!* [yuck!], which is simply a swearword; the cultural element derived from the religious joke in the TT has been culturally neutralised. In the next section, cultural foreignisation will be examined.

Example 18: Diane Mott Davidson, *The Last Supper*, 1995: 179

"Doesn't have an answering machine!" Arch cried when I paused to read a street sign. "Man! She doesn't have cable! She doesn't have remote control! Not to mention that she doesn't have any video games! Where has that woman been for the last fifty years? Brother!"

Japanese TT: translated by Katō Yōko, *Kukkingu • Mama no Shōkanjō*, 1996:77	
「留守番電話ないんだって！」交通標識を読むために車を停めると、アーチが叫んだ。「まいるね！ケーブルーテレビにも入ってないんだよ！リモコンもないんだ！ビデオ・ゲームがないのはもちろんだけどさ！あの人、この五十年間どこで暮らしてたんだろ？ゲゲーだ！」	"Rusubandenwa naindatte!" Kōtsūhyōsiki o yomu tame ni kuruma o tomeru to, Aāchi ga sakenda. "Mairu ne! Kēburu • terebi ni mo haittenainda yo! Rimokon mo nainda! Bideo • gēmu ga nai no wa mochiron da kedo sa! Ano hito, kono gojūnen doko de kurashitetandaro? Gegē da!"

6.2 Cultural Foreignisation

A SL culture-specific item sometimes travels to, and semantically remains in, the TT without losing its potential "otherness" for the TL culture. As stated in section 3.3, otherness as used in this book signifies an easily recognised and different characteristic possessed by an individual or group, which are different from "the self".

6.2.1 Potential for Expansion of the TL Culture

A limited number of newly created items ultimately enter the original TL vocabulary; the rest remain either commonly or rarely used as translational vocabulary. When this happens, their foreign, sophisticated image recedes in the TL. Yanabu (1982) argues that a newly created *kango* word tends to give the impression of expressing an obscure – but refined and important – concept in Japanese. Precisely what the translator means by the new word is never clear to the receptor. He calls this phenomenon *kassetto kōka* [cassette effect] and says that some *kango* terms which emerged through translation during the Meiji period still retain this effect (ibid. 36–37). Very similar cases in the shape of Western-originated words have emerged through transcription or *katakana*-isation. Here, I will focus on how translated popular fiction is culturally foreignised (that is, culturally alien items are received via various means including via *katakana*-isation, which identify them to be of foreign origin) and will examine what happens to the original items in the process. As Yanabu (2002) discusses, expressing foreign concepts or items using a newly created *kango* or a *katakana* word in Japanese translation has an effect of mystification, and thus has an important function.

6.2.2 Loan Translation and Katakana-*isation*

Example 19, taken from *Anne of Windy Willows*, contains an instance of cultural foreignization.

Example 19: Lucy M. Montgomery, *Anne of Windy Willows*, 1994/1936: 100

"I'd get someone to stay with you, of course, Ma," said Pauline. "You see," she explained to me, "my cousin Louisa is going to celebrate her silver wedding at White Sands next Saturday week, and she wants me to go. I was <u>her bridesmaid</u> when she was married to Maurice Hilton. I *would* like to go so much if Ma would give her consent."

Japanese TT: translated by Muraoka Hanako, *An no Kōfuku*, 1981/1958: 130

「もちろん、だれかに頼んで母さんのそばにいてもらいますよ、母さん」と、ポーリーンは言い、あたしに説明しました。「あのね、わたしの従姉いとこのルイーザが来週の土曜日にホワイト・サンドで銀婚式のお祝いをすることになっているのです。で、ルイーザはわたしに来てほしいと言うんですよ。ルイーザがモーリス・ヒルトンのところへ嫁いだとき、わたしは<ruby>付添娘<rt>ブライズメイド</rt></ruby>をつとめたものでね。母さんさえ許してくれれば、わたしは行きたくて仕方がないんですよ」	"Mochiron, dareka ni tanonde kāsan no soba ni itemoraimasu yo, kāsan" to, Pōriin wa ii, atashi ni setsumeishimashita. "Anone, watashi no itoko no Ruiiza ga raishū no doyōbi ni Howaito • Sando de ginkonshiki no oiwai o suru koto ni natteirunodesu. De, Ruiiza wa watashi ni kite hoshii to yūndesu yo. Ruiiza ga Mōrisu • Hiruton no tokoro e totsuida toki, watashi wa tsukisoimusume (buraizumeido) o tsutometa mono de ne. Kāsan sae yurushitekurereba, watashi wa ikitakute shikata ga naindesu yo."

Both the term "bridesmaid" and the custom of having a young female assistant to the bride at a wedding seem to have been unfamiliar in Japan at the time when the novel was first translated in the 1950s. An unfamiliar word, *tsukisoimusume* [attending girl], clearly derived from *tsukisoinin* [attender], has been used as a compromise, since the semantic meaning, or at least the function of *tsukisoimusume*, is clear to the reader, thanks to the *kanji* used: 付添娘. This is an example of loan translation or calque (Hervey and Higgins 1992: 33), whereby lexical items in the ST English force the translator to devise new compounds, or to form unfamiliar-sounding new words.

An interesting point here is that Muraoka has put *buraizumeido* in *katakana* just above the Chinese characters for *tsukisoimusume* written in *ruby* so that the TT receptor can see both the unfamiliar Japanese word and a word close to the original English term. As it happens, the concept is widely known nowadays, especially among young people, by the name *buraizumeido*, although the custom itself is rarely practised.

Furigana, also referred to as *ruby*, is a miniaturised version of *hiragana/katakana or kanji* placed close to a *kanji*, usually to provide phonetic guidance regarding its pronunciation. In translations, *furigana* are often used to indicate the corresponding original term or to provide extra information alongside the word, providing the reader with the opportunity to encounter the new concept in both forms. *Furigana* or *ruby* are an important target of research because of their uniqueness and serviceability in translation. As a result, many scholars have discussed their effect; for example, Mizuno (2007) studies linguistic stylistic norms of the early Meiji period, including the use of *ruby* to clarify reading and meaning to readers, which highlights deviation from the dominant *kanbun kundoku* style of translation language. In Suzuki (2013), the translation of wordplay based on name, character, grammar, form and pun are discussed and the significant role that *ruby* plays as a tool in dealing with wordplay is explored.

The impact of imported words received via *katakana*-isation on Japanese has been immense. Yonekawa (1991) examines the steady increase in imported words [*gairaigo*] in Japanese between 1945 and 1991, and analyses the relationship between this phenomenon and economic growth, commercialism since the Second World War, and the avid taste for Western culture and trends among the Japanese. In areas such as service industries, media, sports, fashion, marketing and computing, a vast number of English words have been *katakana*-ised and brought into use in Japanese. Summing up the result of his research, he comments as follows:

> While decorative and commercial foreign words whose meaning is unclear are increasing in number, following the tendency (encouraged by business) towards preference for European and American culture in people's minds, difficult technical foreign words are also multiplying because of increasing professional specialisation. Many alphabetic acronyms are also used. Both are characteristic of current Japanese. (ibid. 43–44, my translation)

Indeed, modern Japanese contains a vast number of *gairaigo* from languages like modern English, and they play an essential role in everyday language.

Some are compounds of existing words of Japanese or foreign origin (often *kango*) and thus do not sound like the original English word (for example, *chokorētoiro*, meaning chocolate colour). With others, the sounds were simply imported and written down, using *katakana*, with the result that they are phonetically similar to the original, and traceable from it, as in the case of *demokurashii*, meaning "democracy".

The effect of translation on newly imported words is complex. The *katakana*-ised item immediately acquires an alien image because the script has the very function of indicating its foreign origin. There is a paradox: new words are alien to the TL culture in most cases, but as soon as they are *katakana*-ised, they fall into the well-established category of "foreign terms within the Japanese language system". In other words, their alienness is lost or reduced by being systematically marked. Thus, words of foreign origin incorporated into the TL and written in *katakana* have a particular translational nuance.

Such cases can be regarded as cultural foreignisation. A foreign item, or the word which refers to it, is incorporated into Japanese to make the text more exotic, but at the same time, this results in a conventionalisation of the item, because the word becomes an available lexical item in the TL. The foreign effect the reader originally receives may thus depend on longevity (how long the term has been used in Japanese) and the word involved. Indeed, nowadays *katakana* has become so frequently used for a variety of effects, that some of it may not appear foreign at all. Some of the words which were originally created for a specific translation need continue to be used in translation. In the longer run, some obtain proper status as items of vocabulary within Japanese, beyond serving merely as emergency items available only for translation. Newly imported Western words often sound refined when they are still new to the receptors, and even after the freshness has gone, they often retain a complex, sophisticated image. The modern tradition of loading Western concepts with value in an uncritical way is obvious here: the image lasts for some time and then, as people become accustomed to the word and firmly grasp its meaning, the incidence of the word increases while its freshness and prestige decrease. The next two examples include the substantive "tapestry" or "tapestries" in the ST, but they are translated in different ways:

Example 20: Lucy M. Montgomery, *Anne of Windy Willows*, 1994/1936: 12

The whole place was engoldened by the light that came through the corn-coloured curtains, and there was the rarest <u>tapestry</u> on the whitewashed walls where the shadow patterns of the willows outside fell – living <u>tapestry</u>, always changing and quivering.	
Japanese TT: translated by Muraoka Hanako, *An no Kōfuku*, 1981/1958: 19	
とうもろこし色のカーテン越しにそそぎ込む光で部屋じゅうが金色になっており、白塗りの壁には外の柳がおとす影の模様が世にも珍しい<u>壁掛け</u>を織りなしています―たえず変化し、震えている生きた<u>壁掛け</u>です。	Tōmorokoshiiro no kātengoshi ni sosogikomu hikari de heyajū ga kin'iro ni natteori, shironuri no kabe ni wa soto no yanagi ga otosu kage no moyō ga yo ni mo mezurashii <u>kabekake</u> o orinashiteimasu – taezu henkashi, furueteiru ikita <u>kabekake</u> desu.

Example 21: Lilian Jackson Braun, *The Cat Who Knew a Cardinal*, 1991: 118

"Why don't you come over for dinner tomorrow night? I could prepare chicken divan."	
"I wish I could, but Fran is hanging the new <u>tapestries</u> at five o'clock, and I don't know how long the operation will take or how many problems we'll encounter."	
Japanese TT: translated by Hata Shizuko, *Neko wa Tori o Mitsumeru*, 1995: 146	
「明日の夜、夕食にいらっしゃらない？ チキン・ディヴァンを作るわ」 「できたら行きたいんだが、五時にフランが新しい<u>タペストリ</u>ーをかけにくるんだ。その作業に時間がどれぐらいかかるか、あるいはどういう問題が生ずるか、わからなくてね」	"Asu no yoru, yūshoku ni irassharanai? Chikin • divan o tsukuru wa." "Dekitara ikitainda ga, goji ni Furan ga atarashii <u>tapesutorii</u> o kake ni kurunda. Sono sagyō ni jikan ga dore gurai kakaru ka, arui wa dōyū mondai ga shōzuru ka, wakaranakute ne."

The translation of *Anne of Windy Willows*, in Example 20, dates back to 1958, while the translation of *The Cat Who Knew a Cardinal*, in Example 21, was published in 1995. In the former, "the rarest tapestry" and "living tapestry" have become *yo ni mo mezurashii* [rarest] *kabekake* and *ikita* [living] *kabekake* in the TT. *Kabekake* is a word for any ornamental piece which can hang on a wall, including tapestries. However, the receptor of the TT at that time probably did not form a picture of a tapestry with a colourful pattern from the word *kabekake*, since covering a wall with a large piece of fabric was not common then. However, this is obviously the ST author's intention, based on the use of the phrases "the shadow patterns of the willows outside fell" and "always changing and quivering" (12 in the ST). So, the item is linguistically and culturally domesticated in this TT. In Example 21, on the other hand, "tapestries" in the ST is translated into *tapesutorii*, a loan word which refers to tapestries in the Western sense. Later in the story, one of the tapestries mentioned here falls onto the head of the murderer and this helps the main character capture him. The readers are given information on the item at this earlier juncture. In the ten years or so since Example 20, when this novel was translated, both versions of the word have become relatively common in Japan. Thus, its use does not noticeably function as foreignisation.

In the next example, the foreign term is *katakana*-ised and an additional description is included in brackets. This is a frequently used strategy, like the provision of *ruby* in Example 19.

Example 22: Agatha Christie, *The Adventure of the Italian Nobleman*, 1991/1924: 173

"The order was given from the à la carte menu – for three," he explained. "<u>Soup [sic] julienne, filet de sole normande, tournedos of beef</u>, and <u>a rice soufflé</u>. What time? Just about eight o'clock, I should say. No, I'm afraid the plates and dishes have been all washed up by now. Unfortunate. You were thinking of fingerprints, I suppose?"
Japanese TT: translated by Ogura Takashi, *Itariakizoku Satsugaijiken*, 1978: 248–249

| 「御注文は一品料理のメニューからで、三人前でした」とその男は説明した。「<u>ジュリエンヌ・スープ（こまかくきざんだニンジン、ネギなどのすましスープ）</u>に、<u>ノルマンディーひらめの切身</u>に、<u>ひれ肉料理</u>に、<u>ライス入りのスフレ</u>です。時間ですか？ちょうど八時ごろだったでしょう。いえ、その食器類はもう全部洗っちゃっただろうと思います。まずかったですねえ。指紋でしょう？」 | "Gochūmon wa ippinryōri no menyū kara de, sanninmae deshita" to sono otoko wa setsumeishita. "<u>Juriennu・sūpu (komakaku kizanda ninjin, negi nado no sumashi sūpu)</u> ni, <u>norumandii hirame no kirimi</u> ni, <u>hirenikuryōri</u> ni, <u>raisuiri no sufure</u> desu. Jikan desu ka? Chōdo hachiji goro dattadeshō. Ie, sono shokkirui wa mō zenbu aracchattadarō to omoimasu. Mazukattadesu nē. Shimon deshō?" |

The ST in Example 22 includes the names of several dishes unfamiliar to the Japanese reader. The key item is "soup Julienne". It would have been possible to replace it with the more conventional *yasai sūpu* [vegetable soup] to domesticate it, but the idea here is very similar to Muraoka's, as seen in Example 19: both have introduced a foreign cultural item in the form of a foreign-sounding expression, but have added a note to assist the receptor in obtaining as precise an idea as possible of the original meaning. The note in brackets is a rewording of the term, instead of an alternative short term such as *yasai sūpu*. The presence of notes or *ruby* can distort the rhythm or style of the text because they are usually written independently of the text: they are always read immediately after the new item and before the next word in the main text, but can be lengthy and explanatory. They also visually emphasise that the text is a translation. Thus, strategies for lexical foreignisation can affect the language itself. There are three other names of dishes in the same line: "filet de sole normande", "tournedos of beef" and "rice soufflé". The first two have been translated into *norumandiihirame no kirimi* [fillet of Normandy sole] and *hirenikuryōri* [fillet meat dish], using words that are common in Japanese, apart from the proper name *Normandii*. The third, "soufflé", has simply become *sufure* [soufflé] in the TT, without any description. The concept of "soufflé" has been judged to be familiar enough for the receptor not to require additional help, unlike the concept of "soup julienne".

The next example represents another instance of the introduction of an alien-sounding term through cultural foreignisation:

The setting in *Banker* is an executive meeting at a prestigious merchant bank. At this directors' meeting, the main character, a young banker, is suggesting to his senior colleagues that a loan be given to a racehorse breeder. The ST unit in question is "the Turf". It is understood from the context that executives of the bank are discussing whether they should make an investment in English horse racing. There is a horse racing community in Japan as well and there is indeed a word for it – *keibakai*. However, the ST word is not "horse racing" but "the Turf", a word with various connotations, sometimes (but not necessarily) conveying a prestigious image and a certain mystique. Kikuchi takes the strategy of using *keibakai* together with *za Tāfu* in *katakana* to mark its significance when the term occurs for the first time in the TT. From the second time onwards, he uses only the

Example 23: Dick Francis, *Banker*, 1982: 62

Someone down the far end complained that it would be a waste of time and that merchant banks of our stature should not be associated with <u>the Turf</u>$_{(1)}$. "Our own dear Queen," someone said ironically, "is associated with <u>the Turf</u>$_{(2)}$. And knows the Stud Book backwards, so they say."	
Japanese TT: translated by Kikuchi Mitsu, *Meimon*, 1988: 110	
テイブルの端の方の誰かが、時間の浪費に終わるだろうし、うちのような格式の高いマーチャント・バンクは、<ruby>競馬界<rt>ザ・ターフ</rt></ruby>$_{(1)}$ などにかかわり合うべきではない、と反対意見を述べた。 「わが親愛なる女王陛下は」誰が皮肉な口調で言った、<u>「ザ・ターフ</u>$_{(2)}$ にかかわっておられる。それに、血統書に精通しておられる、ということだ」	Tēburu no hashi no hō no dareka ga, jikan no rōhi ni owarudarō shi, uchi no yōna kakushiki no takai māchanto・banku wa, <u>keibakai (za・Tāfu)</u>$_{(1)}$ nado ni kakawariaubeki de wa nai, to hantaiiken o nobeta. "Waga shin'ainaru joōhēka wa" dareka ga hinikuna kuchō de itta, "<u>za・Tāfu</u>$_{(2)}$ ni kakawatteorareru. Soreni, kettōsho ni seitsūshiteorareru, to yū koto da"

katakana-ised *za Tāfu*. His strategy adds the linguistic information in the ST unit but says nothing about the connotation. This allows the readers to comprehend the original word, which would otherwise have no meaning unless they had some background knowledge. For most readers, the term is just like the mysterious "cassette" (Yanabu 1982) discussed in section 6.2.1.

6.2.3 *Dealing with Proper Names*

Since the way proper names are handled is one of the major factors characterising the translational dialect of the text-type, the strategies that are frequently selected in the text-type will be particularly closely examined (see also Nohara 2006 in which the argument of this section was originally developed).

A. TYPES OF TRANSLATION METHODS FOR PROPER NAMES

First, I will look at the generally recognised translation methods. Hermans (1988: 13–14) identifies six methods of dealing with proper names in literary translation: (1) name copies, (2) name transcription, (3) name deletion, (4) name substitution, (5) semantic translation and (6) combination of any of these. Although no list of translation methods or techniques should be regarded as exhaustive, the six types suggested by Hermans seem to cover most cases. Similarly, in discussing the various kinds of cultural transposition that take place in interlingual translation (from exoticism to cultural transplantation), Hervey and Higgins (1992: 29) claim that:

> (i)n translating a name there are, in principle, at least two alternatives. Either the name can be taken over unchanged from the ST to the TT, or it can be adapted to conform to the phonetic/graphic conventions of the TL. [...] A further alternative in translating names is cultural transplantation.

Taking over a name unchanged can produce the highest level of exoticism if the name is completely alien to the TL community. On the other hand, cultural transplantation (which includes at least two methods that Hermans cites: name substitution and semantic translation) can be regarded as more extreme cultural transposition. The common factor in their classifications of the ways of dealing with proper names is that transcription is perceived as cultural transposition to a milder degree – at least when compared to pragmatic/cultural substitutions.

Next, the ways in which foreign names and words can be transcribed in Japanese in general (both in translations and elsewhere) are explained.

B. THE JAPANESE WRITING SYSTEM

As often mentioned in this book, the Japanese language includes *katakana*, a phonetic syllabary that is normally used for names or terms of foreign origin, and this lends a rather distinctive flavour to the measures that are taken to handle proper names and to the resulting effect of their use. Take a look at the following example: the names of the detective Hercule Poirot and his companion, Arthur Hastings, are transcribed using *kata-kana*, according to the conventional system of phonetic correspondence. Predictably, in most of the (published) Japanese translations by various translators, these names become エル キ ュ ー ル・ポ ア ロ and ア ー サ

一・ヘイスティングス respectively.[1] Possible romanised (or *rōmaji*) versions would be Erukyūru・Poaro and Āsā・Heisutingusu. The above versions could technically be written in *hiragana* as well: える きゅーる ・ ぽ あ ろ and あーさー・へ い す て ぃ ん ぐ す. Romanisations of these names would be identical to those of the *katakana* versions, since they are, phonetically speaking, a perfect match. Owing to the foreign (and particularly Western) nature of the two names, however, it would be very rare for *hiragana* to be used to transcribe them, regardless of the text-type, unless the text was aimed at very young children who have not yet learned these syllabaries (in the course of standard school education in Japan, children learn *hiragana* first), or some particular impact or emphasis by means of such unconventional writing was intended. By the same token, neither *kanji* nor *rōmaji* (neither the foreign name's originally spelling, nor its romanisation according to the Japanese system) are used to transcribe proper names in a normative literary situation. Only when some particular communication is intended are *kanji* or *rōmaji* ever applied to a proper name in a translation. This can, for example, reveal the significance of its spelling in the literary context which would otherwise be hidden in *katakana*, or have a humorous or sarcastic impact by hinting at a semantic connotation by virtue of the idiographic *kanji* selected. To summarise, in translations from English into Japanese, most representation of proper names falls into the category of transcription.

C. PROPER NAMES IN TRANSLATED POPULAR FICTION

In this linguistic environment, transcription exhibits fairly diverse methods, which have different effects. I will now attempt to present a general overview of how proper names are usually treated in the current standard Japanese

---

1   It is the convention to insert a・between someone's first name and his/her other names (including the surname), or between two semantic units in a word in which a foreign name or word has been transcribed. It should also be pointed out that both the "r" and the "l" in *Hercule* are transcribed as ル (ru), and that the "th" (in "the") and "s" have respectively become サ (sa) and ス (su) in Arthur Hastings. This is simply due to the lack of corresponding allophones in modern Japanese.

discourse used on translated popular fiction, by examining the ways in which Hermans's six methods are put into practice (using as my source the same series of ST and corresponding TT selected throughout this book). The numbers and symbols in Table 2 show how frequently the various methods are used. Here, rather than conduct a statistical survey on a more substantial and systematic set of literature, I will merely seek to identify translation patterns usually found in translated fiction on an intuitive scale, and will discuss further in Chapter 8 and 9 a hypothesis that the patterns work as devices for creating a mode of narration appropriate for introducing Western fiction to the Japanese community. Table 2 illustrates the degree of diversity in the way personal names are transcribed in Japanese, reflecting the translator's attitude towards conventional transcriptions, that is, towards the particular degree of foreignness to be transferred to the TT. It is intriguing to see semantic meanings in streets, shops and restaurants. Semantic names for food and periodicals are prized, while town names are simply regarded as referential and not to be translated. These points are discussed in detail in section E.

Table 2: Frequency of use for Hermans's six methods of dealing with proper names in literary translation

Strategy \ Type of proper name		People	Towns	Streets	Shops and Restaurants	Food and Periodicals
Name Copies		X	X	X	X	X
Name Transcription	Established way	O	O	O	O	O
	Unconventional way	●	X	X	△	X
Deletion		X	X	X	X	X
Substitution		△	X	X	X	X
Semantic Translation		X	X	O	O	O
Combination		△	△	O	O	O

Key: O = frequently used, ● = used more of late, △ = occasionally used, X = not in use.

The frequent use of combination in handling place names and product names is due to their original formation from generic terms, such as "– Avenue", "– Lane", "–'s Deli", "Café –" and "The Daily –". Three of the six methods, which play a particularly important role (name copies, name transcription and name substitution) are discussed in the following sections D–G in which some examples will also be investigated. Combinations of these methods are also touched upon whenever necessary.

D. NAME COPIES

This method involves the original name appearing in an unchanged form in the TT. Newmark (1988: 214) states that "(n)ormally, people's first and surnames are transferred, thus preserving their nationality, and assuming that their names have no connotations in the text", although he goes on to list a rather wide range of exceptions, including the names of saints and monarchs, and prominent figures in classical Greece and Rome. Thus, it seems that it is not at all unusual for an English TT to have a proper name implanted in it without any spelling or phonological adjustment. Newmark (ibid. 70–71) also points out:

> In belles-lettres, names are normally translated only if, as in some plays, the characters and milieu are naturalised. Neubert (1972) has pointed out that in the best German translation of *Tom Jones*, the characters' surnames are translated, since they "mean" as well as "name", but I do not think they would be translated in a modern version, since this would suggest that they change their nationality.

This would indicate that less transposition of personal names is taking place nowadays. In the case of translation from English into Japanese, name copies would involve a proper name in the English alphabet being transferred from the ST and placed unchanged in the Japanese TT. This hardly ever happens under the current writing system. Although *rōmaji* is available as one of the four character sets, its use is still restricted and its status is peripheral. It is rather rare, as far as literary texts are concerned, for English names (other than acronyms such as "MIT" and "IRA") to be inserted in their original form into Japanese script, which is basically a mixture of the two *kana* systems and *kanji*.[2] The name copies method is a technique positioned at one of the poles of the literal-free continuum for translation into languages that use the Latin alphabet, but is essentially not used for translation into Japanese.

The use of *rōmaji* for a proper name is occasionally found in literary translation, for instance, if the spelling of the name itself has some significance in the story. The original form is usually presented only once or twice to the reader and elsewhere in the literary work, the transcribed version is used, which falls under the sixth method cited by Hermans – that is, a combination of other methods. In the popular US whodunit series *Catering to Nobody* (1992), by Diane Mott Davidson, the main character, Goldie's ex-husband, is nicknamed "Jerk", from the initials (and sounds) of his name (John Richard Korman) – and hinting of course at his past much-less-than-respectable behaviour. Throughout the stories, *Jerk* is translated into *gesuyarō*, which is a reasonable semantic equivalent (although a more vulgar word for women to use in the TL linguistic and social settings than "Jerk" in the ST settings). To translate the narration in which the origin of this nickname is explained, which happens every now and then through the series, the spelling of his names in the Latin alphabet needs to be clarified, thus the name "Jerk" in its unchanged form turns up in the TT in isolated cases. *Rōmaji* also appears when the initial(s) in a person's name need to be shown, such as ミス . J. M. カルヴァ for *Miss J. M. Calver* on the nameplate on the staff desk in a bank (*Make Death Love Me*, 1979, Ruth Rendell, translated by Obi, 1985).

E. NAME TRANSCRIPTION

This seems to be the most frequently utilised method in the genre in question. To transcribe a foreign name into *katakana* is to mark it as foreign

---

2   The use of English names or acronyms (including personal, geographical and institutional names) with their original alphabetical spellings is also seen – especially when there is as yet no conventional *katakana*-isation for them. This is also occasionally the case (for the same reason) in informative works such as scientific articles or books, both native-written and translated.

among all the lexical items in the text. When *Peter Wimsey* (which can clearly be romanised as Pita · Wimuji), in Dorothy Sayers's classic mystery series, *Lord Peter Wimsey Mysteries*, is transcribed into ピーター・ウィムジイ by Asaba (1998), it immediately looks treated as somebody "alien" because of the use of *katakana* – even before the question arises as to whether the name is indeed alien or familiar to the TL culture.

In terms of conformity to TL naming conventions outside translation, naturalisation through transcription is barely possible, for two main reasons: first, as described above, *katakana* script labels the name as "foreign", and thus no naturalising effect, in terms of attunement to TL name culture, can be expected; second, the two languages, English and Japanese, do not share the same pool of "normative" personal names.[3] The most obvious point, but one which still must be mentioned, is the lack of the convention of giving biblical names in Japan. There is no equivalent of Peter, compared to the way Jean, Juan and Giovanni are recognised as the French, Spanish and Italian forms of John. By the same token, "Wimsey" cannot be "translated" as such, and so is only transcribed, giving a clear indication of its "outside" nature. In Japan, the social distance between people is traditionally gauged in terms of *uchi/soto* [inside/outside]. This gauge is also the basis for the way in which people behave towards each other in linguistic terms (Bachnik and Quinn 1994). Therefore, foreignising translation can arouse the feeling of "outside" and affects people's attitude towards it. The obvious semantic hint that "Wimsey" conveys in the ST is lost in the TT, apart from when the lexical resemblance to "whimsy" is verbally touched upon in the story: "Do you mind saying that again ... Whimsy? ... Oh, no H ... just so ... Wimsey with an E ..." (Tylor 1982: 80). To indicate the difference in spelling between the adjective and the name, *ruby* are placed alongside the translation of "Whimsy" and the transcription of "Wimsey" (translated by Asaba, 1998: 126).

---

3   In Japan, unusual names can be created, as demonstrated by a trend since the end of
     the twentieth century, whereby some families give their child a very unconventional
     name, particularly dramatic names, which are known as *kirakira nēmu* [glittering
     names].

Transcribing a foreign name using *katakana* certainly has a mechanical, unimaginative aspect to it because (1) *katakana*-isation of foreign words and names is usually performed according to an established method based on how the English word or name sounds, or used to sound at one point, to the Japanese, and how this can be written down in *rōmaji*; and (2) many ordinary Western names, such as those of biblical or major historical characters, or of celebrities, have their own conventionalised *katakana*-isation. This gives us ジョン (Jon) for John, メアリー or マリー (Meari or Mari) for Mary, and アラン (Aran) for Alan. Translators are expected to follow one of these two existing norms. When they conflict with one another (that is, if the name does not sound to the translator like the conventionally *katakana*-ised version), the standard version tends to be more prized than other possible versions and is therefore adopted. In discussing the transliteration between European languages of place names, such as Luik – Liège – Lüttich, Hervey and Higgins (1992: 29) state: "Where such conventional equivalents exist, the translator may feel constrained to use them. Not to do so would either display ignorance, or be interpreted as a significant stylistic choice". Translators generally follow Japanese conventions, so when somebody does not, it is taken as a deliberate challenge to convention. Kikuchi, renowned as the translator of Dick Francis's horse racing adventure series, uses a transcription closer to the original pronunciation than the established versions: ヘンリイ (Henrii) for Henry, rather than ヘンリー (Henri), and マイクルズ (Maikuruzu) for Michaels, rather than マイケルズ (Maikeruzu) (*Banker*, 1982, translated by Kikuchi, 1988). Likewise, in translating Ruth Rendell's mysteries, Obi transcribes Nigel as ナイジル (Naijiru), rather than ナイジェル (Naijeru), and Sharon as シャラーン (Sharan), rather than シャロン (Sharon) (*Make Death Love me*, 1979, translated by Obi, 1985). One point to note is the co-presence of other linguistic features, in which the ST English structures and lexemes outshine these norm challenging cases of transcription of personal nouns. Also, in the contemporary Japanese community where linguistically foreignising translations are well tolerated and Englishness is one of the features commonly found in literary translations, the degree of linguistic foreignness surrounding unconventional *katakana*-isation tends to be much higher. Long noun-modifiers, sentences with a clear subject indication, many conjunctions, conjunctive particles and pronouns are some of the other characteristic features of anglicised Japanese used in translations.

There are broad attitudes in the translation community towards conformity with conventional *katakana*-isation. Some translators and linguists claim that Japanese translations have been blindly following the conventions established during a time when people had no idea of the real pronunciation of particular words and names, and that it is high time that they be adjusted to match reality. Miyawaki (2000: 77, my translation) touches upon an anecdote in which the Japanese mass media changed the *katakana*-isation of *Ronald Reagan* from リーガン (Riigan) to レーガン (Rēgan) overnight, once they realised that the latter was closer to reality, and he claims that a translator needs the courage to "correct" the conventionally established *katakana*-isation of names, based on their actual pronunciations:

> Thus, it is desirable to avoid writing ジョアン (Joan) for Joan, or アルトマン (Arutoman) for Altman. For Andrew, アンドルー (Andorū) is closer to the original pronunciation than (the conventional) アンドリュー (Andoryū), if the character is British. Katakanising [sic] サラ (Sara) for Sarah is wrong. (ibid. 38)

Likewise, Tobita (1997: 171, my translation) states: "Even if there is a conventional writing (for a name), in a case where it is obviously wrong, we should change it to a writing more faithful to the original pronunciation", although he adds that what the name refers to must be clear to the reader. On the other hand, Kodaka (1991) recognises the recent development of a trend towards *katakana*-ising against convention, and warns translators to stick to the established way and not to produce translations which put the translator's ego on display.

Regarding place names, as the chart indicates, most town names in fiction are transcribed according to the *katakana*-isation convention (which is common both in and out of translation) and the sound, regardless of their semantic meaning. Country and city names are also written in this way: ワイルドキャット (Wairudokyatto) for "Wildcat" as a place name (*The Cat Who Knew a Cardinal*, 1991, Lilian Jackson Braun, translated by Hada, 1995); and アスペン・メドウ (Asupen・Medou) for "Aspen Meadow"

(*The Prime Cut*, 1998, Diane Mott Davidson, translated by Katō, 2000). When dealing with street names, however, there are options available among the different translation norms: transcription, such as エッジウェア・ロード (Ejjiwea・Rōdo) for "Edgware Road" (*Make Death Love Me*), グッドウィンター・ブルヴァード (Guddowintā・Buruvādo) for "Goodwinter Boulevard" (*The Cat Who Knew a Cardinal*), and semantic translation or combination, which are examined in the next section.

Names of shops or restaurants are also sometimes transcribed, as in マークス・アンド・スペンサー (Mākusu・ando・Supensā) for "Marks & Spencer" (*Make Death Love Me*) and サムズ・スープ (Samuzu・Sūpu) for "Sam's Soup" (*The Main Corpse*, 1996, Diane Mott Davidson, translated by Katō, 1997), and sometimes translated semantically. With names of magazines and periodicals, both transcribed and semantically translated cases are evident, but there is clearly a greater inclination to translate such terms as an overall unit, unless the original words are already loanwords in Japanese (so that their meaning is obvious) or the periodical itself is known to the Japanese. Examples would be: ウーマン (Ūman) for *Woman* (*Make Death Love Me*) and コスモポリタン (Kosumoporitan) for *Cosmopolitan* (*Indemnity Only*, 1982, Sarah Paretsky, translated by Yamamoto, 1986). Unlike personal and proper names, there are very few instances in which places or products are transcribed using unique *katakana*-isation in contravention of the norms. It seems that challenging convention to amplify the tone of foreignness which readers find new is largely confined to proper names.

F. NAME SUBSTITUTION

Name substitution used to be carried out regularly in the adaptation of foreign literature. In the late Edo period, playwright Kawatake Mokuami adapted *The Money* by Bulwer-Lytton into a stageplay entitled 人間萬事金世中 (Ningen Banji Kane no Yononaka, 1879), following the conventional pattern of *gesaku* or *kabuki*, Japanese popular fiction and theatre of the time. The name of the main character, Evelyn, in the original is transformed into a Japanese name in *kanji* – 惠府林之助 (Efurin-nosuke). This is not an existing Japanese name, but the domesticated original name (Efurin) is

combined with a conventional male name-suffix *nosuke*. The name is unusual and hints at the fact that it has a foreign origin although the form with
nosuke fits within the Japanese cultural framework. Similarly, in an early
Japanese version of Shakespeare's *Hamlet*, adapted by Kanagaki Ronbun
into a kabuki script in 1886, the name of Hamlet is changed into 葉村丸
(Hamuramaru). This is also a combination of part of the original name,
Hamul..., and ... *maru*, another name-suffix (Haga 2000: 168–169). This
type of substitution is mainly carried out in adaptations of foreign literature,
to move the whole literary setting into Japan. In contemporary translations,
adaptation of this kind is rarely performed – instead substitution is carried
out to adjust names to ones that resonate better with the general reader.
In the most recent Japanese translations of *Sense and Sensibility* by Jane
Austen, the names of the two sisters, Elinor and Marianne, are substituted
by names more familiar to the Japanese, with the former becoming エ リ
ナ (Erina) – which would theoretically be more appropriate as a transcription of *Erina* or *Elena* – instead of the conventional エ レ ノ ア (Erenoa).
マ リ ア ン (Marian) is used for Marianne, which sounds less French than
マ リ ア ン ヌ (Marriannu).[4] It is interesting that エ リ ノ ア と マ リ ア ン
ヌ (Erinoa to [and] Mariannu) is used in the translation of *Elinor and
Marianne: A Sequel to Sense & Sensibility* written by Emma Tennant in
1996 and translated in Japanese by Mukai and Kuzuyamai in 1996. The
incorporation of this classical work into mass fiction in the 1990s by means
of translation will be discussed in section 7.2.2.

G. SEMANTIC TRANSLATION

Personal names are usually transcribed in quite diverse ways when they are
katakana-ised, but there are cases in which the obvious semantic quality
is focused upon and dealt with. Most of these examples are in combination with transcription: "Potty Peak", a nickname, is transformed into

---

4   エ リ ナ (Erina) and メ ア リ ア ン (Mearian) in the early translation of *Sense and
    Sensibility* with the title *Funbetsu to Takan*, by Ise 1952, but エ リ ナ (Erina) and
    マ リ ア ン (Marian) in the translation *Itsuka Hareta Hi ni*, by Mano 1991.

変ちきピーク (Henchiki Piiku), in which the meaning of "potty", as being "crazy", is clearly expressed as *henchiki* means strange or weird (*The Nine Tailors*, 1934, Dorothy L. Sayers, translated by Asaba, 1998). Nonetheless, the literary connotations of a name, including suggestions about the character's family background, social position or religion, are not regarded as something to be transferred and are normatively flattened by transcription into *katakana*.

A variety of examples of semantic translation can be found in the handling of place names and product names. In the case of streets, semantically transparent names are seldom left alone: 幽霊小路 (Yūrei Kōji) for "Ghost Lane" and 恋人たちの古径 (Koibitotachi no Kokei) for "Lovers' Lane" (*Anne of Windy Willows*). When meaning-opaque street names are translated into Japanese, they are often *katakana*-ised and then combined with translated generic terms, such as … *Kokei* (Lane), … *Dori* (Street), … or *Kaidō* (Avenue) for consistency – that is, even semantically untranslatable ones are not just simply transcribed. The ironic fact is that translated street names do not naturalise the text (in terms of native, non-translational linguistic or literary standards) since streets in Japan do not usually have names – apart from main roads or streets in particularly touristic spots. Translated or transcribed, therefore, the verbalisation of street names itself usually functions as a foreigniser or a sign of translation. The translation of street names offers a semantic clue to the names: it is like an attached dictionary which is open for the receptors and explains the meaning of the name, but the receptors are not given the feeling that they are in the literary setting in which the street names really exist.

Names of restaurants, pubs and periodicals are the most prone to be translated. 〈古い水車小屋〉亭 (〈Furui suishagoya〉 tei; the suffix – *tei* denotes an inn, pub or restaurant) for "The Old Stone Mill", 麦束亭 (Mugitaba-tei) for "The Wheatsheaf" (*The Nine Tailors*), and ムース郡なんとか (Mūsugun Nantoka) for "The Moose County Something", a local newspaper (*The Cat Who Knew a Cardinal* by Lilian Jackson Braun, 1991). However, when the item referred to is well known, it tends to be transcribed as seen in section 6.2.3.B, and the two methods – semantic translation and transcription – are both used, even within the same piece of fiction: 朝刊明星 (Chōkan Myōjō) for

"The Morning Star", and タイムズ (Taimuzu) for "The Times" (*The Nine Tailors*). It is worth mentioning that "Frog Bridge", the name of a bridge also in *The Cat Who Knew a Cardinal*, is translated into its semantic equivalent 蛙橋 (Kaeru-bashi), just as "The Wheatsheaf" is translated into 麦束亭 [Mugitaba-tei], even though most of the other geographical names are simply transcribed in the translation of this novel by Hata, 1995. Thus, semantically transparent names may be translated and others simply transcribed – even if it results in inconsistency in the handling of proper names in a literary work.

As in the case of street names, names of restaurants or periodicals therefore rarely function as a factor in domestication. The reason for this is the way in which they are translated. Products of semantic translation seem to be rather unrealistic actual names in Japan. Among the examples given above, the only possible item which could be genuinely Japanese is *Mugitaba-tei*, for "The Wheatsheaf". 〈*Furui Suishagoya*〉 *tei* is translational because of the unusual use of the brackets. *Mūsugun Nantoka* is impossible because of the obscure, casual tone of the word *nantoka* [something or somehow]. Also, it is obvious that *Chōkan Myōjō* is a word-for-word translation, as there is no *Chōkan* [morning paper] construction in Japanese that is used for the name of any newspaper (it is usually *Shimbun* [Newspaper] or *Nikkan* [Daily]).

Semantic translation is often used for place or product names. The pattern whereby proper names are translated and emerge in the TT is one of the main constituents of the translationalness commonly found in translated popular fiction. As demonstrated above, these names tend not to satisfy the normative form of names of pubs, restaurants or periodicals, and thus it is obvious that they are "semantic translations". Again, most of them work not as a naturaliser but as a foreigniser in terms of the naming norms of non-translational Japanese. This is not to say that classic novels are always outside the scope of this phenomenon: any novel can be translated again, resulting in a new version with a distinctive flavour that makes it more accessible and more suited to popular taste. This was the case with a new translation of Jane Austen's *Sense and Sensibility* which was published after successive films based on her novels became Hollywood hits.

Proper names, modified and transferred according to the established patterns of translation of popular fiction, clearly mark the foreign nature of the name in a fixed manner, by means of transcription or semantic translation – albeit in somewhat diverse ways. Translators, by marking them, paradoxically accept them into the established Japanese linguistic and cultural domain, and thus reduce their foreign nature.

6.3 Summary

While translators struggle to decide how audacious they can or should be in using linguistic devices to domesticate translation, there is another aspect to take into consideration: cultural domestication. When the ST includes a concept which would sound unfamiliar and would not fit smoothly in the Japanese TT, translators sometimes change the concept itself into another concept. Something semantically or functionally close to the original, but familiar in the TL cultural environment, is usually sought. In employing this method, the translator is trying to remove unnormative factors so that the TT receptor will not receive an impression of otherness – just as the receptor of the original is not exposed to otherness in the ST. Foreign factors can simply be dropped, or replaced by a more culturally neutral concept or a more TL culture-specific concept. Considering the wide cultural distance between English and Japanese and the sharply contrasting images and connotations of their cultures, the simple replacement of a translation unit can create a complicated challenge. For example, one substitution using a Buddhist term might undermine the whole literary setting. The precariousness caused by cultural inconsistency leads to a major source of translationalness that is specific to the text-type. This will be discussed further in Chapter 7. By contrast, when translators decide to leave an unfamiliar concept or expression in the TT, they take on the task of inventing a linguistic device to convey the new concept (cultural foreignisation): *katakana*-isation is one of the most recurrent strategies for introducing foreign terms into the TL.

Transcription of foreign (and particularly Western) names has a rather delicate function in Japanese translation of Western fictional works, in that it constructs a text-type specific to the genre, which acts as a special container into which otherness in the text can be moulded. Since it is mostly carried out using *katakana*, whose fundamental task in current Japanese is to mark words and names of foreign origin, transcribed and transferred names fall into a well-established category within the Japanese language system. Although their origins are clearly indicated by the script, it is significant that the otherness of these proper names is paradoxically lost (or at least reduced) in the process of their being systematically incorporated into the Japanese system. In other words, whatever emerges from *katakana*-isation in the TT tends to be accepted in the target culture. These proper names visually foreignise the text at the surface level, as they are in *katakana* (and the number of transcribed words is bound to be higher in a translation), but perhaps counter-intuitively, this has the effect of domesticating the names, and assimilating them into the established domain of Japanese. This operates as familiarisation, especially within the recent trend for more cafés, restaurants and periodicals to be given English-, French- or Italian-sounding names (often heavily domesticated) in *katakana*, and these provide a linguistic norm for translation to follow.

When a translator deviates from a conventional pattern of transcription for *katakana*-isation and is more faithful to the original pronunciation when dealing with a name, the effect is defamiliarising – especially in terms of the transcription norms outside translation. In the case of the American film star, Sharon Stone, the transcription that is usually used is シャロン・ストーン (Sharon Sutōn) and nobody in the media would try to come up with an unconventional version using *katakana*-isation like シャラーン (Sharān), as seen in the translation of Ruth Rendell's *Make Death Love Me* by Obi, 1985. Attempts to make the *katakana*-isation phonetically closer to the original pronunciation are more prevalent within the practice of translation – especially literary translation – than outside it. This also means that a change of *katakana*-isation can quietly be advocated through written translation, although no effect whatsoever can be guaranteed on ordinary Japanese. As the use of unconventional *katakana*-isation is generally found in more linguistically foreignised texts, the

Table 3: Strategies for cultural domestication and cultural foreignisation

	Cultural Domestication		Cultural Foreignisation
1	Replacing a culturally neutral item with a TT cultural item.	1	Introducing a new TL term through *katakana*-isation to refer to the ST unit.
2	Replacing a SL cultural item with a TL cultural item.	2	Providing *ruby* or a note in brackets to indicate the reading/meaning of the ST expression in the TT unit.
3	Replacing a TL cultural item with a culturally neutral item.	3	Transcribing/semantically translating proper names.

technique can be regarded as a device for amplifying clear defamiliarising foreignness or otherness in terms of *uchi/soto* [inside/outside] perspectives. Nevertheless, even challenging *katakana*-isation is a frequently witnessed translation norm in popular fiction and therefore has very little defamiliarising effect on the text-type. Overall, not even the simplest form of transcription – conventional or unconventional – avoids shaping names into the normative shape of otherness conveyed to the TL community.

Note that, once they are *katakana*-ised in the text, newly imported words and names fall into the well-established category of "foreign terms" within the Japanese language system. Their otherness is lost or reduced by being systematically incorporated into Japanese. These imported words – including proper names – possess a particular translational tone designed for the text-type. The strategies of cultural domestication and foreignisation that have been discussed can be summarised in Table 3.

CHAPTER 7

Stylistic Features of the Texts

7.1 A Translation-Specific Writing Discourse?

In this chapter, Japanese translated texts of popular fiction are examined together with the variety of strategies adopted for handling particular problems posed by the gap between English and Japanese.

7.1.1 Translated Popular Fiction as a Text-Type

Traces of foreignisation and domestication are sought at both linguistic and cultural levels. Translators engage in very intricate craftwork, balancing the two main options – domestication and foreignisation – to achieve the selected degree and type of closeness in the TT (for example, semantic, structural or functional) to the ST for each unit. Comparing whole texts from different genres, translations exhibit starkly distinctive stylistic features which are common across many works even if each has its own characteristics as well. This indicates that there exists a certain way of writing – a loose bind of linguistic elements – that is regularly produced by translators.

Returning to the discussion of a special type of language that is used in translation, Toury (1995: 2008) states that:

> Whether deliberate or accidental, a so-called "translationese" initially comprises *ad hoc* phenomena. However, it is quite possible for it to undergo a certain institutionalization. Thus, a group of translators may behave in much the same way, and hence produce translational replacements of a similar kind. In the long run, a habitualized translationese may even acquire some distinct markers, which would set it apart from any other mode of language use within the same culture, translational or non-translational. In fact, the more noticed (and accepted) such a differentiation is, the

more justified one would be in regarding such a translationese as a *distinct variety* of the target language. As Pedersen (1983: 7) so nicely put it, "translation itself helps to create its medium".

In other words, a set of common features in translation can differentiate a particular "translationese" from "non-translationese" or from other kinds of "translationese" within the same language. They may be institutionalised over time and may even be accepted as a distinct variety of the language. Robinson (1991: 60–61) also states that:

> Perfectionist programming also lies behind the mainstream arguments against "translationese" – against letting the translation sound like a translation (this is specifically a bourgeois tradition that I explore in the next chapter, but it is about time to start moving in that direction anyway). Only bad translations sound like translations. Usually this happens accidentally, through the translator's weak somatic feel for the TL; but even when it happens intentionally, or perhaps especially when it happens intentionally, as in Nabokov's *Eugene Onegin*, it is deplored by mainstream translation theorists. Good translations sound like the (or an) original. [...] Strive for the impossible. To succeed would in fact be presumptuous: it would raise to the level of divine revelation the scratchings of a mere mortal translator.

He criticises the "mainstream argument", which attributes a translation which sounds like a translation simply to incompetent work by the translator, and argues that, "(t)he closer you come without actually succeeding, without actually supplanting the original in the TL receptor's mind, the better your translation" (ibid. 61). If a translation does not sound like a translation, it might even be mistaken for an original in the TL culture; however, translations are rarely this natural.

Spivak (1993: 399–400) discusses the political implications of the use of "translationese" in translation from English and calls it "a betrayal of the democratic ideal into the law of the strongest", saying that, as a result: "The literature by a woman in Palestine begins to resemble, in the feel of its prose, something by a man in Taiwan". This argument against "translationese" is that it can neutralise or obscure the ST's politically or emotionally driven strong language, rendering it colourless.

The issue of "translationese" is also fully recognised in modern Japanese literary writing. In this respect, Isoya (1980: 173, my translation) claims that:

Translation has at least two functions. On the one hand, it demonstrates to us how various languages and écritures in foreign countries generate styles, and urges the generation of a "new language" in Japan; on the other hand, it weakens our awareness of style by changing the original style into a characterless, uniform translational style or language. [...]

The distortion of Japanese as a result of translation has been assailed as *hon'yakuchō* (translationese). However, we ourselves are now so fully immersed in translationese that it is hard to discern what is translationese and what is not. The national language is in confusion and is descending into anarchy. Some (like Fukuda Tsuneari) are now telling us what proper Japanese is, and textbooks instructing us how to straighten out our distorted Japanese are now appearing.

The stylistic uniformity of translations – often affecting original Japanese writing – tends to be treated simply as "translationese", as in the above quotation, but exhibits diversity in itself. Translators are known to struggle to achieve semantic precision, stylistic readability and sometimes even formal parallelism, but the degree of readability desired seems to be standardised by the translational language conventionally used in the genre: each text-type has some sort of default style, however loose the institutionalisation might be. Too much readability in terms of authentic Japanese writing can be incompatible with the text-type. It is intriguing to consider the properties that can be identified in the normative discourse used in a specific genre, as so far, few systematic attempts have been made to list them. In this chapter, I would like to discuss the overall features that are characteristically observed in some Japanese translations of popular literature (as the starting point for a larger investigation of many other genres), and how the community receives them, and at the same time produces them. The examples dealt with in Chapters 5 and 6 sharply illustrate the privilege of text-type manipulation exercised by translators by means of adjusting the stylistic mode, and in this research these works are regarded as translations of popular fiction, sometimes even despite the text-type of the ST. It needs to be emphasised that the word manipulation is utilised not necessarily to refer to their intentional conduct but to translation that results in changing the ST into the style relevant to the genre involved.

7.1.2 *Generally Recognised Translationalness*

A closer look is now warranted at the concept of what critics call "translationese" or what I call the translational dialect, which the Japanese are conscious of as it relates to their own language. Despite its persistent presence, English translational language (together with its various SL-dependent features) has not been given much attention as a research topic. However, among the Japanese general public, and among highly educated Japanese, there seems to be recognition of the idiosyncrasies of the language used in translation – regardless of the text-type (literary or non-literary) – produced under the influence of Western languages. Yanabu (1979) takes note of the presence of the text-type in contemporary Japanese and of the immediate foreign influences observed in the lexical and structural usages. Some linguistic features that are known to be typical of Japanese "translationese", and which preserve linguistic characteristics of Western SLs, are shown in the following quotations from Yanabu (ibid. 235–237, my translation):

> The visual impression made on most Japanese people by translationese Japanese – before they even start reading – is that there are many *kanji* (Chinese characters) in it. Many of the *kanji* are nouns or noun-like words, as discussed above. Depending on the features of the text, it may include many foreign words written in *katakana* instead of *kanji*. Many of the foreign words are also nouns or noun-like words. [...]

> When we look structurally, there is almost always a subject in each sentence. In ordinary Japanese, there is sometimes a subject and sometimes none; in particular, the "something + *wa*" type of subject appears at certain intervals and this creates a natural rhythm in the sentence flow. [...]

> Another structural feature of translationese is that it contains many long noun-modifying clauses – the type of phrasing in the quotation above: "A concept about the emotion which caused those prototypes to be born". [...]

> Generally speaking, sentences are said to be longer in Western languages than in Japanese. People also say that this is the reason why translationese tends to be longer than ordinary Japanese. Since important predicates or modified words come later in the sentence in Japanese, it is difficult to understand long sentences. Hence, in translation, the ST is cut up and the parts are connected using conjunctions,

conjunctive particles and pronouns. This is also a characteristic of translationese Japanese.

Nomoto (1968: 215, my translation) prescriptively claims that the language used in translation should be identical with the domestic language:

> Translation is to transfer what is written in a foreign language to another language –
> in this case Japanese.
>
> If we say we translate into "Japanese", the completed text has to be real Japanese. In
> other words, the language used in the translation should ideally be real Japanese. It
> should not be at all necessary to set aside a separate chapter to discuss the language
> used in translation. It is necessary, however, and I have to write about it here.

According to Bekku (1985: 11), it is quite usual for a writer to use two styles – one without a touch of "translationese" and the other with. Even if somebody can produce good original writing, this does not prevent them from translating an English text into pronounced "translationese".

The number of works in Japanese contemporary writing identified with the use of translational dialect in published translations (with a mostly negative tone) is indeed large (Kodaka 1991, Yanase 2000, Miyawaki 2000, Yanabu 2004 et al.). It seems a highly popular intellectual activity to identify translational word usages, stiff and tiring discourse, and mistakes in translated literature or academic articles. The paradox is that Japanese translations remain stylistically idiosyncratic (often with an abundance of simple, careless mistakes), despite the public awareness of the problems presented in these commentaries. Grootaers (1979: 110) states that:

> [I]n France, a poor translation work would not sell at all. In Japan, however, many
> copies of translated works are sold (maybe more than in any other country) – despite
> the fact that the quality of the translations into Japanese is far from high.

He explains the mysterious situation in which terrible translations are not only published but reprinted repeatedly without being improved, using the term "extraterritoriality" (ibid. 201). The works produced by translators (often famous professors or writers themselves) are so respected that no reader, student, publisher or colleague dares to impeach the quality – at least in a concrete manner. This situation was described by Grootaers as long ago as 1979 but there has been little fundamental change since then. Although criticised here and there, "translationese" continues to prevail. This dualist structure is a precarious balance: the persistent presence of "translationese" provides intellectuals with opportunities to criticise it without attacking particular figures, and also provides a text-type that is specific to translation. This point will be discussed again in section 7.2.

7.1.3 Greater Tolerance for Translationalness in Non-Literary Texts

Before the translational properties found in translated popular fiction are examined, it is worth taking a quick glance at how the quality and quantity of translationalness differ, depending on the text-type of the material. More interlinear translation has traditionally been valued in non-literary translation, and also for language learning in Japan (see section 3.1). Mizuta (in Bekku 1985: 142, my translation) claims that "so-called fluent Japanese often sacrifices the logical precision of foreign languages" and calls domesticated translation into question. Although faithful and read-able also remains a valid theoretical goal for informational texts, substan-tially more linguistic inconsistency is tolerated in the field of non-literary translation. Translation and original writing in science and engineering in Japan, and the translational styles used in them, are other very important issues, which are related to Japanese people's scientific literacy and the development of academic research; but this will be discussed on another occasion.

In original Japanese informative texts, a more formal style of lan-guage is expected, and this style coincides with certain properties of translationalness in question, as discussed in section 7.2. One factor which makes a particular piece of text sound more formal in Japanese is the prominence of more *kango* or Chinese-derived words. Many of these characters have abstract meanings, and complicated content is com-pressed into a short word, which often consists of only two characters. Compound *Kanji* can express subtleties in nuances which are sometimes not translatable to English words. In other words, the abstract meanings together with particular nuances are a product of there being two *kanji* characters. Their presence can give the text the impression of being difficult to understand, and therefore make it academic or official-sounding. Another feature is the sentence-ending styles, or *buntai*. In informative texts, the ending *de aru* [copula, formal or written form] is more commonly used (Sakanashi 1990). It lends a more serious, informational tone than *da* [copula, plain form], which is used more often in a literary narrative context, and *desu/masu* [copula, polite form], which is often used in letters, informal essays and children's literature. Also, conjunctive words with a formal tone, such as *soreyueni* [therefore], *shikashi* [but], *to wa yū mono no* [having said that], and *shikaruni* [so], are used, since Japanese requires the presence of such connectors – especially in a scientific text (particularly in the fields of humanities and social sciences), in which logical connection is emphasised. Example 24 is quoted from original Japanese writings and uses the *de aru* ending.

Example 24: Kajita Takamichi, *Tōgō to Bunretsu no Yōroppa*, 1993: 175

これらの<u>見解</u>を<u>参考</u>にして<u>説明</u>すれば、「<u>統合</u>」とは、フランス<u>内部</u>に<u>共存</u>している<u>異質</u>な<u>諸集団</u>が、その<u>文化的特殊性</u>を<u>否定</u>されることなく<u>相互</u>に<u>交流関係</u>をもち、「<u>平等</u>」「<u>人権</u>」などの<u>理念</u>を<u>前提</u>にしつつ<u>相互</u>に<u>融合</u>し合い、フランス<u>社会</u>に<u>積極的</u>に<u>参加</u>することを<u>意味</u>する。	Korera no <u>kenkai</u> o <u>sankō</u> ni shite <u>setsumeisureba</u>, "<u>tōgō</u>" to wa, Furansu<u>naibu</u> ni <u>kyōzonshiteiru</u> <u>ishitsuna</u> <u>shoshūdan</u> ga, sono <u>bunkateki</u> <u>tokushusei</u> o <u>hiteisareru</u> koto naku <u>sōgo</u>ni <u>kōryūkankei</u> o mochi, "<u>byōdō</u>" "<u>jinken</u>" nado no <u>rinen</u> o <u>zentē</u> ni shi tsutsu <u>sōgō</u>ni <u>yūgō</u>shiai, furansu<u>shakai</u> ni <u>sekkyokutekini</u> <u>sanka</u>suru koto o <u>imisuru</u>.
English TT: my translation	
"Unification" means, if I explain it taking this view into consideration, that idiosyncratic groups co-existing within France have mutual relations without their cultural uniqueness being denied, integrate with each other taking for granted principles such as "equality" and "human rights", and participate positively in French society.	

Example 24, taken from an academic book on politics, clearly exhibits the features of informational text. The *de aru* style is seen throughout. Many Chinese loanwords, underlined, are used. It is evident that the text abounds with verbs with a *kango* noun + *suru* construction, such as *kyōzonshite* [to co-exist, *te*-form] and *hiteisareru* [to deny, passive form]. There are also many abstract nouns, such as *byōdō* [equality] and *rinen* [principle]. *Furansunaibu ni* [...] *sankasuru* is a long clause which modifies *koto* [thing] and eventually defines the term *tōgō* [unification] found at the very beginning of the sentence. This piece of text is, in fact, one long sentence. The length of the sentence is not extraordinary for the text-type, but it does mean that the sentence is not reader-friendly. Such a serious tone is highly regarded and commonly used, especially in academic circles. Although the text is original, these features do satisfy Yanabu's (1979) description of "translationese".

The norms observed in original informational writing allow the language used in translation in the corresponding genre to be, to a large extent, formal, difficult and translational. The translator is able to manipulate the informational tone in the texts by adjusting the amounts of *kango* and abstract nouns, the ending style, and the connectors (among other features), which are factors that originally arose out of linguistic foreignisation. In a situation in which a translator has more than one available counterpart for an ST expression, a *kango* word, which has a more serious tone, tends to be selected. Again, this tendency is persistent, but never free from condemnation. Tanizaki (1977: 45, my translation) recognises clear foreign features in the language used in the translation of academic articles in the Taishō and early Shōwa periods, and criticises such writing, calling it "a ghost":

> I frequently find papers written by economists in first-class journals such as *Chūōkōron and Kaizō* and always wonder how many readers understand them. The language used in these texts presupposes that the readers have some knowledge of foreign languages. It looks like Japanese but is in fact a ghost of a foreign language. Because it is a ghost, it is more incomprehensible than a foreign language and it should be called an example of bad writing.

Concerned with the same tendency seen in modern Japanese, Yanabu (1979: 69–70, my translation) similarly argues that:

> There are abundant examples of translation in certain types of material which have clear translationese features. Drop in at a bookstore and have a look at a translation of an academic book. If it is difficult to read and understand, the reason is very likely to be that it is a word-for-word translation. The misunderstanding that a word-for-word translation is faithful to the original has dominated studies and thought in modern Japan.

Thus, Yanabu attributes the common use of "translationese" in academic materials to the habit of word-for-word translation. "Translationese" in non-literary texts is more tolerated than it is in literary texts, and is theoretically justifiable because of the already stable norm for the former. Still, the word-for-word approach in a non-literary text is itself criticised as above, and the duality of an existing standard, and criticism aimed at it, is observed. The relationship between translated non-literary works in Japanese and non-translated texts is straightforward, unlike the case in literary translations (special features in translated popular literature, for instance, are almost never seen in original Japanese popular fiction). Now, the discussion will return to literary texts.

7.1.4 Distorting the Original Style

When a translational discourse is independent of the style of the ST, its properties are bound to impede reception by the reader of the same (or similar) literary effect produced by the original. Even if the semantic content has been mainly expressed from the ST, the strangeness of the language used takes firm control of the reader's overall literary experience, thus affecting the content itself. Certainly, the language used in literature, whether a translation or not, often exhibits certain oddities, features unfamiliar in everyday language. Translational strangeness can ironically overwhelm such individual oddities in the ST into the unified style of the TT language. Bekku (1985: 12) focuses on the impact that linguistic Englishness – the main component of translationalness in his, and most critics', analyses – has on the stylistic effect:

A style is an appearance, shape and form of writing. In other words, it is the writer's character expressed by his/her word usages. This piece of translation, however, does not have any form as a piece of writing: it does not express the writer's individual character. If we must give such writing a name, we can call it "the characterless style of direct translation".

He describes a text with uniform translationalness as "translationese", "a text with no recognisable style" (ibid.), and this paradoxically indicates the presence of the commonly used, but unnoticed, writing style. Example 25, taken from an adventure story written by Dick Francis, is a good example of "no recognisable style", which contains an abundance of factors that

Example 25: Dick Francis, *Rat Race*, 1972: 183

"Matthew, throw me the tin." It was a whisper, nothing more.
I began to walk towards him, holding out my right arm. Stumbled. Swayed. Frightened him.
The others were closing to him.
No more time. I took a breath. Straightened up.
"Matthew," I said loudly. "<u>To save your life, throw, me that tin. Throw it now. At once.</u>"

Japanese TT: translated by Kikuchi Mitsu, *Konsen*, 1977: 290	
「マシュー、その罐をこちらへ投げるんだ」囁くような声だ。	"Mashū, sono kan o kochira e nagerunda" Sasayaku yōna koe da.
私は、右腕を差し出したまま、彼の方へ歩いて行った。つまずいた。よろめいた。彼が怯えた。	Watashi wa, migiude o sashidashita mama, kare no hō e aruiteitta. Tsumazuita. Yoromeita. Kare ga obieta.
ほかの連中が彼に近づいている。	Hoka no renchū ga kare ni chikazuite iru.
もはや時間がない。私は、息を吸い込んだ。体を伸ばした。	Mohaya jikan ga nai. Watashi wa, iki o suikonda. Karada o nobashita.
「マシュー」私が大声で言った。「<u>きみの命を救うために、その罐を私の方へ投げるんだ。いますぐ。ただちに。</u>」	"Mashū" Watashi ga ōgoe de itta. "<u>Kimi no inochi o sukū tame ni, sono kan o watashi no hō e nagerunda. Ima sugu. Tadachini.</u>"

have the effect of disrupting the tone in the original text, which needs to be transmitted to the translated text.

Here, the sentences focused upon are uttered by the narrator, the main character, an intelligent civilian pilot in his thirties, to a ten-year-old boy, Matthew. We understand from the context that the tin which young Matthew is holding is actually a bomb inside a canister. Only the narrator is aware of this, and he tries to make the boy throw the tin of chocolates to him so that he can deal with it safely. The bomb might go off any moment – hence the atmosphere is tense. The original lines are very short and are thrown at the reader crisply, one after the other. By describing the situation and people's movements in the scene this way, the author successfully enhances the tension. It is a style recognisable in Francis's work, but the crispness is particularly noticeable in this piece. The question is, whether the sharp, hardboiled tone has successfully been transferred to the TT. In the translated version, some unusual word usages are observed. *Kimi no inochi o sukū tame ni* [to save your life] and *tadachini* [immediately] are semantically corresponding translations, which also reflect the ST's structural features, but both convey an unfitting tone: they sound too formal or even official – especially when spoken to a young child in such an extraordinary situation. Although the original language is also stiff because of the sequence of short, terse, monotonous sentences, the unnaturalness observed in the TT is of a different nature and of a different extent. The use of the words actually interferes with the TT and prevents it from maintaining a tone similar to that of the ST, since the reader's attention is distracted from the situational tension by the translationalness of the sentences. The piece of text is certainly "different" in terms of original Japanese conversation or its depiction in literature. It is, however, not unnatural in any evaluative sense. It might even be argued that Japanese readers are used to this type of translationalness, that this does not bother them (even at the climax of the story), and that they get to the essence of the ST and enjoy the literary experience through the translational veil. But do they really? What they enjoy is, after all, wrapped in this veil, and they cannot know where the veil ends. We will return to this point later.

7.2 Properties

It has been seen in section 7.1.2 that the presence of "translationese" in
Japanese translations in the traditional sense (generally regarded as having
negative connotations) is widely recognised, accepted and criticised at the
same time, and is largely attributed to the linguistic elements inherited from
physically observable features of the SL, regardless of the text-types. A closer
look at translationalness, however, reveals a situation that appears more
complicated. It is high time that the composition of the style be identified
at the micro level, taking account of how foreignised and domesticated elements are mixed in the text, and not just looking at the foreignised part of
the text. It will address the question of how to single out the translational
discourse specifically used in translated popular fiction. As with any other literary translation, various domestication and/or foreignisation operations –
both linguistic and cultural – are made in the process of translation of
the genre, but the specific way they interweave seems to be the key to the
composition of translated works of popular fiction.

Some strategies identified in the reconstruction of the process were
presented in the analysis of the texts carried out in the previous chapters.
The texts examined all display a rather chaotic mixture of the results of the
attempts to domesticate or foreignise them, and the discourse certainly
makes them distinguishable from any non-translational material. This unites
texts whose originals might be on different bookshelves in the bookshop.
Returning to Wakabayashi's (2009: 20) remarks, as introduced in Chapter 4:

> The question is whether translational language in the Japanese context lies between
> the source language(s) and Japanese (that is, external to both) or whether it is a part
> of the Japanese language. I suggest that translational language does not constitute
> a language "between" the source and target languages; rather, it is an integral part
> of the Japanese language and an innovative force that has contributed to the mod-
> ernization of the Japanese language, literature and thinking, while translation as a
> whole elides the boundaries that artificially demarcate source and target languages.

Wakabayashi thus regards translational language as an innovative force
which helps the Japanese language adapt and modernise, through interaction with Western writings and cultures. The book also argues that the

translational dialect, which comes across as highly unnatural, has an unusual but rather positive function by creating a virtual Western literary world which does not exist outside the system of Japanese translation. It is innovative indeed, as the act of translation into this style does not only create the TT, but gives birth to a virtual ST world too.

Before exploring further this argument for the positive role of otherness observed in translation, let us formally confirm the spontaneous use of the translational style by identifying the most conspicuous components of translationalness. This question must be asked through this attempt: do translations acquire these features without strong pressure from the stylistic features of the ST – that is, do these features come into existence in the TT even if the ST is free of them? What I will attempt to do next is to present six categories into which many cases of translation of this kind fall, together with one or two text examples that demonstrate how the characteristics of such language can be found without the ST being the real source of the features.

7.2.1 *Situational Mismatch: A Tone Out of Character with the Scene*

Thorough investigation suggests that this text-type of translationalness often displays a tone, unsuitable in particular scenes in the literary context. So, the first point raised as a stylistic trait is not structural Englishness itself – this is prominent in almost any translation text-type – but a distorted, misleading tone that is frequently caused by it. As a demonstration, I quote from the well-known short story, *The Adventure of the Christmas Pudding*, from the Detective Poirot series by Agatha Christie. In this scene, a girl's body is lying in the snow in front of some people. Poirot's main purpose is to catch the man who has stolen a famous piece of jewellery, and he knows that Lee-Wortley is the perpetrator. Poirot is deliberately accusing him of murdering the girl, which in fact has nothing to do with Lee-Wortley's actual crime (she is in fact only pretending to be dead). Lee-Wortley cannot see through this trick and is desperate to prove that he did not kill the girl. At the same time, however, he is afraid that his theft will be revealed during the investigation. It is a suspenseful scene, because the reader believes that the girl is dead and is supposed to be wondering who the murderer is:

Example 26: Agatha Christie, *The Adventure of the Christmas Pudding*, 1994/1960: 45–46

"There is no pulse …" he stared at Poirot. "Her arm's still. Good God, she really *is* dead!"

Poirot nodded. "Yes, she is dead," he said. "Someone has turned the comedy into a tragedy."

"Someone – who?"

"<u>There is a set of footprints going and returning.</u>(1) A set of footprints that bears a strong resemblance to the footprints *you* have just made, <u>Mr Lee-Wortley,</u>(2) coming from the path to this spot."

Desmond Lee-Wortley wheeled round.

"What on earth – <u>Are you accusing me?</u>(3) *ME*? You're crazy! <u>Why on earth should I want to kill the girl?</u>(4)"

Japanese TT: translated by Hashimoto Fukuo, 1985: 67

「まるっきり脈がない…」彼は呆然とポアロの顔を見つめた。「腕も硬ばっている。こりゃ、ほんとうに死んでいるぞ！」	"Marukkiri myaku ga nai …" kare wa bōzento Poaro no kao o mitsumeta. "Ude mo kowabatteiru. Korya, hontōni shindeiru zo!"
ポアロはうなずいた。「そう、死んでいる。何者かが喜劇を悲劇に変えたわけだ」	Poaro wa unazuita. "Sō, shindeiru. Nanimono ka ga kigeki o higeki ni kaeta wake da"
「何者かって―誰が？」	"Nanimono katte – dare ga?"
「<u>往復している―一組の足跡があります。</u>(1) それが<u>リーウォートリイさん、</u>(2) あなたが小径からここへ来られた時の足跡と、非常によく似ていますよ」	"<u>Ōfukushiteiru hitokumi no ashiato ga arimasu.</u>(1) Sore ga, <u>Riiwōtoriisan,</u>(2) anata ga komichi kara koko e korareta toki no ashiato to, hijōni yoku nite imasu yo"
デズモンド・リーウォートリイはくるりと向き直った。	Dezumondo • Riiwōtorii wa kururito mukinaotta.
「なんだって―<u>あなたはぼくのしわざだと言うのか？</u>(3) このぼくが？ 気ちがいざただ！ <u>ぼくがこの少女を殺したがる理由なんかないじゃないか？</u>(4)」	"Nandatte – <u>Anata wa boku no shiwaza da to yū no ka?</u>(3) Kono boku ga? Kichigaizata da! <u>Boku ga kono shōjo o koroshitagaru riyū nanka naijanai ka?</u>(4)"

The first noteworthy point in the TT is that, compared to the ST, Lee-Wortley sounds surprisingly composed, considering the situation in the last two lines. The point will now be examined in detail. *Anata wa* [you] in (3) would have been omitted in non-translational Japanese, since it is obvious from the context to whom Lee-Wortley is speaking. Its presence – an irregular verbalisation of the sentence subject – suggests that there must be a good reason why he wants to emphasise "you". *Tagaru* [want to] in *koroshitagaru* [to want to kill], in (4), is usually used in the third person. The use of the auxiliary verb in *Boku ga kono shōjo o koroshitagaru riyū* [the reason why I want to kill this girl] imparts the impression that Lee-Wortley is intentionally treating himself as a third person. These points ascribe an unnaturally analytical, objective tone to a person who has suddenly been accused of a murder and is in a panicky state, which the ST counterpart clearly suggests.

Several more expressions that produce an incongruous tone can be observed in the TT. The insertion of "Mr Lee-Wortley" in (2) is normative in a conversation in English but the lexically corresponding translation is not so in Japanese. *Ōfukushiteiru hitokumi no ashiato ga arimasu* [there is a pair of back and forth footprints] in (1) is also a good example of odd Japanese, a long noun-modifier resulting from word-for-word translation. Instead, *ashiato ga hitokumi ōfukushiteimasu* or *kite mata modotteimasu* [a pair of footprints is there back and forth *or* a pair of footprints comes and goes back again] would be possible, with *hitokumi* [a pair] then functioning as an adverb. As mentioned in the previous example, sometimes Poirot deliberately speaks with obviously French-influenced English, but that is not the case here (see section 2.1.4.H). The ST sentences consist of fairly standard English and Poirot's flawless accusation and Lee-Wortley's panicking tone present a good contrast, whereas in the Japanese TT, the stiffness gives the whole conversation a dull uniformity.

Next, an example is presented in which the ST tone is severely distorted by linguistic foreignisation together with extensive linguistic domestication (see also section 7.2.4) in the TT. In the ST of Christie's short story, Lou has witnessed Miss Greenshaw, for whom she is working as a secretary, being shot by somebody in the garden: she has observed the feathered shaft of an arrow protruding from her breast. Immediately after

Example 27: Agatha Christie, *Greenshaw's Folly*, 1994/1960: 228–229

"Come and let me out, Mrs Oxley. I'm locked in.₍₁₎"

"Come and let me out, Mrs Oxley. I'm locked in.(1)"

"So am I.(2)"

"Oh dear(3), isn't it awful?(4) I've telephoned the police. There's an extension in this room,(5) but what I can't understand, Mrs Oxley, is our being locked in. I never heard a key turn, did you?"

"No. I didn't hear anything at all. Oh dear, what shall I do?(6) Perhaps Alfred might hear us.(7)"

Lou shouted at the top of her voice, "Alfred, Alfred."

"Gone to his dinner as likely as not.(8) What time is it?(9)"

Japanese TT: translated by Uno Toshiyasu, *Guriinshōshi no Abōkyū*, 1985: 345

「おねがいだわ、オクスリーさん。ドアをあけていただきたいの。わたし、しめられてしまったのよ(1)」

「わたしも、おなじ目にあっていますわ(2)」

「あら、そうなの?(3) 困りましたわね。(4) 警察へは、電話しておきましたけれど、ええ、この部屋には、電話がありますのよ。(5) でも、なぜわたしたちがとじこめられたのか、わからないわ。錠のかかる音も、聞こえなかったんだけれど —」

「わたしもよ。そんな音、聞かなかったわ。どうしたら、いいのでしょうか。(6) たぶん、アルフレッドが、そこらにいると思いますが(7)」

ルーは、できるだけ声をはりあげて、庭番を呼んだ。

「アルフレッド、アルフレッド!」

「食事にでも、でかけたのかしら?(8) いま何時なんでしょう?(9)」

"Onegai da wa, Okusuriisan. Doa o aketeitadakitai no. Watashi, shimerareteshimatta no yo.(1)"

"Watashi mo, onaji me ni atteimasu wa.(2)"

"Ara, sō nano?(3) Komarimashita wa ne.(4) Keisatsu e wa, denwashiteokimashita keredo. Ē, kono heya ni wa, denwa ga arimasu no yo.(5) Demo, naze watashitachi ga tojikomerareta no ka, wakaranai wa. Jō no kakaru oto mo, kikoenakattanda keredo –"

"Watashi mo yo. Sonna oto, kikanakatta wa. Dō shitara, iinodeshō ka.(6) Tabun, Arufureddo ga, sokora ni iru to omoimasu ga.(7)"

Rū wa, dekiru dake koe o hariagete, niwaban o yonda.

"Arufureddo, Arufureddo!"

"Shokuji ni demo, dekaketa no kashira?(8) Ima nanji nandeshō?(9)"

that, she has discovered that the door is locked from outside and that she cannot get out of the room. Lou assumes that Mrs Oxley has also heard Miss Greenshaw calling for help earlier. It is clear from the context that this is another scene involving extreme shock and panic. Lou restlessly keeps on telling Mrs Oxley about the situation – how she has telephoned the police, how she did not hear a key turn in the lock, and about the possibility that Alfred, the gardener, has gone.

In the TT, by contrast, the discourse between the two ladies' speech seems very relaxed and elegant. The TT gives the reader no hint of Lou's fevered desperation. The presence of an unnecessary subject *watashi* [I] – a trace of linguistic foreignisation – contributes to this relaxed impression, in that she takes the trouble to make clear who the subject is. Another aspect of stiffness caused by foreignisation is the frequent use of commas. There are two in (1), one in (2), one in (3), four in (5), one in (6), two in (7) and one in (8). Most of them indicate an unnecessary pause in speaking and it would be more natural if they were omitted in such a desperate situation. The question marks in (3), (8) and (9) also disturb the hasty, desperate tone of the TT: in Japanese, question marks are normally used to emphasise the rising tone of an utterance. Domestication also affects the tone of the sentence endings: *da wa*, *no* and *no yo* in (1), *wa* in (2), *Ara, sō nano?* in (3), *Komarimashita wa ne* in (4), and *no yo* in (5) are all most peaceful-sounding statements, because of their feminine and elegant tone.

It is not difficult to remain closer to the original tone, and it does not require much semantic adjustment, nevertheless, translational style has been employed to disturb the transfer. The ample use of such devices, including an interrogative mark and sentence-end particles, play an important role in building up this kind of style. Obviously unforced but steady use of these devices lead us to think that the text must have a different tone from the ST, and at the same time must sound unreal within any Japanese setting.

7.2.2 *Absence of Rhythm*

Rhythmical effects observed in the ST tend to be lost. Here I use the term "rhythmical" to mean how well the text flows, achieved by the regular use of certain words. According to Attridge (1996: 1) rhythm is "the continuous motion that pushes spoken language forward, in more or less regular waves, as the musculature of the speech organs tightens and relaxes, as energy pulsates through the words we speak and hear, as the brain marshals multiple stimuli into ordered patterns". People often enjoy literature, especially poetry or stage plays because of rhythm, and translating this presents a particular challenge. When attempting to translate rhythm, Jones (2011: 96) says "(t)rying to reproduce patterns of rhymes and rhythm [...] risks changing or losing this. Other risks are of 'padding' (expanding otherwise succinct target-text lines) to replicate source-text rhymes, and that such rhymes might 'sound extremely weird' in the target language". Clearly the difficulties of reproducing rhythm in translation are widely recognised. Many translated texts are monotonous or colourless because they have lost their original rhythm. This is also usually triggered by linguistic foreignisation. Example 28 is from the latest translation of *Sense and Sensibility* by Jane Austen.

The status of Austen's novels, which are generally recognised as classical, intellectual nineteenth-century English literature, is reflected in the manner in which Japanese translations are carried out, and in the category in which they are placed. Most Austen translations were published in a particularly prestigious series of world literature, such as *Iwanami Bunko*. The latest Japanese translation, by Mano (1996), in contrast, appears to be a model case of successful popularisation of literature through translation. It came out immediately after the hit Hollywood film adaptation, and was published in hard cover by *Kinema Jumpōsha*, including elaborate photographs of the scenes from the film. It successfully attracted and satisfied a large number of readers, including fans of Hugh Grant, who starred in the film. To achieve the aim of popularising the work, the language in the TT includes many of the stylistic flavours of translated fiction – unlike the translation by Ibuki Chise in 1948, in which, for example, proper names are treated in a different manner (see section 6.2.3).

After a long separation, Marianne has met Willoughby, a man she greatly admires, at a dance party. His attitude towards her was surprisingly cold and later she receives an even more disappointing letter, which says that he has never been interested in her and that he is engaged to somebody else. Marianne still tries to justify his behaviour. In deep grief and desperation,

Example 28: Jane Austen, *Sense and Sensibility*, 1995/1811: 159

"Dearest Marianne, who but himself? By whom can he have been instigated?"
"By all the world, rather than by his own heart. <u>I could rather believe every creature of my acquaintance leagued together to ruin me in his opinion, than believe his nature capable of such cruelty.</u> (1) <u>This woman of whom he writes – whoever she be – or any one, in short, but your own dear self, mama, and Edward, may have been so barbarous to bely me.</u> (2) Beyond you three, is there a creature in the world whom I would not rather suspect of evil than Willoughby, whose heart I know so well?"

Japanese TT: translated by Mano Akihiro, *Itsuka Hareta Hi ni – Funbetsu to Takan –*, 1996: 192	
「ねえマリアン、彼以外に誰がいて？ いったい誰が彼をそそのかしたっていうの？」	"Nē, Marian, kare igai ni dare ga ite? Ittai dare ga kare o sosonokashitatte yū no?"
「彼自身の悪意じゃなくて世の中全体よ。<u>わたしの知り合いが一人残らず結託して彼の目に映るわたしのイメージを台無しにしたというほうが、彼の気性でこんなむごいことができるっていうより、むしろ信じられる気がする。</u>(1) <u>彼が書いてるあの女性にしろ―誰なのか知らないけど ― 誰にしろ、要するに、姉さんとママとエドワード以外はみんな、わたしを中傷するような残忍さがあったのかもしれないわ。</u>(2) 姉さんたち三人は別として、わたしから見れば、気心のよくわかっているウィロビーよりよっぽど邪心を疑いたくなるような人たちばっかりだわ」	"Kare jishin no akui janakute yononaka zentai yo. <u>Watashi no shiriai ga hitori nokorazu kettakushite kare no me ni utsuru watashi no imēji o dainashi ni shita to yū hō ga, kare no kishō de konna mugoi koto ga dekirutte yū yori, mushiro shinjirareru ki ga suru.</u>(1) <u>Kare ga kaiteru ano josei ni shiro - dare na no ka shiranai kedo - dare ni shiro, yōsuruni, nēsan to mama to Edowādo igai wa minna, watashi o chūshōsuru yōna zanninsa ga atta no kamo shirenai wa.</u>(2) Nēsantachi sannin wa betsu to shite, watashi kara mireba, kigokoro no yoku wakatteiru Wirobii yori yoppodo jashin o utagaitaku naru yōna hitotachi bakkari da wa"

she is far from being fair towards her acquaintances. In this fragment of text, she emotionally describes her thoughts to her sister. She is not hysterical, however, and somehow retains her composed manner. Considering the context, the underlined parts of the TT are rather stiff. Her emotional, unstoppable flow of speech in the ST is changed into tedious, unrhythmical sentences. In (1), first of all, *hō* [way, one of the options] is preceded by a very long modifying clause: *Watashi no shiriai* [acquaintances] *ga hitori nokorazu* [without exception] *kettakushite* [conspiring] *kare no me* [his eyes] *ni utsuru* [to be reflected] *watashi no imēji* [my image] *o dainashi ni shita* [ruined] *to yū* [(we) say]. There are four pronouns in one sentence, *watashi* (I) twice and *kare* (he) twice, which is extraordinary by native Japanese standards. *Kettakushite* is a formal word (*kango* noun + *suru* [to do]) which does not fit a casual conversation between two young sisters. In addition, *Kare no me ni utsuru* [is reflected in his eyes] appears to be an "unsuccessful" attempt at linguistic domestication of the ST unit "in his opinion" into a fixed expression. However, it simply makes the TT sentence more foreign because yet another pronoun is used.

In (2) in Example 28, the combination of the abstract noun *zanninsa* [cruelty] and the modifier *watashi o chūshōsuru* [to speak ill of me] *yōna* [like, as such] collects attention. *Zanninsa ga attanokamo shirenai wa* [there may have been a cruelty] is a translation of the ST unit "may have been so barbarous". A formal-sounding word of Chinese origin, *chūshō* [slander], is combined with the pronouns *kare* [he] and *watashi* [I] into a long modifier and applied to another abstract word, *zanninsa* [brutality], making the sentence stiff.

It is worth taking a look at another example of a rhythmical ST, taken from Ruth Rendell's mystery *Make Death Love Me* and its translation (see Example 29).

The policeman is interrogating Dr Bolton in the investigation of a bank robbery case. Dr Bolton has come back from holiday to find a Ford used in the robbery in his garage, and the police want to find out who hid the car there. The policeman's answer to Dr Bolton's complaint, "Our friends are not the kind of people who rob banks" is ironical and comical in the original, as he explains in patronisingly clear, logical language the reason why the police need to investigate their social connections, despite their "respectability". Owing to the effective repetition of the words "know", "people", "friends", "have" and "respectable", the line in question is obviously rhythmical. This effect is lost in the TT as the translator used synonyms for the words rather than retaining the originals to achieve a similar rhythm: *shitteiru* [to know] and *shiriai da* [to be acquainted] for "know", *jinbutsu* [person] and *ningen* [human being] for "people", and *jinkakukōketsu* [noble-minded] and *hinkōhōsei* [well-behaved] for "respectable". A more straight-forward translation – with the same repetition of words – would create

Example 29: Ruth Rendell, *Make Death Love Me*, 1994/1979: 180

They were with him in half an hour. Dr and Mrs Bolton were asked to make a list of all the people who knew they had no lock on their garage and also knew they were to be away on holiday. "Our friends," said Dr Bolton, "are not the kind of people who rob banks." "I don't doubt that," said the detective inspector, "<u>but your friends may know people who know people who are less respectable than they are, or have children who have friends who are not respectable at all</u>."

Japanese TT: translated by Obi Fusa, *Shi no Karutetto*, 1985: 256	
警察は三十分でやってきた。ボルトン博士夫妻は、いつもガレージには鍵をかけないという事実と、自分たちが休暇で家をあけるという事実を知っている人間のリストを作るよう警察から依頼された。	Keisatsu wa sanjuppun de yattekita. Borutonhakase fusai wa, itsumo garēji ni wa kagi o kakenai to yū jijitsu to, jibuntachi ga kyūka de ie o akeru to yū jijitsu o shitteiru ningen no risuto o tsukuru yō keisatsu kara iraisareta.
「わたしの友人に」とボルトン博士は言った。「銀行強盗をするような人間はいませんよ」	"Watashi no yūjin ni" to Borutonhakase wa itta. "Ginkōgōtō o suru yōna ningen wa imasen yo."
「それはわかっていますが」と刑事は言った。「ご友人が、<u>人格高潔とは言えないような人物を知っている人間と知り合いだとか、まったく品行方正とはいいかねるような友人をもっているお子さんがおありの方と知り合いだとか、そういうこともありますんでね</u>」	"Sore wa wakatteimasu ga" to keiji wa itta. "Goyūjin ga, <u>jinkakukōketsu to wa ienai yōna jinbutsu o shitteiru ningen to shiriai da toka, mattaku hinkōhōsei to wa iikaneru yōna yūjin o motteiru okosan ga oari no kata to shiriai da toka, sō yū koto mo arimasunde ne</u>"

a stylistic effect close to that of the ST. The cause of the loss of rhythm in Examples 28 and 29 is partly linguistic foreignisation, and partly "unsuccessful" linguistic domestication, in which the translator chose not to reflect the original structure as she constructed the sentences in Japanese.

7.2.3 *Extensive Use of Institutionalised Dialects*

An eminent feature of the text-type is the mechanical, exaggerated application of social, regional, occupational or class dialects to the TT – especially

in conversation. Given that the reasonable use of certain dialects is normative in native Japanese, the translationalness is created by the dramatic effect
caused by the exaggeration. Thus, this qualifies as extensive domestication
(see section 6.1). The Japanese language has a number of clearly identifiable
written social dialects known as *yakuwarigo* (Kinsui 2003). Female speech,
for instance, differs from male speech to some degree in most languages,
but the institutionalised differences are more substantial in Japanese than
in English. Kinsui (2014) also argues that *yakuwarigo* in fiction does not
necessarily reflect reality in Japanese society and sometimes is rather different. When a character is in a trivial role compared to the main character,
or someone who takes a decisive role around the main one, he/she tends
to talk in a strong social dialect, which comes across as unrealistic. Such
effects are widely seen in fiction works in general.

In the translation of literature, such variants are also overused. Kōno
(1999: 188–189, my translation), claims that more attention should be paid
to the use of "*ikanimo* [hackneyed] language" or *yakuwarigo*, as well as to
trendy slang in literary translations:

> I coin the term "*ikanimo* language". There are translators who automatically assign a
> typically farmer-like rough dialect to every farmer in a literary piece – for example,
> "*Tomokaku, ore no itta toki nya, miyako de nakatta da – chinkoi katame no, henpina
> shonbokunai basho dayo*" [...]

> I repeat: conversational style should not be determined by a character's race, profes-
> sion, sex or age. It is the translator's job to devise the most appropriate conversational
> style for each literary work.

Typical cases of the extensive use of dialects in translation of popular fiction can be seen in Example 30.

In this scene from a short story, again by Christie, an old and eccentric millionaire is describing the mysterious dream he has every night: in
the dream, he kills himself with a revolver at exactly twenty-eight min-
utes past three in the afternoon. *Ja* [ending particle] in (1), (6), (8) and
(9), *washi* [I] in (2) and (4), *osorosyū* [horrified, euphonically changed
from *osoroshiku*] instead of *osoroshiku* [horrified] in (2), *shitoru* [doing,
euphonically changed from *shite iru*] instead of *shite iru* [doing] in (5),
chigawan [not different, euphonically changed from *chigawanai*] instead

Example 30: Agatha Christie, *The Dream*, 1994/1960: 192–193

<table>
<tr><td colspan="2">"It's the same dream(1) – night after night. And I'm afraid(2), I tell you – I'm afraid … It's always the same.(3) I'm sitting in my room next door to this.(4) Sitting at my desk, writing.(5) There's a clock there and I glance at it and see the time – exactly twenty-eight minutes past three.(6) Always the same time, you understand.(7)
"And when I see the time, M. Poirot, I know I've got to do it.(8) I don't want to do it(9) – I loathe doing it(10) – but I've got to …"</td></tr>
<tr><td colspan="2">Japanese TT: translated by Ogura Takashi, Yume, 1985: 286</td></tr>
<tr><td>「同じ夢なんじゃ(1)…毎晩毎晩。で、わしも恐ろしうなった(2)…いや恐ろしい…いつも同じ夢だからな。(3)わしはこの隣りの自分の部屋で(4)…デスクに向って書きものをしとる。(5)時計が置いてあるんだが、目をあげて時間を見ると…きまって三時二十八分きっかりなんじゃ。(6)いつも一分一秒ちがわんのだよ。(7)それにポアロ君、時間を見るとどうしてもやらずにおれなくなるんじゃ。(8)やりたくないのにじゃ(9)…したくなんかありゃせん(10)…が、せずにおれなくなる…」</td><td>Onaji yume nan ja(1) … maiban maiban. De, washi mo osorosyū natta(2) … iya osoroshii … itsumo onaji yume dakara na.(3) Washi wa kono tonari no jibun no heya de(4) … desuku ni mukatte kakimono o shitoru.(5) Tokei ga oite arunda ga, me o agete jikan o miru to … kimatte sanji nijuppun kikkari nan ja.(6) Itsumo ippun ichibyō chigawan noda yo.(7) Sore ni Poarokun, jikan o miruto, dōshitemo yarazu ni orenaku narun ja.(8) Yaritakunai noni ja(9) … shitaku nanka aryasen(10) … ga, sezu ni orenaku naru …</td></tr>
</table>

of *chigawanai* [not different] in (6), and *arya sen* [it is not that, euphonically changed from *ari wa shinai*] instead of *ari wa shinai* [it is not that] in (10) are devices to indicate or hint that the speaker is an old man. Here, domestication according to the institutionalised social dialect has been carried out to such an extent that one cannot imagine a Japanese person speaking that way. It would give the text the feeling of a *jidaigeki* [a period play] or an old tale (if it was original Japanese literature), or of a parody of the theatrical language used in such works.

In *Deadlock*, the second book in the V. I. Warshawski private detective series by Sara Paretsky, a night guard is killed after V. I. told him to look after the apartment more carefully. In this scene, the guard's wife, "a dark, dignified woman whose grief was more impressive for the restraint with which she contained it" (Paretsky 1984: 291), is accusing V. I. of her

Example 31: Sara Paretsky, *Deadlock*, 1984: 294

"Well(1), he told(2) me, he said(3), 'I don't know(6) who that girl' – that's(5) you(4) – 'thinks is going to try to get into that place. But I got my eye on it(6).' So he plays the hero, and he gets killed(8). But you(9) say(10) you weren't expecting anything special."

Japanese TT: translated by Yamamoto Yayoi, *Rēkusaido • Sutōrii*, 1986: 91	
「いいかい(1)、うちの人はあたしにいったんだよ(2)。こういったんだ(3)。「あの女―あんた(4)のことだよ(5)―いったい誰があすこに忍びこむと思ってるのか、おれにはわからねえ(6)。けど、しっかり見張ってやらあ(7)」ってね。そうして、英雄のまねなんかして、殺されちまった(8)。それなのにあんた(9)、特別なことが起きるとは思ってなかったっていうんだね(10)」	"Ii kai(1) uchi no hito wa atashi ni ittanda yo(2). Kō ittanda(3). "Ano onna – anta(4) no koto da yo(5) – 'ittai dare ga asuko ni shinobikomu to omotteru no ka, ore ni wa wakaranē(6). Kedo, shikkari mihatteyarā(7),"tte ne.' Sō shite, ēyū no mane nanka shite, korosarechimatta(8). Sore nanoni, anta(9), tokubetsuna kono ga okiru to wa omottenakattatte yūnda ne(10)."

husband's death, quoting what he said to her. In her complaint, vulgar, uneducated-sounding language (often employed automatically for blue-collar workers or farmers, and for coloured people) is used. This includes ending particles that create a rough or informal tone, such as *kai* (1), *da yo* (2) and (5), *da* (3), *yarā* (7) and *da ne* (10), as well as *anta* [you] (4) and (9), instead of the more neutral *anata*, and *korosarechimatta* (8) [has been killed, euphonically changed from *korosareteshimatta*] instead of *korosareteshimatta* [has been killed]. The ST does not exhibit any sign of dialect of this kind. Even if the woman's lines were expected to include some accent that demonstrated her and her husband's social status, it would not imply vulgarity to this extent. Extensive use various kinds of social dialect, such as dialects for the aged, for men, for women, for uneducated people or for provincial people, is a commonly seen type of over-domestication.

7.2.4 *Traces of Attempted Domestication*

An attempted – but not ultimately "successful" – domestication ironically renders a text more unusual in terms of the original Japanese. Considering that it does not produce domesticness, it is perhaps logically misleading to call the attempt a domestication in the first place. Yet there are occasions where the translator's intention is clearly to boost the native qualities of the text. This can go astray in various ways: When it is carried out to an excessive degree, the result is never satisfactorily smooth. Also, when an expression is utilised simply for its idiomaticity or Japanese exoticism, it often leads to a sense of incongruity in the context, regardless of the fact that it does not fit the situation. This widens the stylistic gap between the ST and the TT; it is not the semantic gap but the incongruity which functions as a translational factor.

A. EXTENSIVE DOMESTICATION

The utilisation of hackneyed expressions is a frequent example of extensive domestication. When a whole raft of these expressions (commonly known, but not used in real life) occurs in a short text, it gives readers the impression that they are, in fact, reading a work of fiction. An intriguing point is that the abundant employment of fixed expressions does not cause the translation itself to fail, nor does it reduce its value as translated fiction. Rather, it solidifies the stylistic character of the text-type and its position within the entire body of literary translations. Example 32, taken from *Prime Cut*, contains an interesting example of the overuse of trite expressions.

Example 32: Diane Mott Davidson, *Prime Cut*, 1998: 309

"Oh, Marla. I've missed you so much. And there's something I have to tell you, but you weren't feeling well, and I wanted to wait until your audit was over, because –" "Calm down, will you? I can't listen to whatever it is until I've had some food"	
Japanese TT: translated by Katō Yōko, *Kukkingu・Mama no Shinhannin*, 2000: 376	
「ああ、マーラ、会いたかった。話したいことがあったんだけど、あなたはとてもそんな気分じゃないだろうと思ったから、税務調査が終わるまで待とうと思って、だってー」 「ハイ、ドードードー、落ち着いてよ。話をするのは、あたしがなにか食べてからにしてちょうだい」	"Ā, Māra, aitakatta. Hanashitai koto ga attanda kedo, anata wa totemo sonna kibun janaidarō to omotta kara, zēmuchōsa ga owaru made matō to omotte, datte –" "Hai, dōdōdō, ochitsuite yo. Hanashi o suru no wa, atashi ga nanika tabete kara ni shite chōdai"

A caterer, who is also the mother of a teenage boy, encounters a murder mystery, which she then solves. Her catering business plays an important role in the storyline. Some cooking recipes are introduced to add fun to this breezy whodunit. In the TT, which is part of a conversation between Goldie the caterer and her best friend Marla, *Hai, dōdōdō*, is inserted. *Dōdōdō* or *dōdō* is a sequence of sounds made to tame a horse [whoa] or [whoooa]. Using this phrase to calm down an excited person is a classic joke to ease the tension between close friends in casual dialogue. Although there is no joke (or, in fact, anything else) that represents a corresponding unit in the ST, this is inserted to add an extra comical tone. Marla, a middle-aged woman, does sound rather silly and playful making this utterance, and this, in fact, matches her character. The point here is that the joke does not function as a joke because of its hackneyed nature. The text does not convey the fact that "Marla is a dear character who comes up with such a cheap joke" (Davidson 1998: 77) either, because the text does not create the impression that the joke is inserted here for its "worn-out" effect at a meta level, but simply that it is used as a joke. This is probably due to the presence of many other expressions with a similar tone. Instead of perceiving humour, the reader of the TT receives the impression of being in a uniquely constructed imaginary theatre, within which the jokes are supposed to be funny but are not actually funny. This is another important factor of the discourse, which makes readers conscious of the fact that they are reading a translation and that the translator is striking a good balance of domestication and foreignisation.

B. DOMESTICATION OUT OF CONTEXT

Example 33 illustrates an attempt at domestication in which a supposedly Japanising expression is employed in a non-normative context.

Me o kubaru is an idiom which means to take care of, or to mind, several things simultaneously. Due to the presence of *kubaru* [to distribute], the idiom indicates that there is more than one thing to take care of. This does not fit the ST context, as the only issue is "Robbie". The use of *kubaru* suggests the presence of other objects, but driving is not the objective of *me o kubaru*. For the same reason, it is unusual that this takes a singular

Example 33: Lilian Jackson Braun, *The Cat Who Knew a Cardinal*, 1991: 161

"I'm sorry I didn't meet you during the run of the play," he said, "but you always disappeared right after the curtain."
"I had a long drive home," she explained, "and then … ummm … <u>I have to keep an eye on Robbie</u>."

Japanese TT: translated by Hata Shizuko, *Neko wa Tori o Mitsumeru*, 1995: 202	
「芝居の上演中にお知り合いになれなくて、残念でしたよ」クィラランはいった。「だが、幕が下りるとすぐに姿がみえなくなってしまったから」 「家まで長距離を運転しなくちゃなりませんでしたから」彼女はいいわけした。「それに…そのお…<u>ロビーにも目を配らなくちゃならなかったんです</u>」	"Shibai no jōenchū ni oshiriai ni narenakute, zannen deshita yo." Kuiraran wa itta. "Daga, maku ga oriru to suguni sugata ga mienaku natteshimatta kara." "Ie made chōkyori o untenshinakucha narimasendeshita kara." Kanojo wa iiwakeshita. "Soreni … sonō … <u>Robii ni mo me o kubaranakucha naranakattandesu</u>."

person as the object: *Robii no suru koto* [the things Robbie does] would make more sense. In addition, the expression has a slightly business-like tone to it and sounds odd in this conversation. This is a typical case in which an idiomatic expression is utilised in an "unfitting" environment. Fixed expressions can potentially domesticate the text, if their usage satisfies the target-language norm. The abuse of idiomatic expressions to a large degree exemplifies the tendency towards the growing standardisation suggested by Toury (1995: 267). What is noteworthy, however, is that in many cases their use deviates from normative usage and thus fails to normalise the text. This is despite the fact that the appropriate use of an expression of high idiomaticity can be effective in naturalising the TT, which might otherwise be pulled more towards linguistic foreignisation.

7.2.5 *Joint Appearance of Linguistic Domesticness and Foreignness*

Next, another major constituent of translational style is the patchy appearance of the results of linguistic and cultural domestication and foreignisation. This frequently disturbs the transfer of the tone or rhythm of the ST. The inconsistent appearance of clear traces of the two options is itself a distinct stylistic property, which I will focus on here. Example 34 is taken from Hata's translation of *The Cat Who Knew a Cardinal*. In her translation, colloquial Japanese (including honorifics and AMAs, that is, attitude-marking adverbs) is used in conversation, and plentiful instances of linguistic domestication can be observed. Many of the domestications are successful in themselves. Nevertheless, distinct translationalness is sensed from the text as a whole, because of the traces of Englishness that are often adjacent to the domestications. Also, it is evident that the translator has – in a semantically close manner – transferred most of the cultural elements in the story, such as the details of the characters' lives in an American village. Much more cultural foreignisation than domestication has been employed.

Judging from the TT, the translator seems to have linguistically erased potential structural and lexical Englishness to some extent, for instance, by using an adverb and a simple verb *kichinto kanrishiteru* [is properly controlling] for "runs a tight ship" in (2), deleting the ST idiomaticity and inserting

Example 34: Lilian Jackson Braun, *The Cat Who Knew a Cardinal*, 1991: 41–42

Brodie grunted an affirmative. "What were they all doing here besides eating pizza?"

"Drinking beer and soft drinks and coffee ... hashing over the run of the play_(1)... celebrating its success ... making a lot of noise."

"Were they smoking anything they shouldn't?"

"No. Carol puts the clamps on that. She runs a tight ship._(2) Fran can tell you."

"Any arguments? Any brawls?"

"Nothing like that. Everyone was in a good humor."

"Did you see anybody hanging around the orchard that didn't belong?"

"Not tonight, but we've had curiosity-seekers prowling around ever since we moved in."

"How come Van Brook_(3) honored the party with his presence? He was an unsociable cuss."

"He had an ulterior motive," said Qwilleran. "He wanted to bring the entire student body tramping through my barn on field trips. He didn't ask me: he told me!"

"That sounds like him, all right._(4) How popular was he in the club?"

Japanese TT: translated by Hata Shizuko, *Neko wa Tori o Mitsumeru*, 1995: 47	
ブロディはうなり声で肯定の返事をした。「連中はピザを食うほかに、ここで何をやってたんだ?」	Burodii wa unarigoe de kōtei no henji o shita. "Renchū wa piza o kū hoka ni, koko de nani o yattetanda?"
「ビールやソフトドリンクやコーヒーを飲んで...<u>公演について、ああでもない、こうでもないと討議し</u>₍₁₎...成功を祝い...騒々しい音を立ててた」	"Biiru ya sofutodorinku ya kōhii o nonde ... <u>kōen ni tsuite ā demo nai, kō demo nai to tōgishi</u>₍₁₎ ... seikō o iwai ... sōzōshii oto o tateteta."
「禁止されているものを吸っていたかね?」	"Kinshisareteiru mono o sutteita kane?"
「いや。そいつはキャロルが厳しく取り締まってたからね。<u>彼女はメンバーをきちんと管理してる。</u>₍₂₎フランに聞けばわかるよ」	"Iya. Soitsu wa Kyaroru ga kibishiku torishimatteta kara ne. <u>Kanojo wa menbā o kichinto kanrishiteru.</u>₍₂₎ Furan ni kikeba wakaru yo."
「口論は?けんか騒ぎは?」	"Kōron wa? Kenkasawagi wa?"
「そういうのはないな。全員がご機嫌だった」	"Sō yū no wa nai na. Zen'in ga gokigen datta."
「関係ない人間がりんご園をぶらついているのを見かけなかったか?」	"Kankei nai ningen ga ringoen o buratsuiteiru no o mikakenakatta ka?"
「今夜はね。ただ、ここに引っ越してきてから、好奇心旺盛なのぞき屋が敷地内をしじゅう徘徊してる」	"Kon'ya wa ne. Tada, koko ni hikkoshite kite kara, kōkishin ōseina nozokiya ga shikichinai o shijū haikaishiteru."
「<u>ヴァンブルックのやつ、</u>₍₃₎よくパーティーに顔を出したな。人づきあいが悪いのに」	"<u>Vanburukku no yatsu,</u>₍₃₎ yoku pātii ni kao o dashita na. Hitozukiai ga warui noni."
「秘めた動機があったんだよ」クィラランは説明した。「彼は校外学習の一環として、生徒全員をひき連れて、わたしの納屋を踏み荒らそうという魂胆だったんだ。許可を求めたんじゃない、そう宣言したんだ!」	"Himeta dōki ga attanda yo" Kuiraran wa setsumeishita. "Kare wa kōgaigakushū no ikkan to shite, seitozen'in o hikitsurete, watashi no naya o fumiarasō to yū kontan dattanda. Kyoka o motometanjanai. Sō sengenshitanda!"
「<u>いかにも彼らしいね、まったく。</u>₍₄₎クラブでの評判はどうだった?」	"<u>Ikanimo kare rashii ne, mattaku.</u>₍₄₎ Kurabu de no hyōban wa dō datta?"

the AMA *ikanimo* [at any rate] in (4). Also, she adds ~*no yatsu* [bloody ~]
after *Vanburukku* [Van Brook] in (3) to show Chief Brodie's antipathy
towards Van Brook. Despite such carefully trimmed craftwork, the language does not look domestic in the sense of non-translational Japanese.
This example is a conversation between two educated, middle-aged men –
Qwilleran and Chief Brodie – who are close to each other. Van Brook has
been shot after the party at Qwilleran's barn, and the chief is trying to obtain
the details from him. Both the questions and answers are concise, factual, and
sarcastic. For instance, line (1) in the ST, "Drinking beer and soft drinks and
coffee [...] hashing over the run of the play [...] celebrating its success [...]
making a lot of noise" is nicely rhythmical as well as informative. Qwilleran
is deliberately listing trivial matters in order to explain that nothing unusual
happened during the party. The TT does not maintain the crisp, rhythmical
tone of the ST (section 7.2.2). The tone is explanatory, due to the presence
of some misplaced, formal-sounding words, such as *kōen ni tsuite* [about the
play], *tōgishi* [to discuss] and *iwai* [to celebrate]. The original structure can
almost be discerned from their counterparts in this linguistic foreignisation.
Several colloquial, idiomatic expressions, such as ā *de mo nai, kō demo nai
to* [in various ways] and *tateteta* instead of *tateteita* [to make], are mixed
in. This mélange of linguistic domestication with formal words results in a
hodgepodge and increases the overall effect of translationalese.

7.2.6 Abrupt Appearance of Cultural Domestication

Japaneseness resulting from cultural domestication, which is placed at
random within a foreign setting, is also characteristic of the dialect. While
cultural domestication is seen in literary translations of any genre, arbitrarily
distributed domesticness seems unique to translated popular fiction. Thus,
although cultural foreignness is not a characteristic of the style by itself,
unlike linguistic foreignness, cultural Englishness emphasises translationalness by stressing the abruptly inserted domesticness. Examples 35 and
36, taken from Sheridan Le Fanu's classic short horror story *Squire Toby's
Will*, include not only cases of cultural domestication but also a number
of culturally domestic items that are irrelevant to the rest of the story or
the cultural settings.

Example 35: Joseph Sheridan Le Fanu, *Squire Toby's Will*, 1994/1868: 20

"It's not a great deal, Cooper, but it troubles me, and I would not tell it to <u>the parson</u>(1) nor the doctor; for, God knows what they'd say, though there's nothing to signify in it. But you were always true to the family, and I don't mind if I tell you."

"'Tis as safe with Cooper, Master Charles, as if 'twas locked in a chest, and sunk in a well."

"It's only this," said Charles Marston, looking down on the end of his stick, with which he was tracing lines and circles, "all the time I was lying like dead, as you thought, after that fall, I was with the old master." He raised his eyes to Cooper's again as he spoke, and with an awful oath he repeated – "I was with him, Cooper!"

"He was a good man, sir, in his way," repeated old Cooper, returning his gaze with awe. "He was a good master to me, and a good father to you, and <u>I hope he's happy</u>(2). <u>May God rest him!</u>(3)"

Japanese TT: translated by Yokoyama Jun, *Yuigon*, 1990: 193–194

「たいしたことではないのだが、それが気がかりになっているのに、<u>牧師</u>(1)にも医者にも話す気になれない。かれらがなんというか分らないが、どうせ碌なことは言うまい。しかし、お前はいつもわたしらに忠実だったから、お前にだけなら話してもいい」

「旦那さま、櫃(ひつ)に入れて鍵をかけ井戸に沈めたと同じことで、わたしならご心配ご無用でございます」

線や円をたどっていたステッキの先端を見つめながらチャールズは言った。

「実はな、落馬したのち、お前も知っての通り死人のように眠りつづけていた間中、わたしは父と一緒にいたんだよ」

そう語りながら再びクーパーの顔をみつめ、怖ろしい呪いを口にするかのように、くりかえして、

「父と一緒にいたんだよ」

かしこまって主人を見かえしながら、クーパーはこたえた。

"Taishita koto de wa nainoda ga, sore ga kigakari ni natteiru noni, <u>bokushi</u>(1) ni mo isha ni mo hanasu ki ni narenai. Karera ga nan to yū ka wakaranai ga, dōse roku na koto wa yūmai. Shikashi, omae wa itsumo watashira ni chūjitsudatta kara, omae ni dake nara hanashite mo ii."

"Dannasama, hitsu ni irete kagi o kake ido ni shizumeta to onaji koto de, watashi nara goshinpai gomuyō de gozaimasu."

Sen ya en o tadotteita sutekki no sentan o mitsume nagara Chāruzu wa itta.

"Jitsu wa na, rakubashita nochi, omae mo shitte no tōri shinin no yōni nemuritsuzuketeita aidajū, watashi wa chichi to issho ni itanda yo."

Sō katari nagara futatabi Kūpā no kao o mitsume, osoroshii noroi o kuchi ni suru ka no yōni, kurikaeshite, "Chichi to issho ni itanda yo."

Kashikomatte shujin o mikaeshi nagara, Kūpā wa kotaeta.

| 「ご先代もあの方^{かた}なりに良い方でご ざいました。わたしには良いご主人 でしたし、旦那さまにも良いお父さ までしたよ。きっとご成仏なさって 居られましょう₍₂₎。ご冥福を₍₃₎」 | "Gosendai mo ano kata nari ni yoi kata de gozaimashita. Watashi ni wa yoi goshujin deshita shi, dannasama ni mo yoi otōsama deshita yo. <u>Kitto gojōbutsunasatte oraremashō.</u>₍₂₎ <u>Gomēfuku o.</u>₍₃₎" |

In Example 35, Charles is terrified that his brother and father, who are both dead, have placed a curse on him because of their past rows. In the TT, there are two religious modifications: *gojōbutsunasatte* [entering Nirvana] in (2) and *gomēfuku o* [wishing for the repose of his soul] in (3). Both of the ST expressions, "I hope he's happy (in heaven)" and "May God rest him", obviously have Christian beliefs as their background, so the translator has substituted Buddhist expressions for them. It should be noted that the word "parson" (1) is used only a few lines earlier in the ST and has been allocated the semantically and culturally straightforward translation *bokushi* [clergyman] – not an ambiguous, neutralising term like *bōzu* [priest]. It is absolutely impossible to interpret the term *bokushi* as meaning anything other than a Christian clergyman. Thus, items of both Christian and Buddhist language are embedded in a single literary setting. This imparts a peculiar sense of incongruity and of cultural mixture to the discourse. Similar cases are to be found in the next example, which is taken from the same work:

Example 36: Joseph Sheridan Le Fanu, *Squire Toby's Will*, 1994/1868: 21

| "But he did, he swore he'd hang me yet for it. He said it in them identical words – he'd never rest till he *hanged* me for it, and I think it was, like enough, something about *that*, the old master was troubled; but it's enough to drive a man mad. I *can't* bring it to mind – I can't remember a word he said, only he threatened awful, and looked – <u>Lord a mercy on us!</u>₍₁₎ – frightful bad."

"There's no need he should. <u>May the Lord a-mercy on him!</u>₍₂₎" said the old butler. |

Japanese TT: translated by Yokoyama Jun, *Yuigon*, 1990: 195	
しかし、兄貴はたしかに言ったんだ、きっとわたしを縛り首にしてやるぞと。かれはまさにそう言ったのだ。わたしを縛り首にするまでは安心がならぬと。やっぱり、このことと関わりがあるのかなという気がするな。父も気に病んでいたし。でも、大の男が気も狂わんばかりになるなんて―一思い出せない、父が語った言葉が一言も思い出せない。わたしをはげしく脅迫し、<u>ああ神よ</u>(1)、そのときの顔色もひどく悪かった」	"Shikashi, aniki wa tashikani ittanda, kitto watashi o shibarikubi ni shiteyaru zo to. Kare wa masani sō ittanoda. Watashi o shibarikubi ni suru made wa anshin ga naranu to. Yappari, kono koto to kakawari ga aruno kana to yū ki ga suru na. Chichi mo ki ni yande ita shi. Demo, dai no otoko ga ki mo kuruwan bakari ni naru nante – omoidasenai, chichi ga katatta kotoba ga hitokoto mo omoidasenai. Watashi o hageshiku kyōhakushi, <u>ō kami yo</u>, sono toki no kaoiro mo hidoku warukatta."
「ご先代がそのようなことをなさるはずがありません。どうぞ<u>ご成仏なさっておられますように</u>(2)」	"Gosendai ga sono yōna koto o nasaru hazu ga arimasen. <u>Dōzo gojōbutsunasatte oraremasu yōni</u>."

Again, *gojōbutsunasatte* [attain Buddhahood, polite form] is used for the ST Christian expression "May the Lord a-mercy on him", while the word *kami* [God in general, in either a Christian or a Shintoist sense] remains as the counterpart of "Lord". The functions of the expressions correspond. Yokoyama did not use *hotokesama* [Buddha], for instance, as a possible TT unit to match *gojōbutsu*. *Kami* is a convenient term which can cover any sacred figure in Japanese religious contexts, including Buddhism, Shintō, and Christianity. Given the Japanese cultural environment, in which ordinary people visit both Buddhist temples and Shintoist shrines as part of everyday life, the use of *kami* here does not particularly represent a mismatch for *gojōbutsu*. The term is simply less specific than *hotokesama*. Still, this local ambiguity does not ease the tension caused by the scattered presence of items related to multiple religions.

The story is undoubtedly based in Christianity. The discord among the father and the two sons is an obvious reminder of the Parable of the Prodigal Son (Luke 15: 11–32). The appearances of various literary tools, such as a bulldog which ran around "like the infernal dog in 'Faust'" (Le Fanu 1994: 22); "King Herod's Chamber" (ibid. 25); and the dead father's voice which Charles hears in his dream, "The time's nigh up, it's going to strike" (ibid. 24); all suggest a Christian backdrop, and cultural domestication is not applied to them. In this setting, TT items such as *gojōbutsu* [attaining Buddhahood] in Example 36 and *Namuamidabutsu* [I worship Amida Buddha and follow his doctrine], a part of a Buddhist chant (ibid. 212), have a complex literary impact. Although the reader will understand the Western Christian context from the overall setting (it is unlikely that anyone would think Charlie was a Buddhist), it must be pointed out that this work of fiction is presented through a uniquely atmospheric filter created by the obvious inconsistency in the handling of religious items. It is difficult to obtain a solid visual impression throughout the entire TT, because it vacillates between Christianity and Buddhism whenever a religious expression comes up. This does not mitigate the positive literary impact of this original ghost story's excellent plot but rather envelops it in a peculiar translational tone. This instance shows that, with respect to religion, Japaneseness (as evoked by random fragments of domestication) looks out of context and thus stands out. Because of this effect, the TT is not domesticated as a whole and deviates from normative native Japanese. It can be argued that this way of handling cultural domestication certainly makes it conventional for the text-type. This strong sense of inconsistency and imbalance is typical of the style used in translated popular fiction, of which this text provides a forceful demonstration.

7.2.7 *The Frequent Use of* Ruby *and Notes as Compromise*

Providing a *ruby* is a relatively easy solution for difficult problems in coping with cultural otherness in the ST, as discussed in section 6.2.2. A *ruby* is an aid for the main text and can suggest the reading of *kanji* or indicate what the corresponding ST unit is. Notes are often inserted in the main text in brackets to explain the meaning of the TT unit. *Ruby* and notes seem to be provided as a compromise for units about which the translator is not satisfied or when the translator feels uneasy about the main text. In this text-type, the frequency of their use in cultural foreignisation is rather high. This shows that translators tend to avoid depending on a single solution (that is, the main text) and instead tend to distribute the responsibility of conveying the meaning of the ST cultural item in a manner comprehensible to the reader through more than one device. It is worth looking at a few strategies for using *ruby* that are often observed.

A. PROVIDING THE READING FOR *KANJI*

A translator sometimes provides another word as *ruby* (in either *hiragana* or *katakana*), signalling an unconventional reading of the word in *kanji*, which are ideographic characters, in the main text. In such cases, the word in *kanji* clearly indicates what it refers to, while a more ordinary – but often ambiguous – term for the meaning is given in *ruby*, as if the reader would not be able to grasp the meaning properly without help. The word in the main text functions as a note. Thus, when the text is read aloud, the word in *ruby* is selected. This strategy makes use of the more conventional function of *ruby* – to provide the reading of a difficult or misleading *kango* word, such as 畢竟 [hikkyō, namely] or a proper name like 服部 [Hattori, a surname]. This device is also occasionally used to provide another word in *kanji* to indicate meaning, as in インターポール [Interpol]. The frequent use of these strategies is not only observed in translated popular fiction but also in some contemporary Japanese literature and

Example 37: Sara Paretsky, *Indemnity Only*, 1982: 33–34

"Vicky, if you know anything that you're not telling me in connection with this <u>murder</u> –" "You'll be the first to know, Bobby," I promise.	
Japanese TT: translated by Yamamoto Yayoi, *Samātaimu • Burūsu*, 1985: 53	
「ヴィッキー、この殺人に関して、今話してくれた以外のことを知ってるのならー」 「まっ先にあなたに話すわ、ボビー」私は誓った。	"Vikkii, kono <u>satsujin (koroshi)</u> ni kanshite, ima hanashitekureta igai no koto o shitteru no nara –" "Massakini anata ni hanasu wa, Bobii" watashi wa chikatta.

Example 38: Agatha Christie, *The Jewel Robbery at the Grand Metropolitan*, 1991/1924: 124

"Absolutely. The real work, that of <u>the brain</u> (ah, those brave little grey cells), it is done."
Japanese TT: translated by Ogura Takashi, *Gurando • Metoroporitan no Hōsekitonan Jiken*, 1978: 182

「ほんとだよ。本当の仕事、<ruby>頭脳<rt>あたま</rt></ruby>の…いや、この勇ましい灰色の脳細胞をはたらかせる仕事はもうすんだ。」	"Hontō da yo. Hontō no shigoto, <u>zunō (atama)</u> no … iya, kono isamashii haiiro no nōsaibō o hatarakaseru shigoto wa mō sunda."

manga. The frequent use of these devices creates a certain light, easy-going impression in the text. This is because there is a flexibility in what can be added in *ruby*, and there is little restriction in its use. It is interesting to see that this carefree impression nicely matches the tone of the writing style of translated popular fiction as a whole. Examples 37 and 38 contain typical *ruby* strategies.

From a linguistic point of view, 殺人, *satsujin* [murder], would not, strictly speaking, be read as *koroshi* [killing], but the reader is instructed to read it this way by the *ruby*. *Koroshi* is jargon for murder, which police, detectives, and journalists may use. As Bobby is a homicide lieutenant and Vicky is a private detective, it is not contextually unnatural for the term to come up in their conversation. Also, the fact that they are asking about the murder case, not the act of killing (*koroshi* is the noun form of the verb *korosu* [to kill]), allows the technical word to be used here alongside the Chinese characters for *satsujin*.

In the example above, the unit in question is about the famous "little grey brain cells" of Hercule Poirot, the genius detective. Ogura uses *atama* [head, brain, intelligence] for "the brain", but puts *zunō* [brains] in the main text in *kanji* to restrict the meaning. The unit written above the Chinese characters is used as a note, although the characters are in the main text in this case, just as in the previous example. This allows the reader to deduce the actual meaning and nuance from among several possible options.

B. INDICATING THE ST UNIT

A TT reader can gain access to limited parts of the original English text when a ST word is *katakana*-ised and placed alongside the corresponding TT expression; the reader is given the opportunity to know which expression is used in the original literature for a particular item. It is, however, difficult to speculate on the motive behind the translator's use of this strategy. Investigation shows that the ST words which are given such *ruby* tend to encompass some factor that is difficult to express in the TL. It is likely that this type of *ruby* is used as a last resort, to soothe the feeling of inadequacy which the translator suffers in knowing that the TT expression is less than satisfactory. Alternatively, it may be intended to add some style to the TT through the use of *ruby* in a creative way that is unique to the translator. This usage also has a clear emphatic function.

Example 39: Sara Paretsky, *Indemnity Only*, 1982: 30

I casually whisked some crumbs off the kitchen table and rummaged in the refrigerator for <u>pumpernickel</u> and cheddar cheese.	
Japanese TT: translated by Yamamoto Yayoi, *Samātaimu • Burūsu*, 1985: 48	
キッチン・テーブルのパンくずを何食わぬ顔で払い落とし、黒パンとチェダー・チーズを求めて<ruby>冷蔵庫<rt>プンパーニクル</rt></ruby>をひっかきまわした。	Kicchin • tēburu no pankuzu o nanikuwanu kao de haraiotoshi, <u>kuropan (punpānukuru)</u> to chedē • chiizu o motomete rēzōko o hikkakimawashita.

In Example 39, "pumpernickel" is reduced to the simple *kuropan* [dark bread] in the main text. However, this covers a wider variety of dark bread and does not necessarily refer to the particular kind of hard bread of German origin. It does not hint at any Germanness or Europeanness which is indicated in the ST scene (Vicky, the private detective in the story, is from an Italian family and shown to be health conscious). That is probably why *punpānikuru* is added. The problem is, however, that the *katakana*-ised ST word is not one which the average Japanese reader knows the semantic meaning of or its association, because the ST item is culturally too foreign. Hence, the *katakana*-ised word does not improve the situation; it only indicates that an item called

Example 40: Agatha Christie, *The Mystery of Hunter's Lodge*, 1991/1924: 79

"but I very much fear, Hastings, that we shall be obliged to leave them to Fate, or *le bon Dieu*, which ever you prefer."	
Japanese TT: translated by Ogura Takashi, *Ryōjinsō no Kaijiken*, 1978: 113	
「だがなあヘイスティングス。ぼくはどうもこいつは運命...いや、<ruby>全能の神<rt>ルボン・デュ</rt></ruby>でもいいが...に任せるより仕方がないんじゃないかと思うんだ」	"daga nā Heisutingusu. Boku wa dōmo koitsu wa unmē ... iya, <u>zennō no kami</u> <u>(ru • bon • du)</u> demo ii ga ... ni makaseru yori shikata ga nainjanai ka to omounda."

"something like" *punpānikuru* exists in English, that it is a kind of dark bread, and that it is probably something good, as suggested in Yanabu's (1982) "cassette effect". However, precisely what it is remains a mystery.

French expressions are often woven into Detective Poirot's English speech, as he is Belgian. To indicate to the reader that the ST unit *le bon Dieu* was originally in French (or at least in a language other than English), a *katakana*-ised version is placed alongside the Japanese translation. This is a frequently observed strategy for indicating the presence of a third language in the literary text.

One further interesting technique seen in the translation of popular novels is the strategic use of a term which normally indicates a Japanese item to describe a Western concept. Since few cases of cultural domestication are found in such novels (unless the entire work is adapted into a

Example 41: O. Henry, *Mammon and the Archer*, 1980/1906: 51

"You may run along down to your club now. I'm glad it ain't your liver. But don't forget to <u>burn a few punk sticks</u> in the joss house to the great God Mazuma from time to time."	
Japanese TT: translated by Ōtsu Eichirō, *Mamon no Kami to Kyūpiddo*, 1979: 31	
「さあ、クラブに行ってもいいぞ。肝臓が本当に悪いんじゃなくてよかった。でもときどきは<ruby>お金<rt>マ</rt></ruby>の<ruby>神様<rt>ズマ</rt></ruby>の神殿に行って、<u>線香をあげる</u>のも忘れちゃいかんぞ。」	Sā, kurabu ni ittemo iizo. Kanzō ga hontōni waruinjanakute yokatta. Demo tokidoki wa okane no kamisama (Mazuma) no sinden ni itte, <u>senkō o ageru</u> no mo wasurecha ikan zo.

Example 42: Diane Mott Davidson, *Catering to Nobody*, 1992: 247

A scalpel, one of the kind that used disposable blades. The blade had dried blood on it.	
Japanese TT: translated by Yagura Naoko, *Kukkingu • Mama wa Mētantē*, 1994: 316	
スカルペル（外科用メス）が一本。使い捨ての刃をつけるタイプだ。刃には乾いた血がこびりついていた。	Sukaruperu (gekayō mesu) ga ippon. Tsukaisute no ha o tsukeru taipu da. Ha ni wa kawaita chi ga kobiritsuiteita.

Japanese context), when such an expression appears in a consistent manner, the reader will assume that the expression is meant to signify something Western. In Example 41, the expression *senkō o ageru* [to offer an incense stick] is supposed to refer to some Western (or at least non-Japanese) style of ritual, that is, burning punk sticks, although it is a common expression referring to a Buddhist custom and is part of everyday Japanese.

It is surely up to each reader as to whether he/she arrives at the original Western concept by decoding the Japanese terms.

C. EXPLAINING THE MEANING OF THE TT UNIT

The last function to be discussed involves describing the meaning of an expression – often an unfamiliar-sounding *katakana*-ised word. Notes in brackets are more often used for this purpose than a *ruby*, as there is more flexibility in the amount of space that can be used for a note.

In this example, the unit in question is "scalpel" and its *katakana*-ised version *sukaruperu*. *Sukaruperu* is not in the average reader's vocabulary, so the note *gekayō mesu* [knife for surgery] is inserted in brackets as a reference.

7.2.8 Summary and Further Analysis

The examples above appear to point to the presence of stylistic properties which plausibly mark one type of translated popular fiction as a text-type. This chapter has attempted to identify these properties and analyse their functions in detail. Due to inevitable limitations on the number of works which can be presented, this conclusion cannot be extended to the way in which all popular fiction works are translated, but our analysis does support the claim that there seems to be a sub-category of translated popular fiction which has the style suggested. The notion is that, whatever the ST literature, once it has been translated into this particular style, it reads like many other translated popular fiction works, with individual differences having been levelled out, or at least with each feature reduced. Thus, popular literature translated in this particular way manages its presentation and controls its afterlife in such a way that some works initially lacking strong similarities with each other are categorised into the same group. As mentioned in section 4.1, Meldrum (2010) fully discusses the characteristic features of Japanese "translationese" and investigates the following items: (1) overt personal pronouns, (2) more frequent loanwords, (3) female-specific language, (4) abstract nouns as grammatical subjects of transitive verbs, and (5) longer paragraphs. Most of these features seem to be the result of the translator's handling of foreignisation, thus they have also been seen in this focus on foreignisation and domestication, including uses out of context. In particular, the following seven properties of the text-type have been identified and highlighted here. Although this is certainly not an exhaustive list of translational properties specific to the text-type, it at least covers some of the main constituents:

(a) A tone out of character with the scene, caused by linguistic foreignisation
(b) Loss of rhythm, also usually due to linguistic foreignisation
(c) Extensive use of institutionalised social, regional, occupational, or class dialects
      These are categorised as excessive domestication and tends to be its most conspicuous symptom. The high frequency of the use of hackneyed expressions is a strong marker of translationalese.
(d) Abundant traces of other kinds of attempted domestication
      These include overdone and out-of-context domestications which cause incongruity. When a domestication attempt is found along with a foreignising unit, the translational effect is also amplified.
(e) Joint appearance of clear traces of linguistic domestication and foreignisation

(f) Abrupt appearances of cultural domestication

The tendency to utilise culturally domesticating items, despite the slightly "unfitting" context, is quite strong.

(g) Frequent use of *ruby* and notes in brackets as a compromise

There are three distinctive functions of their use: (1) providing the reading of the word in *kanji*, (2) indicating what the ST unit is, and (3) explaining the semantic meaning of the TT expression. This can be regarded as foreignising.

Although a quantitative or statistical investigation is not within the scope of this work, I have measured the approximate proportion of each property occurring in ten pages from each of eight literary translation works randomly selected from the genre. Below is the list of the works:

- *Detective story*

  Lilian Jackson Braun (1991) *The Cat Who Knew a Cardinal*. Translated by Hata, Sizuko (1995) *Neko wa Tori o Mitsumeru*.

  Sara Paretsky (1982) *Indemnity Only*. Translated by Yamamoto Yayoi (1985) *Samātaimu-Burūsu*.

- *Science fiction*

  Ray Bradbury (1977/1950) *The Martian Chronicles*. Translated by Ogasawara Toyoki (1976) *Kaseinendaiki*.

  James Byron Huggins (1995) *Leviathan*. Translated by Nakamura Tōru (2003) *Kyōjū Rivaiasan*.

- *Adventure story*

  Dick Francis (1982) *Banker*. Translated by Kikuchi Mitsu (1988) *Meimon*.

  Michael Crichton (1990) *Jurassic Park*. Translated by Sakai Akinobu (1993) Jurashikku • Pāku.

- *Other genres*

  Youth novel

  Lucy M. Montgomery (1994/1936). *Anne of Windy Willows.*
  Translated by Muraoka Hanako (1981/1958) *An no kōfuku.*

  Horror story

  Joseph Sheridan Le Fanu (1994/1868). *Squire Toby's Will.*
  Translated by Yokoyama Jun (1990) *Yuigon.*

It is not possible to quantify these properties through style markers automatically identified by computer, since we are searching for certain type shifts between the ST and the TT, rather than words or phrases. Consequently, the properties need to be identified through reading and interpretation. In Table 4, the numbers of each property found and their frequency, relative to the other sub-genres, are shown as: ◎ frequent, O normal, and △ rarely used. In addition, the overall impact of inconsistently used domestication and foreignisation is indicated, according to the following classifications:

Table 4: Properties observed in popular fiction texts

Properties	How domesticated/ foreignised	Detective story	Adventure story	Science fiction	Others
(a)	LF	92◎	104◎	62O	71O
(b)	LF	51◎	48◎	39O	40O
(c)	ED	28◎	20O	22O	26◎
(d)	AD	29◎	22O	18△	25◎
(e)	F+D	79◎	49O	31△	50O
(f)	CD	14O	9△	16◎	18◎
(g)	LF	19O	14◎	24O	21◎
Inconsistent appearance	F+D	Strong	Medium	Weak	Strong

Note. LD: linguistic domestication   CD: cultural domestication
LF: linguistic foreignisation   CF: cultural foreignisation
ED: extensive domestication   AD: attempted domestication
D: domestication   F: foreignisation

strong (mixed use is strongly detected); medium (mixed use is detected); and weak (mixed use is hardly detected). The latter scores on impact are based on individual interviews in which eight reviewers gave their impressions after reading the same pages of each work. The reviewers all have Japanese as their mother tongue, and their ages range from twenty-one to forty-seven. They were brought up in a range of regions in Japan.

The results of the semi-quantitative analysis in Table 4 provide an indication of the frequency with which the properties (a)–(g) caused by the various forms of foreignisation and domestication may occur in popular fictional novels. For example, property (a), a tone out of character with the scene caused by linguistic foreignisation (LF), is most frequently observed in adventure stories and detective stories. Property (e), the accompanying occurrences of domestication (D) and foreignisation (F) in limited parts of the texts, is found mostly in detective stories but also seen less frequently in other categories. The reviewers noted a strong sense of inconsistency caused by these occurrences (F+D) in the detective stories.

Meldrum (2010) identified a number of features related to translation-alness in popular fiction; namely (1) overt personal pronouns, (2) more frequent loanwords and (4) abstract nouns as grammatical subjects of transitive verbs. I consider these as part of property (e) – the joint appearance of clear traces of linguistic domestication and foreignisation. In addition, Meldrums category (3) (female-specific language) can be regarded as part of (c) (the extensive use of institutionalised social, regional, occupational, or class dialects). Item (5) (longer paragraphs) has not been identified as a specific stylistic feature in these samples of popular literature, but is more or less a general characteristic of all types of translation.

What influences the distribution of the above seven properties includes the storyline, sub-genre, author, translator, and even the editor. These properties are sometimes concentrated in a few pages of text and then more dispersed throughout the other parts.

Figure 3 provides an example of a detective story text which contains an abundance of characteristic features of the text-type marked with underlines, circles and squares, as indicated above. The visual impact the reader receives can be clearly seen. The cases of properties (a), (b) and often (g) rooted in foreignisation, and properties (c), (d) and (f) rooted

「あの青年が過激派の友達とつきあって、ビラを振りまわしてたために、労組がらみの犯罪に巻きこまれたっていうの？いい加減にしてよ、ボビー！」

セイヤー事件からわたしを遠ざけたいとの願いと、捜査上の秘密を口外してはならぬという義務のあいだで、マロリーが苦悩している様子が、その表情にあらわれていた。ついに彼はいった。

「うちでつかんだ証拠だがな、あのガキども、ナイフグラインダーズの印刷物の大部分(a)を引き受けてる業者に、連中のビラの一部を頼んでるんだ」

わたしは悲しげに頭を振った(a)。ナイフグラインダーズ国際労組(e)は暗黒街との結びつきで悪名を馳せている(d)。三〇年代という騒然たる時代(d)に腕っぷしの強い(d)連中を雇い入れ、それ以来どうしても、彼らと縁を切る(f)ことができないのだ。その結果、組合の選挙の大部分と財政業務の多く(a)は腐敗してしまった―そのとき突然、わたしの正体不明の依頼人が何者であったか、アニタ・マグローの名前になぜ聞き覚えがあったか、そして、男が職業別電話帳からなぜわたしを選び出したかが、脳裏にひらめいた(d)。わたしは椅子にさらに深くもたれたが、沈黙を守り続けた。

「ヴィッキー、今度の事件でわし(c)の行く手を横切る(d)ようなまねをしてみろ。」マロリーの顔が赤くなった。「おまえさん(c)のためを思って(a)、監獄にぶちこんでやるからな！」彼は乱暴に立ち上がって(a)椅子を倒してしまった。マゴニガル部長刑事に身ぶりで合図して、二人でドアを叩きつけて(a)出て行った。

わたしは二杯目のコーヒーを持って浴室に行き、それをたっぷり投げこんで、熱い湯を出した。浴槽に身を沈め、深夜の飲酒の後遺症が骨のなかからにじみ出ていく(a)のを感じながら、わたしは二十年以上も前の夜を思い出していた。母がわたしを

ジュリー浴用剤(e)を浴槽

Key: (a): ‗‗‗‗‗   (b): ‗‗‗‗‗   (c): ⊡⊡⊡⊡⊡   (d): ⊡⊡⊡⊡⊡

(e): ⬭⬭⬭⬭⬭   (f): ‗‗‗‗‗   (g): ⬭⬭⬭⬭⬭

「撃ち殺されてたわ(c)、ボビー(b)。死体解剖はしなかったけど」
「ヴィッキー、一セント(e)と引き換えに、そのかわいい小さなケツを蹴っとばしてやりたいよ(a)。きみ
はまともな娘なら見向きもせん(c)ようなことを商売にしとる(c)が、決して抜けちゃいない。あのアパ
ートメント(e)に忍び込んだとき—まあ、どうやって入ったかはこのさい見逃してやるが—育ち
のいいお嬢さんと違って、おまえさん(c)が悲鳴も上げなきゃ、吐きもしなかったろうってことは、
ちゃんとわかってるんだ。アパート(e)をざっと調べたに決まっとる(c)。それから、死体を見てぴんと
きた(d)ことは何ひとつなかったというんなら、きみ(b)、外に出て頭を吹っ飛ばされちまうがいい(a)」
わたしは溜息をつき、椅子にぐったり寄りかかった。「わかったわよ、ボビー(b)。あの子、計画
的に殺されたのよ(c)。麻薬にいかれた過激分子があの弾丸(g)を撃ったんじゃないわ(c)。あの子の知って
る誰か、あの子が椅子を勧めてコーヒーを出そうとした相手が、あの場に居合わせたに違いない。わたし
のにらんだところ、銃を撃ったのはプロね。だって、仕事が完璧で、一発で命中してるも
の。でも、あの子の知り合いが誰かついてきたに違いないわ(c)。あるいは彼と親しい人間で、天才
的な射撃の名手なる人物(a)が殺った(g)のかもしれない……彼の家族のこと、調べてみた？」
マロリーはわたしの質問を無視した。「たぶん、そこまで読んでると思ってたよ。わし(c)はな、
この一件がいかに危険かを悟るだけの頭脳(g)がきみにあると思うからこそ、事件に首を突っこまん
ように頼んでおるのだ(c)」わたしはあくびをした。マロリーは癇癪を起こすまいと固く決心してい
た。「いいか、ヴィッキー、ごたごた(d)から手を引いてくれ(a)。どうも(d)、組織的な犯罪というか、労
組のからむ事件というか、そういう臭いがするんだ。きみには太刀打ち(f)できん大きな組織がから
んでおる(c)かもしれん」

Figure 3: Properties samples from *Samātaimu • Burūsu*.

in domestication are highlighted, and the physical space that they occupy on the sample pages is respectively indicated. While they do not consistently appear over each page, the overall impression may nevertheless be of a sense of incongruity that makes a strong impact on the reader. The feeling of incongruity may well arise from the way the features are physically located; namely how adjacent domesticness and foreignness are to each other (amounting to property (e)), and how domesticness suddenly appears without fitting local settings which would, constitute property (f).

Toury (1995) comments on the law of standardisation in translation, requiring that textual relations in the original be modified or ignored in favour of habitual options characteristic of the target repertoire. The observations in this book in no way contradict Toury's conclusions. The translational discourse has been found to be commonly used and even taken as a standard for a certain group of popular fiction texts, so that it can be utilised even when it disturbs the original stylistic features.

Text-types	Stylistic properties	
	Translational properties rooted in LF, CD and Extensive LD	Translational properties rooted in F + D
Popular fiction 1 (with translation-emphatic stylistic features)		
Popular fiction 2 (with fewer such features)		
High-brow		
Informative		

MORE   LESS

Figure 4: Features of translational discourse used in different text-types.

In order to emphasise the distinctiveness of the translationalness of the genre, a brief account of informative texts and more high-brow literature has been provided, for contrast, in Figure 4 (for popular and high-brow literature in the Japanese literary context, see section 7.1.1). Since it is not the case that all translations of popular fiction fall into this text-type, the kind of popular fiction which has fewer features of translation-emphatic style and is thus closer to original Japanese writing is also indicated in the chart as a different category (popular fiction 2; see Figure 4).

The linguistic domestication which marks the type of translation of popular literature under investigation is rarely observed in these three text-types. Linguistically foreignised texts are accepted more positively in non-literary translations because it is a normative feature that this genre requires in native writing (originally as a result of the influence of Western documents). Translations of high-brow literature seem to have fewer properties of linguistic foreignisation or cultural domestication, and they are much less prone to the effect created by the combination of foreignisation and domestication. This may be the result of the individual styles of the translators rather than a product of the genre – translators may feel encouraged to create more original translations with fewer of the conventional translationalese features that are evident in mass fiction. This is simply a personal impression, however, and more analysis would be required to make a more substantive and scientific comparison.

Due to the distortion's uniform pattern seen in the popular fiction genre examined, the translational properties discussed above function as an obstacle to recreating the style of the original. The literary work often is reduced to a piece of translated popular literature from the West, regardless of the text-type of the original, and it is simply lumped together with many other works that share many of the same stylistic traits. These issues are revisited in detail in Chapter 8.

CHAPTER 8

Cultural Implications

8.1 Recipients' Expectations of Translationalness

The previous section identified some of the main features of translationalness that are commonly found in certain translated popular fiction. The
kind of language seen is certainly not normative from the "native" Japanese
point of view, but its use has become an established convention in the translation of certain literature from English into Japanese. The text-type covers
a rather large proportion of translated fiction. If one goes to the translated
literature section, *kaigai bungaku*, in a bookshop and takes a look at a few
books, one will immediately realise how dominant the conventional style is.
In many works, the particular features of translationalness are in evidence.
Some well-known series of translated classical literature are good resources
for finding different and diverse styles. Prestigious literary works seem to
be given more individual care and attention. Thus, Japanese translations
of Shakespeare, Chekhov, Dostoevsky, Balzac, and Kafka, to name but a
few, have managed to resist being moulded into this style. This does not,
however, mean that the matter is settled for these classics. Any novel can
be translated again, and the new version can gain great popularity, as seen
in the case of Austen's works after the films based on her novels became
Hollywood hits. This section is thus devoted to a discussion of the cultural
background and implications of the prevailing translational style used for
works categorised as popular fiction. I will endeavour to show how the significance of the distribution of the uniform style to diverse types of fiction
in the Japanese cultural context can be systematically studied.

It is a common assumption in Japan, as in many other countries, that
a translation needs to be not only faithful (semantically and structurally
close) to the original but also readable as literature. Translators, critics,

and researchers repeatedly insist upon this as the ideal state of translation. Mainstream criticism cherishes translations written in native-looking
Japanese. Bekku (1983: 28, my translation) emphasises the significance of
conveying the ST contents using only existing, natural Japanese: "So-called
'interlinear translation' does not deserve the name of translation and is only
a preparatory operation before translation". Despite widespread conceptual
agreement on what a literary translation should be, translated popular fiction clearly indicates the presence of translations in the opposite state – that
is, the presence of a text-type specific to translation. This dual reality looks
theoretically precarious but, in fact, continues to exhibit surprising stability
as the supply of translation work steadily continues and is well received by
readers, and it gives rise to a secondary literature criticising "translationese".
As long as the language used in a piece of translation does not greatly deviate from this established norm, the reader will not become aware of the
existence of this unique style. Thus, the community accepts the standard
translational style as a device to provide an alternative readability, without
changing the translational style's theoretical position.

The style is not only tolerated as a necessary evil but is, in fact, sought
after. Its unmistakable, pervasive presence – at least in commercial products –
suggests that they sell anyway, in spite of this. Seidensticker (1962: 213,
my translation), known as the translator of *The Story of Genji*, was aware
of the general tendency for translational language in literary translation,
stating that:

> Even when Western literary works are translated into Japanese, they are usually
> translated word-for-word and literally, as if they were technical translations. In short,
> a queer Japanese, a kind of translationese, is thriving. Yet, Japanese readers do not
> think that these are bad translations, but seem to be satisfied. Moreover, they seem to
> enjoy feeling a taste of exotic cultures from such translationese, in which the literary
> value of the ST has been lost.

Although his phrase "usually translated word-for-word and literally" is an
oversimplification, he correctly points out that "translationese" is enjoyed
by the community – unlike in the West, where people expect a translation to stand as an independent piece of literature (ibid. 214). A number
of social and cultural factors seem to be related to the special demand for,

and tolerance of, the discourse. These will be considered in some detail in the following sections.

8.2 Desired Oddity: Logic and Thought Patterns from the West

First of all, the question needs to be posed: what makes a translation look like a translation to such an extent? A rather superficial (but still important) factor is the value that the Japanese have placed on the otherness of other countries, especially Westernness. I use the terms "the West" and "Westernness" here to refer to any cultures belonging to the American and European realms, which the Japanese can reach through translations from English to Japanese – although, during and after the Meiji Restoration, encounters with the Dutch, Portuguese, Spanish, Germans, British, French, and Americans were particularly emphasised. The collective notion of "the West" will be discussed later in section 8.4.

Japan has repeatedly faced and overcome various identity crises (such as during the opening of the country, followed by the Meiji Restoration in the late nineteenth century; in succumbing to military pressure from the Western countries for trade; and after the defeat in the Second World War, followed by the US occupation) by quickly learning and absorbing the cultures and systems which flowed in. Doi (1973), in his groundbreaking psychological analysis of the Japanese mentality, describes the well-known inquisitiveness which the Japanese tend to show in regard to foreign affairs and which should, in fact, be considered as the surface explanation for their eagerness to translate:

> This curiosity was noticed a long time ago by foreigners visiting this country. As early as the sixteenth century, Francisco Xavier, the first Christian missionary to arrive in Japan, remarked in his letters on the extraordinary desire for knowledge of the Japanese, in which respect they were, he said admiringly, different from any other heathens. This curiosity and lust for knowledge was certainly an important

contribution to the fact that Japan modernized herself at an earlier date than any other Oriental nation. (translated by John Bester, *The Anatomy of Dependence*, 1971: 47)

The way in which the Japanese transformed their hatred and fear towards otherness into sheer admiration, at least on the surface, seemed rather dramatic and unique among non-Western countries – especially to European visitors' eyes (Kawakatsu 1991: 132–133). Surely, there was more behind the scenes. The options that global trends presented to Japan were only two in number: either Westernising itself thoroughly to gain international competence, or withdrawing from the front line. While its positioning in world politics as a nation-state has been repeatedly shaken, Japan has continued to choose the former option, apart from the exceptional period of *sakoku*, the policy of seclusion from the seventeenth to nineteenth centuries. Thus, its willingness to import new skills and knowledge was genuine but always closely linked to a desperate need to re-identify itself. This point will be re-examined in section 8.3.

A national identity re-established (at least on the surface) through a rapid absorption of Western cultures could lead to an uncritical appreciation of these cultures – even in the twenty-first century. Although, during the last fifty years, Japan's attitude towards the rest of the world has varied – reflecting a number of economic and political changes, including the bubble years, the bursting of the bubble, and then the continuing efforts to emerge from the ongoing recession – its constant desire to search for something new to import is at least partially responsible for the state of translation, which is an act of introducing other cultures to the country. Importing fresh concepts, items, or ways of thinking at the surface level and learning about the otherness held within them are two different things. The latter requires a more fundamentally open attitude than the former, and that open attitude may be lacking, as evidenced by the trend for linguistic foreignisation which often imports the content without facilitating a deep understanding or assimilation of its otherness into society. The use of some strategies such as adding a ruby or a short explanation to the translation can of course function as a facilitating device but does not always domesticate the text.

It is useful to look at some related arguments concerning linguistic Anglicisation here, even though it is from a rather different time. Nogami

(1938, in Naganuma 2010, my translation), an influential literary critic and researcher in the field of English literature and also a translator, insists that "a translation of a Western text should look Western", however difficult it might be to understand the product. He argues that translation should be the act of expressing the meaning of the ST (which might, for example, be in English) in Japanese as closely as the ST expresses it, and that this should include structural and lexical similarities. He claims that the Japanese will get used to the way in which Westerners think and come to understand it. He uses the first line of *Hamlet*'s monologue, "to be, or not to be", as an example, and translates it as *Aru ka, aranu ka*. Because of the "be" verbs used in the ST, Nogami believes that *aru* [to be or exist] is the only appropriate Japanese word, even if it creates several possible interpretations of the sentence in the TT (ibid.). Yoshikawa (1974, in Bekku 1983: 93, my translation), a literary critic specialising in Chinese poetry, also suggests word-for-word translation, although his argument is milder:

> I think that translation is after all a means to show the original text to the ignorant. [...]
> If it conveys no more concepts – or fewer concepts – than are contained in the original
> text, it is rather convenient as a means for the ignorant. There is a risk of damaging the
> capability for learning if [we are] excessively concerned about the Japanese readers.

In the view of critics like Yoshikawa, a translation through which the original text shines is supposed to reflect the ST (Western) author's logic, emotions, and thought patterns, and be more informative to the reader than a translation written in more natural native Japanese. Odd language surely does not guarantee any precision, but such a text gives the impression that it is odd because it is likely to be a faithful mirroring of the respected original. A translation faithful to the ST is believed to be unusual anyway, reflecting the otherness of the source culture, and the reader does not imagine the oddity is freshly created through translation. Thus oddity can function as a convenient mark of otherness, embedded in the text. Although products that are linguistically foreignised, as Nogami suggested, are hardly found in contemporary literary translation, it is clear that local structural and lexical Englishness is one of the main properties that make up the translation style of popular fiction, reflecting the deeply rooted preferences that are evident in the commentaries of critics and academics.

Odd texts are thus strongly associated with the presence of otherness coming from a foreign culture. Readers do not necessarily understand or ingest the ST author's thought patterns or writing processes from a foreignised text, but such texts often satisfy readers by giving them the impression that they have at least had some contact with the author's thinking and writing. ST culture-specific items in the text that are brought out through cultural foreignisation, such as proper names ("John Willoughby" or "Arthur Hastings") and daily customs ("a snow shoe tramp" or "Halloween"), undoubtedly create a kind of beloved Western atmosphere. Indeed, even though the Halloween trick-or-treat custom is increasingly being adopted in large Japanese cities, without any religious or anthropological implications, reading about the tradition in the context of real Western life may still be refreshingly foreignising.

The linguistic unsettledness a reader feels through the language can also be effective in this sense. It is even better when the meaning of part of the text is not vividly clear or does not make much sense because of foreignisation: the impact of otherness is simply amplified. It may even be the case that readers enjoy the frustration they feel regarding incomprehensible parts of the text, if the volume of these parts is appropriate. This value given to obscurity in writing style is rather similar to the cassette effect argued by Yanabu (1982). It is difficult, however, to say whether or not translators and readers are conscious of the mechanism of their supply of, and demand for, such foreignness, although at a minimum, the reader's acceptance influences translators and functions as a driver of partial foreignisation.

8.3 The Substitution of Readability in Reality

When considering cultural aspects, it is important to be aware that the translational style in question is produced via a number of strategies, including linguistic/cultural domestication, and is not simply due to linguistic/cultural foreignisation. As repeatedly demonstrated, despite the distinctive appreciation of Western cultures, extreme linguistic or cultural foreignisation is never dominant as a translation method for contemporary popular literature (see section 7.2). Linguistically foreignised sentences remain only part of the discourse. The translating side always suffers from the dilemma of domestication versus foreignisation, and Japanese translators are no exception, as has been shown throughout Chapters 5 and 6. *Rakuchū Shokan*, a collaborative work by Yoshikawa and Ōyama Sadakazu (who has translated a number of major European works by well-known authors, including Rainer Maria Rilke, Goethe, and Kafka) refutes Yoshikawa's argument. Ōyama (1974, in Bekku 1983: 94, my translation) emphasises that the significance of literary translation is more than simply a means to an end, and thus he suggests that there is more scope for flexibility than in a strictly word-for-word method:

> In short, I would like it to be understood that a work of translated literature is itself a work of literature – which ought to have been written by now (in our language), and which is presented in the form of a so-called translation. [...] I want you to accept that what I tentatively refer to as "translated literature" does exist.

Although the value and position of translation within the whole literary system have never been agreed upon, Ōyama's claim that translated literature should be, or indeed is, literature that is itself worth reading – and not purely a means – is widely accepted in the translation community. Yanase (2000: 3, my translation), a leading contemporary translator, quotes *Bunshō Tokuhon* by Mishima Yukio. Mishima (1959) stresses the importance of maintaining the quality of language used in translation:

> As far as the general public's attitude to reading a translated text goes, it is thought to be a show of good etiquette to the original author to throw away the translated version if the text is difficult to understand or if the translation is not well executed. We must give up our slave-like attitude of taking pains to read a text that is incomprehensible as a piece of Japanese – just because it has the reputation of being faithful to the original.

According to Yanase (ibid.):

> We often hear translators complain about their translations, using the original foreign-language text as their excuse. It is simply disgraceful if a translator apologises for publishing something that is incomplete because it is a "translated text".

Thus, in the translators' view, translation should not be a mechanical transfer of the ST and whether the quality of the Japanese language used in translation is maintained at a certain level is a moral issue. It is worth noting that translators have – or at least are believed to have – "native" Japanese as a point of reference for judging the quality of the Japanese language. Yanase (ibid.) states, for example, that: "a translation completed and publicised is an expression through one national language called Japanese. All that matters is the quality of the national language". Yet, curiously enough, a large portion of literary translation – that is, of popular fiction – results in a discourse with a different appearance. This reality seems very much to contradict this notion. The double standard (involving faithful and readable text on the one hand, and the established translational style as the norm to be followed on the other) manages to maintain a unique balance in the Japanese translation community, regardless of its opposing qualities.

It is convenient for the translators that the contradiction seems to have been resolved at least for, and by, readers. They are collectively so used to the normative translational language that they are almost at the stage of accepting it as part of what Yanase (2000) calls "the national language", which is a language or languages that the nation officially has legislated as representative. When a translated detective story, for instance, shows normative translational features, the text is accepted by the reader as safely "readable", since it is not jarring when read. The reader encounters a number of pronouns, top-heavy sentences, *katakana*-ised words whose meanings remain obscure, lots of *ruby* and notes, and Buddhist terms next to Christian expressions – but all these are just as expected.

The texts appear perfectly under control. Only this kind of substitution of the definition of "readability" in the reader's view can explain the mysterious tolerance of translationalese. If this context is assumed, the whole picture can be understood more clearly. There is no double standard concerning the way popular fiction should be translated, only a rather convenient standard: "faithful and readable", meaning "faithful and normatively translational, as the reader expects". Translators instill properties in a Japanese version of science fiction, for example, to make it fit the available text-type which only exists within the system of translation. Critics and researchers often comment on some limited points regarding these properties in translations (the traces of linguistic foreignisation) and criticise them as disturbing readability. This is in theory beside the point, as the properties are contributing to the text and satisfying the conditions for readability. However persistently critics condemn linguistic foreignness in the text, as long as the reader desires it (see section 8.2) and translators provide it, it will remain in the text. It is neither openly admitted nor instructed that the translational style – including linguistic Englishness in place of native Japanese – constitutes a legitimate kind of readability. The reasons behind this are difficult to speculate upon. It might be the case that nobody wants a moral debate on the active use of the translational style as an institutionalised register within the national language. Similarly, it might be too risky to admit that linguistic foreignness is found in the text because it is desired and thus provided. This fact is not brought out into the open, yet at least critics still have something to criticise on a regular basis.

8.4 Translational Style as a Matrix for Otherness

Finally, what are the cultural circumstances behind the presence of the text-type specific to certain translated popular literature? How has such a peculiar writing style established itself as a translation norm – despite the general antipathy towards the third language (the Japanese used in translations)? To speculate on possible answers to these questions, the notions of identification and assimilation (which are known to be core concepts in the analysis of the behaviour and disposition of the Japanese) need to be considered. Japan has absorbed foreign (especially Western) cultures with great enthusiasm whenever its identity has been shaken in an international setting, so let us consider further the behavioural pattern that the Japanese have exhibited in each contact with otherness. Doi (1971) argues that the Japanese treat strangers with stark indifference as long as they present no threat. Once they do, the Japanese will abruptly change their attitude and resort to another strategy:

And the means used at this point is to win favor with (*toriiru*) or take over (*torikomi*) the other side. This process corresponds with what is known in psychoanalysis as identification or assimilation, [...] As this suggests very clearly, identification and assimilation are psychological mechanisms with which the inhabitants of the world of *amae* are very much at home.

The preceding applies, of course, to individuals but interestingly enough it can be also applied to Japan as a whole. This is particularly true of the times in the past when Japan first came into contact with foreign cultures, when its reaction can be explained largely in terms of identification and assimilation. (Translated by John Bester, *The Anatomy of Dependence*, 1973: 45)

Doi focuses on the Japanese word *amae*, for which it is hard to find an appropriate equivalent in English. In the English translation of his book, the word "dependence" is used for this term. Doi claims that *amae*, the affirmative attitude towards the spirit of dependence in a society, is the key to understanding the mentality of the Japanese. One symptom of their dependency is that when they find "somebody" or "something" good, they try to identify themselves with it or to assimilate it. As he hints in the quotation, since this happened to the nation as a whole at the end of the nineteenth century, the Japanese managed to totally depend on the newly arrived Westernness by assimilating it, in all its possible aspects, on the surface. Doi's theory of dependence explains the unbalanced relationship between Japanese culture and Western cultures, and the ever-continuing interest of the Japanese in taking in – almost without fail – anything "good" from the West. In this context, translation can be regarded as part of a widely available scheme of assimilation, arising out of the fact that the Japanese feel uneasy or threatened in regard to their cultural identity. In these circumstances, what would they translate into their own system? One could get rid of people and things that would otherwise bring otherness or threaten national unity in a more straightforward manner, that is, by producing fluent translations, as many contemporary US translators do (Venuti 1995). Instead, the position that the Japanese take towards foreignness looks, at least on the surface, to be much more subordinate.

The term "the West" has been used as if there were one single entity which can be regarded as a source culture. This is exactly the view that the Japanese have adopted in coping with the threat from other countries. In order to handle the ambivalent recognition about their own stance by assimilating the source of the threat, they first need to determine what exactly the threat is. As it is impossible to imitate all the idiosyncrasies of the American and European cultures, homogenisation in the process of their recognition has been inevitable. At the same time, the Westernness needs to be something that is clearly foreign, in order for the reader to take it in. In discussing the framework of the Japan-West comparison utilised in the analytical research of Japanese thought so far, Sakai (1997: 53, my translation) states:

> In using the term "the scheme of vs-configuration", the author wishes to state that the framework of the comparison (for example, between Japan and the West) is basically imaginary. [...] In the desire for Japanese thought – and in order to configure Japan – the West had to be configured.

He also points out that, to Japan, the West is completely alien, and vice versa:

> Many publications in English about contemporary Japan [...] pretend to make a critical study of Japanese society and culture, but are instead obsessed with a desire to recognise the uniqueness of an amorphous entity known as "the West", rather than the uniqueness of Japan. (ibid. 191)

Thus, the Japanese must constantly configure "the West" as clearly "other" in order to assimilate it. Translation as an act of assimilation can easily manipulate the picture of the West to suit this need. Until a text is translated, the TL culture does not usually know what the ST says anyway, so it is not surprising that the recipients do not notice the trick. The uniform image of "the West" is produced in the readings and distributed to the readers of translated novels in a subtle manner. No one expects to sense the individuality of each text. This explains the presence of an established style for translated popular fiction, which homogenises a variety of literary works (which there would otherwise be no reason to lump into the same category), but which seems to fit well into the conventional Japanese way of interacting with Western cultures. Considering the tension between English as an SL, or representative of "the West", and Japanese (whose native speakers harbour an innocent, uncritical enthusiasm for texts from the West) as a TL, the text-type actually fulfils the function of a ready-made framework for works of fiction coming in from the Occident. As long as they arrive neatly and settle into the moulded pattern of Westernness that the Japanese are familiar with, such texts offer no threat to the existing Japanese literary or cultural system. It looks as if a mould or a predetermined shape has been unconsciously established to form the shape of the discourse. The following quotation presents an interesting example of the cultural assimilation carried out in the past by the Japanese, which appears to parallel the case of translation. Doi (1973: 45) states that:

> the following quotation from Nakamura Hajime is illuminating: Generally speaking, in adopting foreign religions, Japanese have already had some practical ethical framework which they regard as absolute, and have taken over and adapted only insofar as the newcomer would not damage, or would actually encourage and develop, what already existed.

It is important to discern what matrix the community has prepared for the inflow of some particular otherness (new religions, laws, cars, or works of fiction) in order to understand how it is modified in the process of assimilation. The points raised can be brought together in a simple argument: Japanese readers can comfortably identify themselves by means of the exclusive otherness in translated fiction produced in the discourse specific to translation, as it is the otherness they already know within their own cultural domain. Otherness is never genuinely "other" after undergoing the process of assimilation. Certainly, different ways of conveying foreignness in the ST have been, and will be, attempted in the translation of foreign literature. Many of the popular fiction works are, however, predominantly standardised in this manner, and these are the texts through which the majority of the general public takes in much foreign information. The influence that these translated texts have on the formation of the image of the West is quite substantial for a certain community, compared to that of the limited number of works of classical literature that are read. The way in which otherness is transmitted to the community is safely and securely controlled.

The state of translation as discussed above matches, at the surface level, the general reader's hunger for the strong conviction that he/she is reading a translated work of literature from the West, which is fuelled by extraordinary word usages and fresh concepts. The texts conveniently satisfy that hunger. The satisfaction that the reader derives from the text is closely related to the prestige associated with reading translated literature, as the reader is vaguely aware of the undeniable historical fact that reading translations is the key to the West, and thus the key to survival. This helps the reader develop a sense of belonging to the illusory circle of translation lovers. The easy accessibility or lightness of the fictional works they read does not deprive them of the prestige of the act of reading translations. This group consciousness not only shows tolerance towards the peculiar translational language but it even seems to espouse the appreciation of it as a secret code. The assimilation of otherness from the West results in the utilisation of a specific set of properties which only have cultural and psychological significance in the TL community. The translationalese properties are presented as the TT in the form of what people casually call *hon'yakuchō* [translationese], but they are much more than that in substance.

8.5 Quasi-Popular Fiction

It is worth expanding on why the particular style of translational Japanese is observed more in popular fiction than in high-brow literature. Translation is always a product resulting from a long, complicated process, and it is impossible to pin down only one or two factors as reasons for the formulation of the target style. It is nevertheless possible, and even meaningful, to identify those factors which function as pieces of the jigsaw, which contribute to the way literary works are conventionally translated – even if identifying them remains a matter of speculation. There are often clear differences in practical situations in which translators of detective stories and those of serious high-brow literature are placed (they are not necessarily different individuals). For instance, there is a simple hypothesis that translators spend less time on works of popular fiction. In a personal communication, one of the contemporary literary translators revealed that professional translators usually cannot afford to take more time when translating popular works because these are plentiful in the market, and translating a single one does not earn them much; thus, taking time over each work simply does not make sense for most translators. Considering this situation, it is probably easier for them to produce a translation that conforms to the standardised style, as they then do not need to work in a consistent mode of either foreignisation or domestication. Assuming that the style identified in this book is an "easy solution" rather than a careful manoeuvering of language and culture, it is not surprising that translators subconsciously shape their work into this style whenever they judge that "it will do". As this option now satisfies one of the contemporary translation norms, it is even more unlikely that they will bother producing something original – a process likely to consume more of their time and energy. A consistent selection of words to achieve appropriate balance usually requires more care than a random translation. It cannot, however, be so easy to hit the normative balance of domestication and foreignisation, which is never consistent but rather mixed in the category of popular fiction, as demonstrated in the earlier chapters. The expression used above, "the style as an easy solution", might be valid paradoxically only when it comes to an experienced translator who is accustomed to producing it.

There may, however, be a more positive factor behind the presence of the style in the popular fiction category. One speculation is that Western popular fiction is turned into something fresh and more domesticated as a whole by wearing these stylistic features. The sample literary works quoted in this book look more subcultural than the ST because of the abrupt, unsmooth language. These works are not as accessible to everyone as other kinds of popular literature which have a less translational Japanese discourse. Since the works in question lack smoothness, they actually look less popular or mass-market and hence rather distinct from major popular writings; although clearly different from high-brow literary writings. If the series of popular fiction which shares the eccentric discourse conveys a unique literary impact to readers due to its style, it is taking the role of creating a not-yet-recognised literary category. In revisiting the polysystem, Even-Zohar's (2005: 40) redefinition is useful to recall: "a multiple system, a system of various systems which intersect with each other and partly overlap, using concurrently different options, yet functioning as one structured whole, whose members are interdependent". The particular way in which translation has been used appears to be a process of subculturalisation of Western popular fiction in the Japanese context – in contrast to authentic writing traditions. This can be regarded at the same time as an emerging or at least prevailing subcategory of translated popular fiction within the Japanese literary polysystem.

The literary world of this category which the reader inhabits thus seems to have a dual structure. There is this stylistic element into which translationalness is fully condensed, and the features easily distract the reader from the original, individual literary effects. The reader can, however, be pleased with this peculiarly edgy, unsmooth style as a translational norm, just as Japanese fans of subcultural products enjoy items such as cartoons, Japanimations, and some underground light novels which are equipped with special codes to be properly interpreted. The reader needs to know a set of traditional rules to enjoy Japanese *manga* cartoons, for example; a certain sign gives onomatopoetic information to the scene or signifies absolute quietness. The readers can reach each work's storyline and the artistic effect only if they know those semiotic rules and work them out – rather like a puzzle. Reading translated popular fiction is somehow similar to this, as it provides the reader with experiences from two sources: translationalese as a mysterious code to interpret and individual literary effect. The stress on a clear-cut storyline in popular fiction, rather than subtle literary nuances or interwoven intertextuality, probably encourages the presence of those translational features. The storyline of a work of popular fiction is usually easy enough to follow without being disturbed by translationalness, whereas subtle literary touches may be disturbed by an unsmooth and inconsistent writing style.

8.6 Summary

It has conventionally been the case that material imported from foreign countries are much appreciated in the Japanese community – especially from the West since the Meiji Restoration, although clearly there were sensitive times, such as during the two world wars. A text that is obviously a translation, nevertheless, often wins respect and attention, as Seidensticker (1962) points out in the passage quoted earlier in this chapter. Some attempt has been made to describe the background to why people seek out, and even enjoy, conspicuous translationalness and the actual presence of such discourse. This may be attributable to several factors.

First, throughout its history, Japan has repeatedly overcome its identity crises by learning from foreign cultures. The traditional enthusiasm for Western cultures, at least on the surface, still leads readers to seek a touch of linguistic or cultural foreignness (Westernness) in translated texts, partly as a means for understanding the author's logic, emotions, and thought patterns, and partly to enjoy the immediate impression that they are experiencing the otherness enclosed in a foreign culture.

Second, readers have by now become used to the normative translational language – a standardised patchwork of foreignisation and domestication – and it is accepted as readable. Thus, readers and translators now recognise an alternative, substitute definition of readability. This is not openly acknowledged, and instead critics sometimes only pick on limited aspects of the translational properties, in the shape of traces of linguistic foreignisation, which they criticise as disturbing the more traditional type of readability. This criticism is in theory ungrounded, as these aspects are contributing to the text and satisfying the conditions for readability which people are used to and are striving for in practice.

Lastly, the presence of the translational text-type was explained on the basis of some analyses of the Japanese mentality that used the classic concept of *amae* or dependence as an example. The way in which translation is carried out can be understood only in the context of the ever-continuing interest of the Japanese in identifying themselves with and assimilating anything "good" from the outside. Translation of popular fiction using the identified discourse can be regarded as part of the Japanese way of assimilation, rooted in the Japanese thirst for foreign information and experiences while, at the same time, seeking a way to identify themselves in relation to other parts of the world. The influence of translations of popular fiction on the formation of the image of the West, and by association of the Japanese, is substantial, as these translations are widely read by a mass audience. The clear translationalness in the text helps the reader develop a sense of belonging to an illusory circle of translation readers (a circle of the learned, in terms of information about overseas) and then the even bigger circle of Japanese in contrast to Westerners. The assimilation of otherness from the West results in its codification through the use of a specific set of properties which only have cultural and psychological significance in the TL community. There is an intriguing analogy between codifications observed in the translationalese and in subcultural discourse, such as *manga* or Japanimations, and one can argue that translation of popular fiction into the translational style is a process of subculturalisation of Western popular fiction, or of producing a subcategory in the popular fiction text-type, in the Japanese context.

CHAPTER 9

Conclusions

The question of what translation is, and what it brings to people in an essentially monolingual society such as Japan, tends to be answered with the assertion that it is a key to cultures outside the country. Even when the issue is specifically limited to contemporary translation from English into Japanese, there is no doubt that translation allows people access to various cultures through the so-called international medium. The act of translation – particularly from Western languages – has been greatly encouraged in contemporary Japan due to its historical background. The Japanese have constantly been facing up to Western cultures, at risk to their own identity, and they have maintained a policy of taking these cultures in rather than excluding them (except during certain historical periods). New types of literature, experiences, values, and perceptions are flowing into Japan in the form of translation, and Japan has absorbed them with tremendous eagerness in many cases. This bears repeating: in the form of translation – not in a form that might nurture a command of foreign languages within Japan that would enable people to understand the original texts. This (most likely involuntary) choice has had many consequences. The questions that need to be asked here are: how have works been translated? And what mechanism has been established for dealing with such a vast amount of Western information flowing in? A certain existing mechanism for the emergence of translated literature into the Japanese literary system is evident. Indeed, certain types of ST tend to be translated with particular stylistic properties and in larger quantities than other types of ST. Those pieces of translation which share a similar discourse constitute one text-type within the TL literary system.

    This book has focused on Japanese translations of (so-called) popular fiction originally written in English, and it has attempted to demonstrate how words are dealt with in the process and to illustrate the properties that these products appear to share. The way in which the text is taken in through translation reveals both the way the society desires it to be and the way in which it is actually perceived by society. The translation of fiction reveals a great deal as the norms guiding how fictional works are translated between the two languages and cultures represent much of the interaction between them. Popular literature itself mirrors people and their lives in a complex manner. It is not that stories or settings illustrate reality, but rather that the way in which they are written reflects the context from which the works arise. By the same token, the way in which they are translated mirrors the way in which the two languages and communities are associated with each other, in a delicate but steady manner. It is therefore meaningful to focus on this genre in order to identify how the otherness found in the ST is manipulated into the TL picture.

The investigation in Chapters 5 and 6 reveals that Japanese translations of the fictional works identified and examined in the textual analysis look rather similar to each other in a peculiar manner – despite the diversity of subgenres, places of origin, storylines, literary effects in the ST, and other attributes. In fact, the originals have very little in common. The novels in Dick Francis's popular horse racing series from England are in a so-called hard-boiled style, with a brave, stoic hero always solving a vicious crime under pressure in a tense environment. In Lucy Montgomery's long-standing hit series *Anne of Green Gables* from Canada, the village life of Anne and her friends is depicted in an innocent tone and usually with a peaceful ending. Diane Mott Davidson's *Goldie the Caterer* series is written in a light, comical tone, although it is an American whodunit featuring a number of brutal murders. Jane Austen's classically renowned novels are loaded with English morals, and an explanatory, calm tone permeates throughout the stories. The majority of the originals, whose translations have these common features, belong to the category of so-called popular light novels, such as detective stories, adventure stories, science fiction, romance and horror stories, in the Western readers' community. Thus the group of texts under investigation has been labelled "translated popular fiction" in this book.

The latter term may be misleading, because it might appear to cover only translations of texts which are categorised under popular fiction within the SL literary system. However, my intention is to refer to a genre into which, theoretically, any original text can be transferred by virtue of the fact that it wears the particular stylistic costume in Japanese as the TL. The discourse of the translational dialect appears to have been rather firmly institutionalised (judging from the fact that it has been so well accepted). It does not appear to have been edited or smoothed out before publication. A translation satisfying the stylistic patterns now appears conservative, even if the individual expressions used are novel and innovative. This facilitates the translator's work of deleting or reducing the uniqueness or individuality of each fictional work. Thus, the translation norms and the translational discourse produced as a result determine the presence of the text-type and define it – despite the fact that the STs include newly created individual expressions. I illustrate this in Figure 5, which shows the two potential primary options in translating popular fiction from English into Japanese: one is a route to a discourse with the translation-emphatic stylistic features I have identified in the earlier chapters, while the other option is for a more nontranslational discourse. The dominant path found throughout this book is the upper one in Figure 5.

It needs to be clearly pointed out that I do not claim that all popular fiction is translated into this discourse. We surely find Japanese translations with fewer signs of the features, even if the STs are obviously from the category of Western popular fiction. More important is that this particular

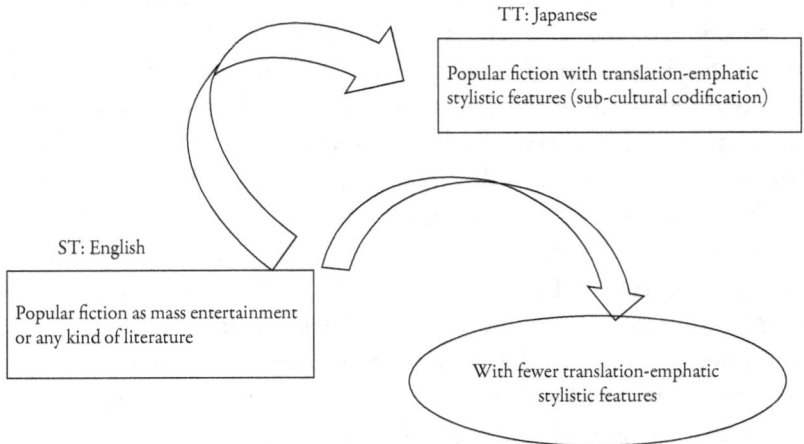

TT: Japanese

Popular fiction with translation-emphatic stylistic features (sub-cultural codification)

ST: English

Popular fiction as mass entertainment or any kind of literature

With fewer translation-emphatic stylistic features

Figure 5: Two options for dealing with popular fiction.

translationalese is identified among, and thus unites, an array of works from random sources and yields an independent category in the Japanese translation context.

To identify the properties found in the texts of the type in question, the following four translational options have been employed as technical yardsticks: (1) linguistic domestication, (2) linguistic foreignisation, (3) cultural domestication, and (4) cultural foreignisation. The definition and the background of the terms were fully discussed in Chapter 4. In the end, the strategy adopted during translation always comes down to a choice between domestication and foreignisation, which are the only options available, and these yardsticks constitute useful analytical tools. In Chapters 5 and 6, the ways in which the texts in the genre are generally dealt with (in terms of the four options) were investigated. For the first stage of the analysis, I assigned the contemporary standard Japanese language and culture as the criteria for judging how each translation unit goes through foreignisation and/or domestication, sometimes with native English speakers' help as necessary. It is difficult to identify normative features of a translation, as it always contains variations. However, it is certainly worth attempting to do so.

The distinctive properties of the discourse used in translated popular fiction – the particular category in question – have been identified in section 7.2. Many instances of linguistic domestication and foreignisation are observed, distributed in a rather chaotic manner within a work, a short section, or even one sentence of a text. As the effects of domestication and foreignisation are fundamentally in a trade-off with one another, the text embodies unmistakable inconsistency and emits a subtle hint of instability. A typical strategy for linguistic domestication involves the frequent introduction of attitude-marking adverbs (AMA), such as *masaka* [surely], *dōmo* [at any rate], and *yappari* [as expected], whose prominence is peculiarly Japanese and which often occur in colloquial settings. Certain strategies involving AMAs, such as *condensation, insertion*, and *substitutive insertion*, are practised (see section 5.1.4). These partially function as effective domesticators when they are used appropriately in a mode which the Japanese non-translational text would require; however, their presence on some occasions (both fitting and unfitting) also contributes to the standardisation of the translational discourse. It is noticeable that translators seem to grasp opportunities to use "uniquely Japanese" expressions such as adverbials, idioms, phrasal verbs, and sayings, rather than letting them go. They do not always end up doing so successfully, however.

There are abundant cases in which these expressions are used in a mildly "unfitting" context, semantically or pragmatically, causing a slight ripple of frustration. The simple fact is that, while the expression does not precisely fit the context, it does enhance the translationalness of the text. This kind of "unsuccessful" domestication can certainly be analysed as a kind of decon-ventionalisation, as this helps the text deviate from the non-translational state. Thus, translators attempt to domesticate texts using various strategies; however, it is unusual for this to be carried out to a degree sufficient to produce original-looking Japanese. Attempts at linguistic domestication are often limited to small units and, most importantly, left adjacent to foreignised/"unsuccessfully" domesticated parts. On the other hand, there are also many cases in which texts are linguistically foreignised, such that clear Englishness remains (see section 5.2.2). Mechanical correspondences to the ST lexical items and structures, such as abstract nouns and long noun modifiers, are often in evidence. These are the features literary critics and linguists traditionally identify as aspects of the so-called "translationese", but in this work, they are recognised only as some of the essential properties of my argument. The more precise state of translational style (or rather, translational discourse tailored for the text-type) is multilayered, and such linguistic Englishness is one of its facets.

Cultural domestication and foreignisation are also frequently adopted in a rather mixed, inconsistent way within a single text. It appears that translators domesticate ST cultural items when a parallel is available in the TL cultural system, just as in some cases of linguistic domestication (see sections 6.1.2 and 6.1.3), and they are not particularly concerned about offering a unified picture to the literary setting. It is not rare, for example, to find Christianity-related and Buddhist-related expressions used side by side in a short piece of translation. This lends an inconsistent image to the whole literary effect, although the fact that the setting of the ST is Western (and often Christian) is clear to the readers, since they know that it is a narrativised Western story in translation. When cultural domestication is consistently observed, it is, of course, possible that the Japanese replacement is transposed there only to signify the corresponding Western concept, regardless of the lack of agreement between the translator and the readers. It is difficult to assess what fictional world readers find themselves in as a result of the TT: it may often be a literary setting covered with a veil of alien smoke, even if it is described with familiar Japanese words.

As already mentioned, one prominent source of translationalness is inconsistency itself, resulting in variability and a sense of instability. It is, in fact, rather unusual to find a work of translated popular fiction controlled by clear principles concerning the way and extent to which domestication and/or foreignisation should be pursued. While this brings about a strong feeling of a lack of uniformity or integrity in the TT, it paradoxically holds the text-type intact. When the criteria for measuring foreignisation and domestication are shifted from normative original Japanese to normative translational Japanese, the picture looks different and possibly simpler. Stylistic patterns of the language used in translated popular fiction have been firmly conventionalised, and a large portion of published products in the genre falls into this category. There are an infinite number of potential tokens of linguistic expressions in existing translational Japanese. Thus, even if fresh expressions or usages actually crop up, the principles on which they are utilised are rarely new. To be genuinely against convention within the Japanese linguistic/cultural writing system (which, of course, includes translational Japanese), a translation must be in the style of an unsuitable text-type or completely innovative, that is, either excessively assimilating to native-sounding Japanese or outrageously translational. It appears rather difficult to produce anything that is totally unconventional. Literary impact, a poetic impression, or any kind of originality or uniqueness which the ST imparts as a piece of SL still needs to be transferred to the TT, which is carried out within the established (and thus comfortably familiar) framework of moulded or loosely formulated oddity which expresses otherness from the ST, unless a radically new style is invented and institutionalised.

One major – and fairly symbolic – strategy for cultural foreignisation is the use of the *katakana* syllabary. The system of *katakana*-isation in Japanese has made the straightforward introduction of otherness in the ST into the Japanese language possible, because one of the functions of the syllabary is to transcribe foreign items, particularly proper names, although it has also been playing a number of other roles, as explained in 6.2. A noteworthy point is that while *katakana*-isation marks the foreign origin of the item, at the same time it demonstrates that the word in the TT is no longer a foreign word but something reformed and incorporated into Japanese. Thus, the otherness of the item is reduced to being of a lower grade in some sense. Still, those newly *katakana*-ised words provide a foreignising impact by their form and lack of familiarity. *Katakana*-isation is widely used in all text-types, and it is also employed in translations of popular fiction, together with other strategies, in loosely fixed patterns (see sections 6.2.2 and 6.2.3). As previously pointed out, Yanabu (2002) argues that imported or newly created terms through translation render the semantic content of the term cryptic, and this *hi* (秘) or the mystery expected with those words has been very much appreciated by the Japanese throughout history. Freshly created translational words, including *katakana*-ised terms, can amplify the enigmatic literary impact of the translationalese. Moreover, in addition to those imported terms, the discourse itself, which is codified to look mysterious, can be appreciated in the Japanese cultural context.

Translation – especially translation of literature – reflects the complexities of reality. The translations that are produced and the ways in which the translations are carried out profoundly reveal the TL attitude at home and abroad. It is not easy to come up with a good explanation for how this way of bringing foreign literary works into the Japanese system (that is, putting the works and the otherness contained within them into a kind of mould, a ready-made style of writing) has come about. The first factor that should be considered is the reader's persistent desire (most likely subconscious) for translationalness. It has conventionally been the case that materials imported from foreign countries are much appreciated in the society, apart from certain historical occasions, and a text that is obviously a translation often wins respect and attention, as was pointed out in passages quoted in the previous chapter (sections 8.1 and 8.2). This is quite an extraordinary situation, which prompts Seidensticker (1962) to refer to Japan as a mysterious country in this respect. The mystery resides in the peculiar way in which the Japanese communicate with Western cultures through translation: importing foreign materials using a strongly standardised third language. The persistence of this third language, which is often seen as a rare phenomenon, has been deconstructed and examined in this work. Readers are after a touch of Westernness in the text – to some extent as a means to understand the author's logic, emotions, and thought patterns on one level, but perhaps also to enjoy the immediate impression that they are experiencing a foreign culture. Nakayama (1988: 241–142) argues that a secret, "typically Japanese essence" is hidden in the way in which people transform each element that they receive from a foreign culture. He calls this *bokashi* [blurring] and points out that imported words are frequently loaded with more meaning during the process of acceptance, so that their core semantic meaning becomes blurred (ibid. 241). This concept of *bokashi*, which is used in an attempt to identify Japaneseness, is useful when thinking about what happens in the process of translation. Wakabayashi (2009) states that Japanese "translationese" does not exist between the ST and the TT, but is instead an aspect of Japanese. I agree with this notion, since stylistic features have already been firmly established within the translational convention (see section 7.1.1).

It is, however, important to be aware that semantic elements are often "blurred" when translated in the translational style since readers, in attempting to read and understand translated literature, cannot refer to the normative Japanese system. Words, expressions, and passage structures are constantly being invented and presented to the reader. Even if the expressions are new, however, the way in which they are created is firmly established. The semantic content is left ambiguous, while the vessel or mould is clearly established – and this seems to be a rather comfortable way for the Japanese to receive otherness. Why this phenomenon surfaces more in the genre of popular fiction than in other kinds of writing is a question that needs to be answered.

Although in the twenty-first century we are living in a so-called information society, this does not seem to have changed the fundamental structure of readers' attitudes towards translation. An intriguing point is that the translational discourse seems to allow readers to experience some group consciousness as they might even enjoy the feeling that they are part of an illusory cultural circle of translation readers (an imaginary subcultural society), rather than suffering from the stiffness of the texts that they encounter. The circle is, in fact, open to everybody due to its easy access. As Kodaka

(1991: 174) puts it, "An uncanny, parallel world has emerged in which people communicate with each other through sketchily translated texts". For this purpose, it is vital that a translation be clearly marked as a translation. This highlights a function that these translations fulfil, that is, they are media through which readers in the inner circle receive enjoyment and satisfaction – not only from reading and interpreting the translated works themselves but also from being aware that they share this experience with their fellow readers. It is understandable that translation texts need to be attuned to these readers' expectations and that the translations are indeed as popular (and popularised) as other items which belong to the category of globally attention-grabbing Japanese subcultures. This explains to some extent why translated popular fiction needs to be distinctively coded in style: it is required to serve an enthusiastic inner group as a commercial item of reverence. So-called *otaku* – people whose identity is defined by their understanding and appreciation of non-mainstream, lowbrow cultural items, such as cartoons, technological gadgets, and collectable character figures – maintain their subcultural world in a rather similar manner. The items they are interested in are strictly required to have a certain shared obscurity (Ōsawa 2006), which repels many sceptics. The outrageousness which characterises these subculture items is diverse on one level; however, they certainly exhibit some common features which indicate their form of "popness".

Schusterman (1994: 145–146) refutes Adorno who claims that popular art lacks justification as it follows a mass standard and is full of clichés. This is immediately related to its commercial and industrial aspects, and popular art is therefore not aesthetically self-controlled. Shusterman (ibid.) criticises such one-dimensional analysis. In the USA, for example, popular culture emerged in reaction to the "aristocracy of culture" (Bourdieu and Nice 1980: 252) which was mainly rooted in Europe, and this background unites the concept of popular art. There is, however, certainly "pop" off the mainstream as well. Writings outside what the community admits as mainstream and regarded as subcultural items may also be allowed to be as "pop" or marginal as they want to be. Japanese popular literature translations and the way in which they are translated – with strongly codified otherness, in contrast to authentic popular writing traditions – demonstrate some parallelism with this.

When translated texts introduce something idiosyncratic into the traditional Japanese cultural system, they sometimes utilise the method of popularising or narrativising it by labelling it accordingly – that is, by giving it a certain uniform style. The more texts are given this style, the more securely the mould becomes consolidated as a text-type. This way of accepting otherness as part of the cultural system – with a unique untidiness – leaves these translations with a popular but also subcultural status. Readers of translations are constantly experiencing different literary effects in each work of fiction, as well as the edgy translationalness that is common throughout the genre. It is almost as if they have been conditioned to regard the dualistic nature of translated works as an indispensable feature of the genre. It should not be forgotten that the usually exciting, easy-to-follow storylines in popular fiction nevertheless help readers to enjoy reading it – despite its eccentric stylistic oddity, which can potentially disturb the reading experience.

Another factor which deserves attention is the Japanese mentality, which has been observed from pre-modern times up until the contemporary period, as originally discussed, for example, by Doi (1973), and which can be regarded as one of the keys to the mystery already talked about. The *amae* argument has been explored and questioned especially with regard to the cultural inherency of *amae* (Johnson 1993, Smith and Nomi 2000) and the argument was later modified by Doi himself, but only the general tendency of *amae* in Japanese culture is relevant here. In their constant need to identify themselves in interactions with Western countries, the Japanese have tried to define the West as a monochromic otherness (see section 8.4). This homogenised image of the West is widely distributed to, and absorbed by, the readers of translated fiction through the established mode of language – the readers believe that they are receiving an individual piece of a fictional entity. While people generally show some respect or favour towards imports from the West, the presence of the translational dialect systematically filters the incoming information. Thus, the otherness they experience in the form of oddity is neither identical nor close to its genuine depiction but rather is reshaped into a ready-made matrix. Translation can be regarded as part of a nationwide scheme of assimilation – possibly originally rooted in feelings of some defensiveness with regard to the Japanese cultural identity. The assimilation of otherness from the West results in its codification, utilising a specific set of properties which only have cultural and psychological significance in the TL community.

It is obvious that the unified concept of the West, which can be abstracted from the writing, does not reflect the semantic content of the ideas of the regions and cultures which the Japanese have in reality. It is more appropriate to think that they have a collective idol image of the West as such, which is handy for stabilising their own identity as non-Westerners. How and to what extent this attitude will change or be maintained through the use of the Internet needs to be monitored in the future.

While the persistent co-presence of foreignisation and domestication traces (including "unsuccessful" attempts at domestication for convenience) is a salient feature of most texts, the Golden Rule – that translation should be semantically faithful and at the same time readable – receives wide theoretical support (Bekku 1983) in Japan, as in most translation communities. The discrepancies between the ideal and the reality here are as wide as in many other aspects of human life. People theoretically value readable translations, but they neither create nor encourage their production in terms of a readability that resembles original Japanese. This fact is undeniably odd, as odd as the style itself. There are obviously two different conceptions of readability at work – one for purposes of criticism and another in practice. When critics produce commentaries on a translation, they do so on the basis of readability 1 – that is, readability with respect to everyday Japanese. Moreover, most readers only tend to be aware of a limited number of the features that make up the translational discourse, such as structural Englishness and neologism.

These individual features are simply helping the text to satisfy the conditions for readability 2 – that is, readability with respect to the established translational discourse. Since readability 2 is accepted (or rather, passes unnoticed) as the norm by readers and the market, it is in a sense pointless to criticise a translation on the basis of readability 1. Thus, as long as the translation sticks to the normatively fluent translationalese, the text is naturally exempt from criticism in this respect. The substitution of the definition (or more precisely, the blurring of the conception of readability that the community desires in practice) needs to be recognised in order for the presence of what might be called a double standard to be understood.

When discussing translation, people often become judgemental and tend to treat the subject as a moral issue (section 8.3). This book takes a purely descriptive approach; it makes the claim that there exists a translationalese and speculates upon its cultural implications. Although some of the translationalese features do overlap with those of "translationese", which conventionally has a negative connotation, I have no intention of being judgemental concerning the existing translational norm in Japanese. Indeed, the translational features such as the "unsuccessful" domestication may be "successful" in terms of contributing to the established translating style. Nevertheless, it must be pointed out that the peculiarly standardised discourse does yield some theoretical problems – the most obvious being the stylistic distortion of the original literature.

On one level, any work is reduced to being just one more item in the familiar category of translated popular fiction from the West – together with hundreds of others with the same or similar stylistic traits. On another level, it is hard to recreate the original tone sufficiently, with regard to aspects such as tension, friendliness, stiffness, and formality, when the TT is steadily narrativised as translational, because this often disturbs those subtle original features. The problem becomes more serious when an ST is not from the so-called popular fiction genre in the SL, or the publisher of the TT or the translator has no intention of reshaping the work into a piece of popular fiction, yet it needs to come out as such on the Japanese market.

I doubt that translators are in fact conscious of the presence and effects of the particular discourse as a communicative, manipulative device. It is rather problematic to leave the discourse in their hands without them being aware of its function to re-narrate literary works in another mode. It is possible, for instance, to insert the stylistic features of popular fiction into a translation of SL high-brow literature or vice versa, and both cases can be observed, albeit significantly less frequently. In the former case, the work seems to be immediately accepted in the market as easy reading. In the latter case, by contrast, a detective story translated with a more high-brow tone cannot easily be upgraded to cultured literary status in the view of the reader – but the possibility needs to be investigated in the future. In any case, English popular fiction as mass entertainment could be translated so that it sounds like authentic Japanese popular literature. As a matter of fact, however, it is often turned into subcultural literary items with the translation-emphatic features described.

Whether readers notice, or react at all differently to, these marginal cases, in which a detective story is translated with unusual stylistic features (with much less linguistic foreignisation and cultural domestication, for example), is an intriguing question. Subculture or pop art is usually produced within its own domain; translated popular fiction, however, has its origin elsewhere. Thus, whether shaping translations in such a mould ought to be encouraged or not is another theoretical – or perhaps ethical – question for future consideration. Translation is a major form of communication with the outside world and with people unfamiliar to the Japanese, and translationalese has been established as a strategic device for identifying both the Japanese themselves and the SL cultures within the constant incoming flow of foreign elements. The presence of the translational discourse seems to act as a restraining force. It prevents Japanese literary translation from going as far in the direction of domestication or foreignisation as it otherwise might. The stagnancy of the translational dialect seems to coincide with the stagnant state of communication and understanding of other cultures, which the Japanese face as a threat, difficulty, and source of joy, and sometimes as a yardstick for measuring where they should be standing in their ever-intricate international interactions.

Bibliography

Abe, Kōbō. 1967. *Tomodachi*. In *Nihon Gendai Gikyoku Taikei*, vol. 7. Tokyo: Sanichi Shobō.

Akiyama, Yūzō. 1998. *Umoreta Hon'yaku. Kindai Bungaku no Kaitakushatachi.* Tokyo: Shindokusho.

Álvarez, Román, and M. Carmen-África Vidal (eds). 1996. *Translation, Power, Subversion*. Clevedon: Multilingual Matters.

Anderson, John. 1983. *The Architecture of Cognition*. Cambridge, MA: Harvard University Press.

Andō, Sadao. 1975. Shakaigengogaku to Hon'yaku. *Gengo* 4, 499–507.

Anonymous. 1896. Zappō Nihonshiika no Shinsō. *Teikoku Bungaku* 4, 63–64.

Ariyoshi, Sawako. 1982. *Kōkotsu no Hito*. Tokyo: Shinchōsha.

Ariyoshi, Sawako. 1983. *Akujo ni tsuite*. Tokyo: Shinchōsha.

Asaba, Sayako (trans.). 1998. *Nain Teirāzu*. / Sayers, Dorothy L. *Nine Tailors: Changes Rung on an Old Theme in Two Short Touches and Two Full Peals*. Tokyo: Sōgensha.

Attridge, Derek. 1996. *Poetic Rhythm. An Introduction*. Cambridge: Cambridge University Press.

Austen, Jane. 1995/1811. *Sense and Sensibility*. London: Penguin Books.

Bachnik, Jane M., and Charles J. Quinn Jr (eds). 1994. *Situated Meaning. Inside and Outside in Japanese Self, Society, and Language*. Princeton, NJ: Princeton University Press.

Baetens, Jan, and José Lambert (eds). 2000. *The Future of Cultural Studies: Essays in Honour of Joris Vlasselaers*. Leuven: Leuven University Press.

Baker, Mona. 1992. *In Other Words. A Coursebook on Translation*. London: Routledge.

Barnstone, Willis. 1993. *The Poetics of Translation. History, Theory, Practice*. New Haven, CT: Yale University Press.

Bekku, Sadanori. 1979. *Hon'yaku Tokuhon. Shoshinsha no tameno Hasshō*. Tokyo: Kōdansha.

Bekku, Sadanori. 1983. *Eibun no Hon'yaku*. Tokyo: Taishūkan Shoten.

Bekku, Sadanori. 1985. *Hon'yaku to Hihyō*. Tokyo: Kōdansha.

Bell, Roger T. 1991. *Translation and Translating. Theory and Practice*. London: Longman.

Berman, Antoine. 1985. Translation and the Trials of the Foreign. In Lawrence Venuti (ed.), *The Translation Studies Reader*. New York: Routledge, 276–289.

Biguenet, John, and Rainer Schulte (eds). 1989. *The Craft of Translation*. Chicago: University of Chicago Press.

Bloom, Alfred H. 1981. *The Linguistic Shaping of Thought. A Study in the Impact of Language in China and the West*. Mahwah, NJ: Lawrence Erlbaum Associates.

Boase-Beier, Jean. 2006. *Stylistic Approaches to Translation*. Manchester: St Jerome Publishing.

Bourdieu, Pierre, and Richard Nice. 1980. The Aristocracy of Culture. *Media, Culture and Society* 2, 225–254.

Bradbury, Ray. 1977/1950. *The Martian Chronicles*. London: Grafton.

Braun, Lilian Jackson. 1991. *The Cat Who Knew a Cardinal*. London: Headline Book Publishing.

Catford, John C. 1965. *A Linguistic Theory of Translation*. London: Oxford University Press.

Chanlat, Jean-François, Eduardo Davel and Jean-Pierre Dupuis (eds). 2013. *Cross-Cultural Management: Culture and Management across the World*. London: Routledge.

Chesterman, Andrew (ed.). 1989. *Readings in Translation Theory*. Helsinki: Oy Finn Lectura Ab.

Chino, Eiichi. 1983. Hony'akuron to Gengogaku. *Gengo Seikatsu* 384, 16–23.

Christie, Agatha. 1991/1924. *Poirot Investigates*. London: Harper Collins Publishers.

Christie, Agatha. 1993/1954. *The Mousetrap and Other Plays*. London: Harper Collins Publishers.

Christie, Agatha. 1994/1960. *The Adventure of the Christmas Pudding*. London: Harper Collins Publishers.

Clements, Rebekah. 2015. *A Cultural History of Translation in Early Modern Japan*. Cambridge: Cambridge University Press.

Cockerill, Hiroko S. 2003. Futabatei Shimei's Translations from Russian: Verbal Aspect and Narrative Perspective. *Japanese Studies* 23(3), 229–238.

Cockerill, Hiroko. 2010. Kaidai 16. In Yanabu Akira, Mizuno Akira and Naganuma Mikako (eds), *Nihon no Hon'yakuron. Anthology to Kaidai*. Tokyo: Hōsei Daigaku Shuppankyoku, 176–180.

Crichton, Michael. 1990. *Jurassic Park*. 1990. New York: Ballantine Books.

Doi, Takeo. 2007. *Amae no Kōzō (zōhofukyūban)*. Tokyo: Kōbunsha.

Doi, Takeo, and John Bester (trans.). 1973. *The Anatomy of Dependence*. Tokyo: Kōdansha International.

Duff, Alan. 1989. *Translation*. Oxford: Oxford University Press.

Even-Zohar, Itamar. 1978. The Position of Translated Literature: Within the Literary Polysystem. In James S. Holmes, José Lambert and Raymond van den Broeck (eds), *Literature and Translation: New Perspectives in Literary Studies*. Leuven: Acco, 117–127.

Even-Zohar, Itamar. 2005. Polysystem Theory (Revised). In *Papers in Culture Research*. Tel Aviv: Tel Aviv University, 38–49.

Fibras, Jan. 1986. On the Dynamics of Written Communication in the Light of the Theory of Functional Sentence Perspective. In Charles R. Cooper and Sidney Greenbaum (eds), *Studying Writing: Linguistic Approaches*. New York: Sage, 40–71.

Florenz, Carl. 1895a. Nihon Shiika no Seishin to Oshū Shiika no Seishin tono Hikakuko. *Teikoku Bungaku* 3, 69–85.

Florenz, Carl. 1895b. Ueda Bungakushi ni Tou. *Teikoku Bungaku* 7, 115–122.

Francis, Dick. 1976/1966. *Flying Finish*. London: Pan Books.

Francis, Dick. 1972/1970. *Rat Race*. London: Pan Books.

Francis, Dick. 1983/1982. *Banker*. London: Pan Books.

Fujinami, Fumiko. 2007. *Hon'yakukōi to Ibunkakan Komyunikēshon. Kinōshugiteki Hon'yaku Riron no Shosō*. Tokyo: Shōraisha.

Fukushima, Masami (trans.). 1985. *Supeinhitsu no Himitsu* / Christie, Agatha. *The Mystery of the Spanish Chest*. In Hashimoto Fukuo et al. (trans.). 1985. Kurisumasu Pudding no Bōken. / Christie, Agatha. *The Adventure of the Christmas Pudding*. Tokyo: Hayakawa Shobō.

Furuno, Yuri. 2002. Nihon no Hon'ayku: Henka no Arawareta 1970 nendai. *Tsūyaku Kenkyū* 2, 114–122.

Furuno, Yuri. 2005. Translationese in Japan. In Eva Hung (ed.), *Translation and Cultural Change: Studies in History, Norms and Image-projection*. Amsterdam: John Benjamins, 147–160.

Grace, George W. 1987. *The Linguistic Construction of Reality*. London: Croom Helm.

Gregory, Michael, and Suzanne Carroll. 1978. *Language and Situation. Language Varieties and Their Social Contexts*. London: Routledge and Kegan Paul.

Grootaers, A. Willem, and Takeshi Shibata (trans.). 1979. *Goyaku Shimban*. Tokyo: Sanshodo.

Gutt, Ernst-August. 1991. *Translation and Relevance. Cognition and Context*. Oxford: Blackwell.

Hada, Shizuko (trans.). 1995. *Neko wa Tori wo Mitsumeru.* / Braun, Lilian Jackson. *The Cat Who Knew a Cardinal*. Tokyo: Hayakawa Shobō.

Haga, Tōru (ed.). 2000. *Hon'yaku to Nihon Bunka*. Tokyo: Yamakawa Shuppansha.

Halliday, M. A. K. 1985. *An Introduction to Functional Grammar*. London: Edward Arnold.

Hara, Takuya. 1979. Tolstoy Hon'yaku no Gendaiteki Imi: Tolstoy cho Kitagami Jirō Yaku Sensō to Heiwa, Anna Karēnina. *Asahi Journal* 21, 65–67.

Hara, Takuya, and Nishinaga Yoshinari (eds). 2000. *Hon'yaku Hyakunen Gaikokubungaku to Nihon no Kindai*. Tokyo: Taishūkan Shoten.

Harker, Jaime. 1999. Contemporary Japanese Fiction & 'Middlebrow' Translation Strategies. *The Translator* 5(1), 27–44.

Hashimoto, Fukuo et al. (trans.). 1985/1960. *Kurisumasu Pudding no Bōken.* / Christie, Agatha. *The Adventure of the Christmas Pudding.* Tokyo: Hayakawa Shobō.

Hatim, Basil, and Ian Mason. 1990. *Discourse and the Translator.* London: Longman.

Hatim, Basil, and Ian Mason 1997. *The Translator as Communicator.* London: Routledge.

Henry, O. 1980/1906. *The Gift of the Magi and Other Short Stories.* London: Dover Publications.

Hermans, Theo. 1988. On Translating Proper Names, with Reference to De Witte and Max Havelaar. In Michael Wintle (ed.), *Modern Dutch Studies: A Volume of Essays in Honour of Professor Peter King.* London: Athlone, 11–24.

Hervey, Sándor, and Ian Higgins. 1992. *Thinking Translation. A Course in Translation Method. French to English.* London: Routledge.

Huggins, James Byron. 1995. *Leviathan.* Nashville, TN: Thomas Nelson.

Ibuki, Chise (trans.). 1948. *Funbetsu to Takan. Erina to Mearian.* / Austen, Jane. *Sense and Sensibility.* Tokyo: Shingetsusha.

Imai, Kunihiko. 1975. Hon'yaku to Gengogaku. *Gengo* 4, 490–498.

Inoue, Ken. 1994. Iwano Hōmei Yaku Arthur Symons Hyōshōsha no Bungaku Undō. In Yoshihiro Ōsawa (ed.), *Text no Hakken.* Tokyo: Chūōkōronsha, 349–363.

Isoya, Takashi. 1980. *Hon'yaku to Bunka no Kigōron.* Tokyo: Keisō Shobō.

Itagaki, Shimpei. 1995. *Hony'akugaku.* Tokyo: Shinzanshashuppan.

Jakobson, Roman. 1997/1959. On Linguistic Aspects of Translation. In Lawrence Venuti (ed.), *The Translation Studies Reader.* London: Routledge, 138–143.

Johnson, Frank A. (ed.). 1993. *Dependency and Japanese Socialization: Psychoanalytic and Anthropological Investigations in Amae.* New York: New York University Press.

Jones, R. Francis. 2011. *Poetry Translating as Expert Action. Processes, Priorities and Networks.* Amsterdam: John Benjamins.

Kajita, Takamichi. 1993. *Tōgō to Bunretsu no Yōroppa. EC, Kokka, Minzoku.* Tokyo: Iwanami Shoten.

Kamei, Shunsuke (ed.). 1988. *Gaikokugo no Kenkyū.* Tokyo: Kōdansha.

Kamei, Takashi, Ōtō Tokihiko and Yamada Toshio. 1966. *Nihongo no Rekishi 6. Atarashii Kokugo eno Ayumi.* Tokyo: Heibonsha.

Katō, Yōko (trans.). 1996. *Kukkingu • Mama no Shōkanjō.* / Mott-Davidson, Diane. *The Last Supper.* Tokyo: Shūeisha.

Katō, Yōko (trans.). 1997. *Kukkingu • Mama no Kenshisho* / Mott-Davidson, Diane. *The Main Corpse.* Tokyo: Shūeisha.

Katō, Yōko (trans.). 2000. *Kukking • Mama no Shinhannin.* / Mott-Davidson, Diane. *Prime Cut.* Tokyo: Shūeisha.

Katz, Jerrold J. 1976. Effability and Translation. In Franz Guenthner and Monica Guenthner-Reutter (eds), *Meaning and Translation*. New York: New York University Press, 191–234.

Kawakatsu, Heita. 1991. *Nihon Bunmei to Kindai Seiyō Sakoku Saikō*. Tokyo: Nihonhōsō Shuppan Kyōkai.

Kawamura, Jirō. 1981. *Hon'yaku no Nihongo. Nihongo no Sekai 15*. Tokyo: Chūōkōronsha.

Kazumi, Mukai, and Hiroshi Kuzuyama (trans.). 1996. *Erinoa to Mariannu – Zoku • Funbetsu to Takan*. / Tennant, Emma. *Elinor and Marianne: A Sequel to Sense and Sensibility*. Tokyo: Aoyama Shuppansha.

Keene, Donald (trans.). 1969. *Friends*. / Abe, Kobo. *Tomodachi*. New York: Grove Press.

Keene, Donald, and Yoshida Kenichi (trans.). 1979. *Nihon no Bungaku*. Tokyo: Chuokoronsha.

Kikuchi, Mitsu (trans.). 1976. *Hietsu*. / Francis, Dick. *Flying Finish*. Tokyo: Hayakawa Shobō.

Kikuchi, Mitsu (trans.). 1977. *Konsen*. / Francis, Dick. *Rat Race*. Tokyo: Hayakawa Shobō.

Kikuchi, Mitsu (trans.). 1988. *Meimon*. / Francis, Dick. *Banker*. Tokyo: Hayakawa Shobō.

Kimura, Naoji. 1975. Hon'yakuron no Kihonteki Shomondai. *Gengo* 4, 482–489.

Kinsui, Satoshi. 2003. *Virtual Nihongo Yakuwarigo no Nazo*. Tokyo: Iwanamishoten.

Kinsui, Satoshi (ed.). 2014. *Yakuwarigo Shōjiten*. Tokyo: Kenkyūsha.

Kodaka, Nobumitsu. 1991. *Hon'yaku to yū Shigoto*. Tokyo: Japan Times.

Konishi, Jinichi. 1993. *Nihon Bungakushi*. Tokyo: Kōdansha.

Kōno, Ichirō. 1999. *Hon'yaku no Okite*. Tokyo: DHC.

Kudō, Hiroshi. 1982. Johōfukushi no Imi to Kinō. *Kokuritsukokugokenkyūjo Kenkyūhōkokushū* 3. Tokyo: Shūeishuppan, 45–92.

Kunihiro, Tetsuya. 1981. Hon'yaku no Gengogaku. *Gengo* 10, 62–67.

Kußmaul, Paul. 1985. The Degree of Semantic Precision in Translation. *Babel* 31(1), 12–19.

Kußmaul, Paul. 1997. Text-type Conventions and Translating. In Anna Trosborg (ed.), *Text Typology and Translation*. Amsterdam: John Benjamins, 67–83.

Lawendowski, Boguslow P. 1978. On Semiotic Aspects of Translation. In Thomas A. Sebeok (ed.), *Sight, Sound and Sense*. Bloomington: Indiana University Press, 264–282.

Le Fanu, Joseph Sheridan. 1994/1868. *Squire Toby's Will*. In M. R. James (ed.), *Madam Crowl's Ghost and Other Stories*. Hertfordshire: Wordsworth Editions.

Lecercle, Jean-Jacques. 1993. The Current State of Stylistics. *The European English Messenger* 2(1), 14–18.

Leech, Geoffrey N., and Michael H. Short. 1981. *Style in Fiction. A Linguistic Introduction to English Fictional Prose*. London: Longman.

Lévi-Strauss, Claude. 1966. *The Savage Mind*. Chicago: University of Chicago Press.

Levy, Indra. 2010. *Translation in Modern Japan*. New York: Routledge.

Levý, Jeri. 1963. Will Translation Theory Be of Use to Translators? In Rolf Italiaander (ed.), *Übersetzen*. Frankfurt: Athenäum Verlag, 77–82.

Lyons, John. 1977. *Semantics I & II*. Cambridge: Cambridge University Press.

Malmkjaer, Kirsten. 2002. (ed.). *The Linguistics Encyclopedia*. London and New York: Routledge.

Malone, Joseph L. 1986. Trajectional Analysis: Five Cases in Point. *Babel* 32(1), 13–25.

Mano, Akihiro (trans.). 1996. *Itsuka Hareta Hi ni. – Funbetsu to Takan –*. / Austen, Jane. *Sense and Sensibility*. Tokyo: Kinema Jyunpōsha.

Meldrum, Yukari F. 2007. Source-Based Translation and Foreignization: A Japanese Case. *Invitation to Interpreting & Translation Studies* 2, 39–54.

Meldrum, Yukari F. 2009. Translationese in Japanese Literary Translation. *traduction, terminologie, rédaction* 22(1), 93–118.

Meldrum, Yukari F. 2010. *Contemporary Translationese in Japanese Popular Literature*. Mauritius: Lambert Academic Publishing.

Milton, John. 2000. The Translation of Mass Fiction. Investigating Translation. In Allison Beeby, Doris Ensinger and Marisa Presas (eds), *Selected Papers from the 4th International Congress on Translation*. Amsterdam: John Benjamins, 171–179.

Miyawaki, Takao. 2000. *Hon'yaku no Kihon*. Tokyo: Kenkyūsha Shuppan.

Mizuno, Akira. 2007. Kindai Nihon no Bungakuteki Tagen System to Hon'yaku no Isō: Chokuyaku no Keifu. *Invitation to Interpreting & Translation Studies* 1, 3–43.

Mizuno, Akira. 2010. Kaidai 4. In Yanabu Akira, Mizuno Akira and Naganuma Mikako (eds), *Nihon no Hon'yakuron. Anthology to Kaidai*. Tokyo: Hōsei Daigaku Shuppankyoku, 74–78.

Mizuno, Akira. 2011. Meijishoki no Hon'yakubuntaikihan: Yobitekikōsatsu. *Invitation to Interpreting & Translation Studies* 5, 1–24.

Mizuta, Hiroshi. 1985. In Bekku Sadanori (ed.), *Hon'yaku to Hihyō*. Tokyo: Kōdansha, 142.

Montgomery, Lucy M. 1994/1936. *Anne of Windy Willows*. London: Puffin.

Morimoto, Junko. 1994. *Hanashite no Shūkan o Arawasu Fukushi ni tsuite*. Tokyo: Kuroshio Shuppan.

Morioka, Kenji. 1968. Hon'yaku ni okeru Chokuyaku to Iyaku. *Gengo Seikatsu* 197, 21–31.

Morioka, Kenji. 1999. *Ōbun Kundoku no Kenkyū. Ōbunmyaku no Keisei*. Tokyo: Meiji Shoin.

Mott-Davidson, Diane. 1992. *Catering to Nobody*. New York: Bantam Books.

Mott-Davidson, Diane. 1995. *The Last Supper*. New York: Bantam Books.

Mott-Davidson, Diane. 1996. *The Main Corpse.* New York: Bantam Books.

Mott-Davidson, Diane. 1998. *Prime Cut.* New York: Bantam Books.

Munday, Jeremy. 2008. *Introducing Translation Studies. Theories and Applications.* London: Routledge.

Muraoka, Hanako (trans.). 1981/1958. *An no Kōfuku.* / Montgomery, Lucy M. *Anne of Windy Willows.* Tokyo: Shinchōsha.

Nae, Niclina. 1999. Concept Translation in Meiji Japan, *Translation Journal* 3(3).

Naganuma, Mikako. 2010. Nogami Toyoichirō no Hon'yakuron. *Interpreting and Translation Studies* 10, 59–83.

Nakamura, Tōru (trans.). 2003. *Kyōjū Rivaiasan.* / Huggins, James Byron. *Leviathan.* Tokyo: Tokyo Sōgensha.

Nakamura, Yasuo. 1989. *Meiyaku to Goyaku.* Tokyo: Kōdansha.

Nakamura, Yasuo. 2009. *Hon'yaku wa doko made Kanō ka.* Tokyo: Japan Times.

Nakau, Minoru. 1980. Bunfukushi no Hikaku. In Tetsuya Kunihiro (ed.), *Nichieigohikaku Kōza 2 Bunpō.* Tokyo: Taishūkan, 157–219.

Nakayama, Osamu. 1988. *'Bokashi' no Shinri.* Tokyo: Sōgensha.

Narumi, Shirō (trans.). 1980. *Nezumitori.* / Christie, Agatha. *The Mousetrap and Other Plays.* Tokyo: Hayakawa Shobō.

Naruse, Takeshi. 1978. *Hon'yaku no Shosō.* Tokyo: Kaibunsha Shuppan.

Newmark, Peter. 1988. *Approaches to Translation. New Edition.* New York: Prentice Hall.

Nida, Eugene A. 1964. *Towards a Science of Translating. With Special Reference to Principles and Procedures Involved in Bible Translating.* Leiden: E. J. Brill.

Nida, Eugene A., and Charles T. Taber. 1969. *The Theory and Practice of Translation.* Leiden: E. J. Brill.

Nida, Eugene A., Charles T. Taber and Noah S. Brannen / Sawanobori, Haruhito (trans.) / Masukawa Kiyoshi (trans.). 1973. *Hon'yaku – Riron to Jissen.* Tokyo: Shinchōsha.

Nida, Eugene A., and Jan De Waard. 1986. *From One Language to Another. Functional Equivalence in Bible Translating.* Nashville, TN: Thomas Nelson.

Nihongo Kokugo Daijiten Dainihan, vol. 5. 1973. Tokyo: Shōgakukan.

Nihongo Kokugo Daijiten Dainihan, vol. 12. 2000. Tokyo: Shōgakukan.

Niranjana, Tejaswini. 1992. *Siting Translation. History, Post-Structuralism, and the Colonial Context.* Berkeley: University of California Press.

Nogami, Toyoichirō. 1938. *Hon'yaku no Riron to Jissen*, Tokyo: Iwanamishoten.

Nohara, Kayoko. 2006. Moulded Otherness: On the Strategic Use of Proper Names in Popular Japanese Literature. *Current Trends in Translation Teaching and Learning* 1, 180–198.

Nohara, Kayoko. 2009. Jōhōfirutā to shite no Hon'yaku. *Nihongobungaku* 44, 133–152.

Nohara, Kayoko. 2014. *Discussion kara Manabu Hon'yakugaku. Translation Studies Nyūmon.* Tokyo: Sanseidō.

Nolan, Liam, and Sakuhara Saeko. 2001. *Nanataki no Chiisana Otoko*. Jiaien Ashi-
nagaojisan no Kai.

Nomoto, Kikuo. 1968. Hon'yaku no Bunshō. *Kokubungaku Kaishaku to Kanshō* 33,
215–222.

Nord, Christiane. 1991. *Text Analysis in Translation*. Amsterdam: Rodopi.

Obi, Fusa (trans.). 1985. *Shi no Karutetto*. / Rendell, Ruth. *Make Death Love Me*.
Tokyo: Kadokawa Shoten.

Ogasawara, Toyoki (trans.). 1976. *Kaseinendaiki*. / Bradbury, Ray. *The Martian Chronicles*. Tokyo: Hayakawa Shobō.

Ogasawara, Toyoki (trans.). 1985. *Makeinu*. / Christie, Agatha. *The Underdog*. In
Hashimoto Fukuo et al. (trans.). 1985. *Kurisumasu Pudding no Bōken*. / Christie,
Agatha. *The Adventure of the Christmas Pudding*. Tokyo: Hayakawa Shobō.

Ogura, Takashi (trans.). 1978. *Gurando Metoroporitan no Hōseki Tōnan Jiken*. / Christie, Agatha. *The Jewel Robbery at the Grand Metropolitan*. In Takashi Ogura
(trans.). 1978. *Powaro Tōjō*. / Christie, Agatha. *Poirot Investigates*. Tokyo: Hayakawa Shobō.

Ogura, Takashi (trans.). 1978. *Itariakizoku Satsugai Jiken*. / Christie, Agatha. *The
Adventure of the Italian Nobleman*. In Takashi Ogura (trans.). 1978. *Powaro Tōjō*. /
Christie, Agatha. *Poirot Investigates*. Tokyo: Hayakawa Shobō.

Ogura, Takashi. (trans.). 1978. *Powaro Tōjō*. / Christie, Agatha. *Poirot Investigates*.
Tokyo: Hayakawa Shobō.

Ogura, Takashi (trans.) 1978. *Ryōjinsō no Kaijiken*. / Christie, Agatha. *The Mystery of
Hunter's Lodge*. In Takashi Ogura (trans.). 1978. *Powaro Tōjō*. / Christie, Agatha.
Poirot Investigates. Tokyo: Hayakawa Shobō.

Ogura, Takashi (trans.). 1978. *Seibu no Hoshi Tōnan Jiken*. / Christie, Agatha. *The
Adventure of the Western Star*. In Takashi Ogura (trans.). 1978. *Powaro Tōjō*. /
Christie, Agatha. *Poirot Investigates*. Tokyo: Hayakawa Shobō.

Ogura, Takashi (trans.). 1978. *Yasu Apāto Jiken*. In Takashi Ogura (trans.). 1978. *The Adventure of
the Cheap Flat*. In Takashi Ogura (trans.). 1978. *Powaro Tōjō*. / Christie, Agatha.
Poirot Investigates. Tokyo: Hayakawa Shobō.

Ogura, Takashi (trans.). 1985. *Yume*. / Christie, Agatha. *The Dream*. In Hashimoto
Fukuo et al. (trans.). 1985. *Kurisumasu Pudding no Bōken*. / Christie, Agatha.
The Adventure of the Christmas Pudding. Tokyo: Hayakawa Shobō.

Ōsawa, Masayuki. 2006. Otaku to Yū Nazo. *Forum Gendaishakaigaku* 5, 25–39.

Ōtsu, Eiichirō (trans.). 1979. *O Henri Kessakusen*. / Henry, O. *The Gift of the Magi
and Other Short Stories*. Tokyo: Iwanamishoten.

Ōyama, Teiichi, and Yoshikawa Kōjiro. 1974. *Rakuchūshokan*. Tokyo: Chikuma Shobō.

Paretsky, Sara. 1982. *Indemnity Only*. New York: Dell.

Paretsky, Sara. 1984. *Deadlock*. New York: Dell.

Phillips, J. B. 1953. Some Personal Reflections on New Testament Translation. *The Bible Translator* 4(1), 53–59.

Popoviç, Anton. 1970. The Concept Shift of Expression in Translation Analysis. In Frans de Haan Holmes and Anton Popoviç (eds), *The Nature of Translation: Essays on the Theory and Practice of Literary Translation*. The Hague: Mouton, 78–87.

Pym, Anthony. 1992a. *Translation and Text Transfer*. Frankfurt: Peter Lang.

Pym, Anthony. 1992b. Shortcomings in the Historiography of Translation. *Babel* 38(14), 221–235.

Pym, Anthony. 1995. Schleiermacher and the Problem of "Blendlinge". *Translation and Literature* 4(1), 5–30.

Radó, György. 1987. A Typology of LLD Translation Problems. *Babel* 33(1), 6–13.

Reiß, Katharina. 1977. Text Types, Translation Types and Translation Assessment. In Andrew Chesterman (ed.) *Readings in Translation Theory*. Helsinki: Oy Finn Lectura Ab, 105–115.

Reiß, Katharina, and Hans J. Vermeer. 1984. *Grundlegung einer allgemeinen Translationstheorie*. Tübingen: Niemeyer.

Rendell, Ruth. 1994/1979. *Make Death Love Me*. London: Arrow Books.

Rieu, E. V., and J. B. Phillips. 1954. Translating the Gospels. *Concordia Theologian Monthly* 25, 754–765.

Robinson, Douglas. 1991. *The Translator's Turn*. Baltimore, MD: Johns Hopkins University Press.

Sager, Juan C. 1997a. Text Typology: Register, Genre and Text Type. In Anna Trosborg (ed.), *Text Typology and Translation*. Amsterdam: John Benjamins, 3–23.

Sager, Juan C. 1997b. Text Types and Translation. In Anna Trosborg (ed.), *Text Typology and Translation*. Amsterdam: John Benjamins, 25–41.

Sakai, Akinobu (trans.). 1993. *Jurashikku • Pāku*. / Crichton, Michael. *Jurassic Park*. Tokyo: Hayakawa Shobō.

Sakai, Naoki. 1997. *Nihon Shisō toyū Mondai. Hon'yaku to Shutai*. Tokyo: Iwanami Shoten.

Sakanashi, Ryūzō. 1990. Yōgakusha no Shisō to Buntai. *Kokugo to Kokubungaku* 67, 122–135.

Sakuma, Agata. 1940. *Gendainihongohō no Kenkyū*. Tokyo: Kōseikaku.

Satō, Miki. 2007. Zasshi Eigo Seinen ni Mirareru Meiji Taishō no Eibungaku Hon'yaku Kihan. *Hokkaido Daigaku Daigakuin Kokusai Kōhō Media Kenkyūka Inseironshū* 3, 48–59.

Satō, Miki. 2009. Shinyaku o Meguru Hon'yaku Hihyō Hikaku. *Media and Communication Studies* 57, 1–20.

Satō, Miki. 2010. Kaidai 2. In Yanabu Akira, Mizuno Akira and Naganuma Mikako (eds), *Nihon no Hon'yakuron. Anthology to Kaidai*. Tokyo: Hōsei Daigaku Shuppankyoku, 62–65.

Satō, Miki. 2015. 1960–70 nendai no Eibeibungaku Hon'yakukan: Eigoseinen to Kikan Hon'yaku no Kyōshin to Kairi. *Invitation to Interpreting & Translation Studies* 14, 21–38.

Sato-Rossberg, Nana. 2012. *Translation and Translation Studies in the Japanese Context*. London: A&C Black.

Savory, Theodore H. 1957. *The Art of Translation*. London: Jonathan Cape.

Sawada, Harumi. 1978. Nichiei Bunfukushirui (Sentential Adverbs) no Taishōgengogakuteki Kenkyū: Speech Act Riron no Shiten kara. *Gengo Kenkyū* 74, 1–36.

Sayers, Dorothy L. 1966/1934. *Nine Tailors: Changes Rung on an Old Theme in Two Short Touches and Two Full Peals*. Boston, MA: Mariner Books.

Schleiermacher, Friedrich. 1813. Über die verschiedenen Methoden des Übersezens. In *Friedrich Schleiermachers sämmtliche Werke, Dritte Abtheilung: Zur Philosophie*, vol. 2. Berlin: Reimer, 207–245. Bartscht, Waltraud (trans.). 1992. From "On the Different Methods of Translating". In Rainer Schulte and John Biguenet (eds), *Theories of Translation: An Anthology of Essays from Dryden to Derrida*. Chicago: University of Chicago Press, 36–54.

Schusterman, Richard. 1994. *Pragmatist Aesthetics. Living Beauty*. London: Blackwell.

Seeley, Christopher. 1991. *A History of Writing in Japan*. Leiden: E. J. Brill.

Seidensticker, Edward G. 1989. On Trying to Translate Japanese. In John Biguenet and Rainer Schulte (eds), *The Craft of Translation*. Chicago: University of Chicago Press, 142–153.

Seidensticker, Edward G., and Nasu Satoshi. 1962. *Nihongo Rashii Hyōgen kara Eigo Rashii Hyōgen e*. Tokyo: Baifūkan.

Shibauchi, Sachiko, and Takai Atsuko. 1967. Ōbunchokuyakutai to Sono Eikyō. *Nihonbungaku* 29, 56–71.

Shuppan Geppō: Hon'yaku Shuppan no Genjo. November 2000. Tokyo: Kōekishadanhōjin Zenkoku Shuppan Kyōkai.

Smith, Herman W., and Nomi Takako. 2000. Is amae the Key to Understanding Japanese Culture? *Electronic Journal of Sociology* <http://www.sociology.org/content/vol005.001/smith-nomi.html> accessed 15 December 2017.

Snell-Hornby, Mary. 1995. *Translation Studies. An Integrated Approach. Revised Edition*. Amsterdam: John Benjamins.

Spivak, Gayatri C. 1993. The Politics of Translation. In Gayatri C. Spivak (ed.), *Outside in the Teaching Machine*. New York: Routledge, 179–200.

Sugimoto, Tsutomu. 1960. *Kindai Nihongo no Seiritsu. Kotoba to Seikatsu*. Tokyo: Ōfūsha.

Sugimoto, Tsutomu. 1996. *Edo no Bun'en to Bunshōgaku.* Tokyo: Sōdaishuppanbu.

Sugimura, Yasushi. 2009. *Gendai Nihongo ni okeru Gaizensei o Arawasu Modariti Fukushi no Kenkyū.* Tokyo: Hitsuji Shobō.

Suzuki, Miyuki. 2013. A Study of Translation of Children's Literature: With Special Reference to Wordplay in the BFG. *Invitation to Interpreting & Translation Studies* 9, 63–79.

Tahara, Mildred (trans.). 1984. *The Twilight Year.* / Ariyoshi, Sawako. *Kōkotsu no Hito.* London: Peter Owens Publishers.

Takeda, Kayoko. 2017. *Hon'yaku Tsūyaku Kenkyū no Shinchihei.* Kyoto: Kōyō Shobō.

Tamamura, Fumio. 1983. Gaikokugo no Fukushi to Nihongo no Fukushi. *Nihongogaku* 10, 47–55.

Tennant, Emma. 1996. *Elinor and Marianne: A Sequel to Sense and Sensibility.* London: Simon & Schuster.

Tirkkonen-Condit, Sonja. 2002. Translationese – A Myth or an Empirical Fact? A Study into the Linguistic Identifiability of Translated Language. *Target* 14(2), 207–220.

Tobita, Shigeo. 1997. *Hon'yaku no Gihō.* Tokyo: Kenkyūsha.

Tokieda, Motoki. 1941. *Kokugogaku Genron.* Tokyo: Iwanami Shoten.

Tokizane, Hiroshi. 1978. *Gen'ei no Dairen.* Osaka: Ōminato Shobō.

Torikai, Kumiko. 2013. *Yokuwakaru Hon'yaku Tsūyakugaku.* Kyoto: Minerva Shobō.

Toury, Gideon. 1980. *In Search of a Theory of Translation.* Tel Aviv: The Porter Institute.

Toury, Gideon. 1995. *Descriptive Translation Studies and Beyond.* Amsterdam: John Benjamins.

Trosborg, Anna (ed.). 1997. *Text Typology and Translation.* Amsterdam: John Benjamins.

Tsujimura, Toshiki. 1991. *Nihongo no Rekishi.* Tokyo: Meiji Shoin.

Tsukishima, Hiroshi. 1963. *Heian Jidai no Kanbun Kunyakugo ni tsukite no Kenkyū.* Tokyo: Tokyo Daigaku Shuppankai.

Twine, Nanette. 1991. *Language and the Modern State. The Reform of Written Japanese.* London: Routledge.

Tytler, Alexander F. 1791. Essay on the Principles of Translation (extract). In André Lefevere (ed.), *Translation / History / Culture: A Sourcebook.* London: Routledge, 128–135.

Uchiyama, Akiko. 2009. Translation as Representation: Fukuzawa Yukichi's representation of the "Others". In John Milton and Paul Bandia (eds), *Agents of Translation.* Amsterdam: John Benjamins, 63–85.

Ueda, Kazutoshi. 1895. Futatabi Florenz-sensei ni Kotau. *Teikokubungaku* 9, 158–162.

Ueda, Kazutoshi. 1895. Hihyō Dichtergrüsse aus dem Osten. Doktor Florenz yaku. *Teikokubungaku* 3, 98–99.

Ueda, Kazutoshi. 1895. Zatsuroku Florenz-sensei no Wakashiikahikakukō o Yomu. *Teikokubungaku* 5, 65–73.

Ujiie, Yōko. 1987. Epistemological Study of Language: Mental Integration Observed in Japanese Adverbs. *Yamagata Daigaku Kiyō* 11, 649–666.

Ujiie, Yōko. 2010. *A Speaker's Cognition Encoded in Japanese – Speech, Mind, and Society*. Tokyo: Sangensha.

UNESCO Evolution of Translation. Index Translationum <http://www.unesco.org/xtrans/bssatexp.aspx/> accessed 24 April 2017.

UNESCO Index Translationum <http://www.unesco.org/xtrans/> accessed 24 April 2017.

UNESCO "TOP 10" Original Language. Index Translationum <http://www.unesco.org/xtrans/bssatexp.aspx/> accessed 24 April 2017.

UNESCO "TOP 50" Target Language. Index Translationum <http://www.unesco.org/xtrans/bsstexp.aspx?crit1L=4&nTyp=min&topN=50> accessed 24 April 2017.

Uno, Toshiyasu (trans.). 1985. *Guriinshōshi no Abōkyū*. / Christie, Agatha. *The Greenshow's Folly*. In Hashimoto Fukuo et al. (trans.). 1985. *Kurisumasu Pudding no Bōken*. / Christie, Agatha. *The Adventure of the Christmas Pudding*. Tokyo: Hayakawa Shobō.

Usami, Takeshi. 1989. Robinson Crusoe no Meijiki Hon'yaku o Megutte: Hyōgenkōzō ga Tsukuridasu Sekai. *Kokugo to Kokubungaku* 66(3), 41–55.

Venuti, Lawrence. 1995. *The Translator's Invisibility. A History of Translation*. London: Routledge.

Vermeer, Hans J., and Andrew Chesterman (trans.). 1989. Skopos and Commission in Translational Action. In Andrew Chesterman (ed.), *Translation Studies Reader*. London: Routledge, 173–187.

Viaggio, Sergio. 1999. The Limitation of the Strictly Socio-Historical Description of Norms. In Christina Schäffner (ed.), *Translation and Norms*. Cleveland, PA, Tronto, Sydney, Johannesburg: Multilingual Matters, 122–128.

Wakabayashi, Judy. 1996. *An Alternative Tradition. Translation Theory in Japan* <http://iias.asia/iiasn/10/Regional/10CECD03.html> accessed 19 June 2017.

Wakabayashi, Judy. 1998. Marginal Forms of Translation in Japan – Variation in the Norm. In Lynne Bowker (ed.), *Unity in Diversity: Recent Trends in Translation Studies*. Manchester: St Jerome Publishing, 57–63.

Wakabayashi, Judy. 2009. Translational Japanese: A Transformative Strangeness Within. *Portal Journal of Multidisciplinary International Studies* 6(1), 1–20.

Watanabe, Minoru. 1983. Fukuyōgen Sōron. *Nihongogaku* 10, 4–9.

Yagura, Naoko (trans.). 1994. *Kukkingu • Mama wa Meitantei*. / Mott-Davidson, Diane. *Catering to Nobody*. Tokyo: Shueisha.

Yamada, Yoshio. 1936. *Nihonbunpōron*. Tokyo: Hōbunkan.

Yamamoto, Masahide. 1965. *Kindaibuntai Hassei no Shitekikenkyū.* Tokyo: Iwanami Shoten.

Yamamoto, Yayoi (trans.). 1985. *Samātaimu • Burūsu.* / Paretsky, Sara. *Indemnity Only.* Tokyo: Hayakawa Shobō.

Yamamoto, Yayoi (trans.). 1986. *Reikusaido • Sutōrii.* / Paretsky, Sara. *Deadlock.* Tokyo: Hayakawa Shobō.

Yamaoka, Yōichi. 2010. Kaidai 21. In Yanabu Akira, Mizuno Akira and Naganuma Mikako (eds), *Nihon no Hon'yakuron. Anthology to Kaidai.* Tokyo: Hōsei Daigaku Shuppankyoku, 221–226.

Yanabu, Akira. 1979. *Hikaku Nihongoron.* Tokyo: Babel Press.

Yanabu, Akira. 1982. *Hon'yakugo Seiritsu Jijyō.* Tokyo: Iwanami Shoten.

Yanabu, Akira. 2002. *Hi no Shisō. Nihon Bunka no Omote to Ura.* Tokyo: Hōsei Daigaku Shuppankyoku.

Yanabu, Akira. 2004. *Kindai Nihongo no Shisō. Hon'yaku Buntai Seiritsu Jijyō.* Tokyo: Hōsei Daigaku Shuppankyoku.

Yanabu, Akira, Mizuno Akira and Naganuma Mikako (eds). 2010. *Nihon no Hon'yakuron. Anthology to Kaidai.* Tokyo: Hōsei Daigaku Shuppankyoku.

Yanase, Naoki. 2000. *Hon'yaku wa Ikani Subekika.* Tokyo: Iwanami Shoten.

Yokoyama, Jun (trans.). 1990. *Yuigon.* In Kimiyoshi Yura (ed.), *Igirisu Kaidanshū.* / Le Fanu, Joseph Sheridan. *Squire Toby's Will.* In M. R. James (ed.), *Madam Crowl's Ghost and Other Stories.* Tokyo: Kawaide Shobō.

Yonekawa, Akihiko. 1991. Gendai no Gairaigo no Ryūnyū. *Nihongogaku* 10, 37–44.

Yukio, Naruse. 2006. *Hon'yaku Kōzakōgiroku* <http://sites.google.com/site/junbi-kakougi/zhun-bei-ke-jiang-yi-lu-1/> accessed 18 June 2017.

Zenkoku Shuppankai Shuppan Shihyō Nenpō. 2016. Tokyo: Shuppankagaku Kenkyūjo.

Name Index

Subject Index

NEW TRENDS IN TRANSLATION STUDIES

In today's globalised society, translation and interpreting are gaining visibility and relevance as a means to foster communication and dialogue in increasingly multicultural and multilingual environments. Practised since time immemorial, both activities have become more complex and multifaceted in recent decades, intersecting with many other disciplines. New Trends in Translation Studies is an international series with the main objectives of promoting the scholarly study of translation and interpreting and of functioning as a forum for the translation and interpreting research community.

This series publishes research on subjects related to multimedia translation and interpreting, in their various social roles. It is primarily intended to engage with contemporary issues surrounding the new multidimensional environments in which translation is flourishing, such as audiovisual media, the internet and emerging new media and technologies. It sets out to reflect new trends in research and in the profession, to encourage flexible methodologies and to promote interdisciplinary research ranging from the theoretical to the practical and from the applied to the pedagogical.

New Trends in Translation Studies publishes translation- and interpreting-oriented books that present high-quality scholarship in an accessible, reader-friendly manner. The series embraces a wide range of publications – monographs, edited volumes, conference proceedings and translations of works in translation studies which do not exist in English. The editor, Professor Jorge Díaz Cintas, welcomes proposals from all those interested in being involved with the series. The working language of the series is English, although in exceptional circumstances works in other languages can be considered for publication. Proposals dealing with specialised translation, translation tools and technology, audiovisual translation and the field of accessibility to the media are particularly welcomed.